MORE FAMILY WALK

MORE FAMILY WALK™

Bruce H. Wilkinson
Executive Editor

Paula A. Kirk
Editor

Calvin W. Edwards
General Editor

Walk Thru the Bible Ministries
Atlanta, Georgia

Zondervan Publishing House
Grand Rapids, Michigan

More Family Walk
Copyright © 1992 by Walk Thru the Bible Ministries
All rights reserved

Published by Zondervan Publishing House

Requests for information should be addressed to:
Walk Thru the Bible Ministries   or   Zondervan Publishing House
4201 North Peachtree Road   Grand Rapids, MI 49530
Atlanta, GA 30341–1362

Library of Congress Cataloging-in-Publication Data

More Family Walk: habits, fairness, stress and 49 other weekly readings for
your family devotions/ Walk Thru the Bible Ministries, Atlanta, GA
    p. cm.
    ISBN 0-310-54571-4 (pbk.)
    1. Family—Prayer-books and devotions—English. 2. Devotional calendars.
3. Bible—Devotional use. I. Walk Thru the Bible (Educational Ministry).
II. Family Walk
BV255.M67   1992
249—dc20   92—8293
                                                    CIP

Cover and interior design by Michelle Beeman
Cover photo by Tony Stone Worldwide
Cartoons by Martha Campbell

Printed in the United States of America

93 94 / DH / 10 9 8 7 6 5 4 3

DEDICATION

In an age that seems to reward "characters" more than "character," it is refreshing to discover people who model the values and character traits rewarded by God. Bill and Nora Bolthouse are examples of Christian believers who have a dynamic testimony in their church, community, and business as they touch the lives of others for eternity. They have supported the ministry of Walk Thru the Bible through their steadfast loyalty, their generous sharing, and their faithful prayers. Therefore, we gratefully dedicate *More Family Walk* to a special couple, Bill and Nora Bolthouse.

Bruce H. Wilkinson

ACKNOWLEDGMENTS

More Family Walk: Habits, Fairness, Stress, and 49 Other Weekly Readings for Your Family Devotions is the second compilation of topical studies from *Family Walk,* a devotional guide published monthly by Walk Thru the Bible Ministries. We are grateful to everyone in Walk Thru the Bible's Specialized Publishing Group who worked so faithfully on this devotional guide during the past 10 years, from those on the leadership and sales teams right down through all the support and production staff.

Special thanks for great ideas and exceptionally fine work on this book go to our *Family Walk* design and production team: Robyn Holmes, Michelle Beeman, Helen Ryser, and Stuart McLellan. May their investment of time, talent, and exceptional teamwork make a lasting difference in families who read this book.

INTRODUCTION

More Family Walk is carefully designed to help parents train their children to apply biblical truths to everyday situations. With this book, parents have a tool to open communication about the vital issues families face today and to find the answers in God's Word.

More Family Walk will help you and your children establish the Scriptures as your foundation for living in this chaotic and insecure world. As you discover practical applications for family problems in *More Family Walk,* your child will see the Bible in a new light. No longer will the Bible simply be a book of exciting stories about things that happened long ago. Instead, your children will see the Bible as a vital resource for a happy and successful life. As you and your children grow spiritually and become confident in God's love, you will become more secure as a family.

We at Walk Thru the Bible Ministries are pleased to join with Zondervan Publishing House to make this Bible reading guide available to you. The common purpose of our ministries is to help Christians become grounded in the Scriptures.

Bruce H. Wilkinson
President and Executive Editor

How to Get the Most Out of *More Family Walk*

More Family Walk is arranged by topics for you and your children to explore together each week. You can start with the first topic or just jump in at any point in the book. Simply put a check in the accompanying box to keep your place.

Day One of each topic brings your family a definition of the topic and a key Bible verse. The primary Scripture portion for Day One is the key verse, and we encourage you and your children to read it aloud several times and perhaps even memorize it. Use the cartoon as a discussion starter or just have a good laugh together.

Days Two–Five are divided into these three sections:

> **An opening story** helps your family focus on the question for the day.

> **Take a Look** guides you to a passage in God's Word that gives insight into the biblical answer to the day's question. Let your children find the passage in their Bibles and read the selection aloud. Or let them read the verse that is printed in italic type. Encourage your children to mark that verse in their own Bibles and reread it at some point during the day.

> **Take a Step** reveals useful ways you can practice what you learn. Through discussion about the Scripture you read, references back to the opening story, and concrete action your family can take, Take a Step is designed to generate conversation about the issues young people face today.

We encourage you to be sensitive to your children's needs and questions. Stop at any point to discuss what you're reading and how it relates to your situation. Spiritual growth is a process that takes place over time. *More Family Walk,* if used consistently, is a tool that will give your family and its individual members opportunities to prepare for the challenges that will come your way.

WALK THRU THE BIBLE MINISTRIES

Walk Thru the Bible Ministries (WTB) began in the early 1970s in Portland, Oregon, when a young teacher named Bruce Wilkinson developed an innovative way of teaching surveys of the Bible. By enabling people to actively participate in the learning process through memorable hand signs, the Word of God came alive for them and lives were changed.

From these small beginnings emerged the multifaceted Bible-teaching outreach that Dr. Wilkinson officially founded as a nonprofit ministry in 1976. In 1978 WTB moved to its current home in Atlanta, Georgia. Since then, WTB has grown into one of the leading Christian organizations in America with an international ministry extending to 30 countries representing 22 languages. International branch offices are located in Australia, Brazil, Great Britain, Singapore, and New Zealand.

By focusing on the central themes of Scripture and their practical application to life, WTB has been able to develop and maintain wide acceptance in denominations and fellowships around the world. In addition, it has carefully initiated strategic ministry alliances with more than one hundred Christian organizations and missions of wide diversity and background.

WTB has four major outreach ministries: seminars, publishing, leadership training, and video training curricula. Since it began its seminar ministry two decades ago, WTB has instructed more than one million people worldwide through seminars taught by more than two hundred highly qualified, well-trained teachers. People of all ages and religious persuasions have developed a deeper understanding of the Bible through these unique Old and New Testament surveys, and many have come to know Christ in a new and more personal way.

WTB's publishing ministry began in 1978 with the launching of *The Daily Walk* magazine. Since then, WTB Publishing has continued to develop additional publications that enable individuals, families, and churches to maintain a regular, meaningful habit of daily devotional time in the Word of God. The publications include *Closer Walk, Family Walk, LifeWalk, Quiet Walk,* and *Youthwalk.* WTB is one of the largest publishers of devotional magazines in the Christian community. The third strategic ministry of WTB is the training of Christian leaders and communicators. Launched in the late 1980s, the Applied Principles of Learning (APL) training conference for teachers, pastors, and parents has rapidly become the most widely used interdenominational teacher training program in North America. Dozens of certified WTB instructors regularly conduct this life-changing course in schools, churches, businesses, and colleges. In addition, WTB's Leadership Dynamics curriculum is an integral part of the regular and ongoing discipleship training in hundreds of churches.

The newest ministry of WTB is the Video Training curriculum. In just a few short years, the WTB creative team has developed a number of leading video courses that have enjoyed widespread distribution. *The Seven Laws of the Learner,* featuring Dr. Bruce H. Wilkinson, focuses on the needs of the student and helps teachers learn to communicate in the most effective and compelling manner possible. *The Seven Laws of the Teacher,* featuring Dr. Howard G. Hendricks, equips church school teachers, parents, and others to effectively prepare and teach Bible lessons that capture attention and change lives. *Master Your Money,* a six-part presentation by Christian financial planner Ron Blue, trains people to maximize their effectiveness as stewards of God's resources. Thousands of churches use these and other fine WTB videos with their congregations each year.

WTB has had a consistent history of strategic ministry from its beginning. The organization strives to help fulfill the Great Commission in obedience to the Lord's call. With this mission in mind, WTB lives out its commitment to excellence with the highest standards of ethical conduct and integrity, not only in the ministry but also in its internal operational policies and procedures. No matter what the ministry, no matter where the ministry, WTB focuses on the Word of God and encourages people of all nations to grow in their knowledge of Him and in their unreserved obedience and service to Him.

For more information about Walk Thru the Bible's publications, videos, or seminars in your area, write to Walk Thru the Bible Ministries, 4201 North Peachtree Road, Atlanta, Ga 30341–1362 or call (404) 458-9300.

CONTENTS

KINDNESS

With class beginning in minutes, Erin and Debra hurried to their seats.

"Oh, Erin. Look who's coming in. It's that new girl, Leslie, and look what she's wearing. Have you ever seen anything so tacky?"

"Debra, not so loud. She might hear you."

"Oh, don't be silly. There's too much noise in here. Besides, she really is a mess. Just look at her. She'll never make any friends!"

"Debra, don't be so mean! Leslie doesn't look all that bad. Why don't we invite her to sit with us at lunch? It must be scary being new in a big school, and she might be really nice once we get to know her."

"Are you crazy or something? I wouldn't be seen anywhere with the likes of her. Hey, she's crying. I wonder what's the matter . . . "

◆ THINKING ABOUT KINDNESS

Carrot-top. Pizza-face. Four-eyes. Names and taunts that none of us likes—especially when we're on the receiving end.

By contrast, there's nothing quite as welcome as a kind word . . . a genuine compliment . . . an expression of friendship that lifts our spirits and makes us feel loved and accepted.

Everyone feels the need to be treated with kindness. It makes us feel special. It encourages us. It motivates us to do our very best.

Kindness is **treating others tenderly, as we would want to be treated ourselves**. In Ephesians 4:32 Paul tells us:

● KEY VERSE ON KINDNESS

Be kind and compassionate to one another, forgiving each other, just as in Christ God forgave you (Ephesians 4:32).

▲ LOOKING AHEAD

This week we'll look closely at kindness.

Go back to the classroom scene for a moment. Debra missed a wonderful opportunity to make a new student feel welcome. What could she have said or done in kindness to Leslie—and in keeping with the command in Ephesians 4:32?

"I followed the golden rule today, but only about three karats worth."

I may not deserve it, but I sure could use it!

Gil and Michael were walking home after basketball practice.

"Hey, Gil, aren't you glad you're not Steve right about now? Can you believe it—Coach kicked him off the team!"

"He had it coming, Michael. Always talking tough to everyone, and hogging the basketball all the time."

"Maybe you're right, Gil, but can you imagine how Steve must feel now? Just think what a ribbing he'll get in P.E. tomorrow. Every guy in the school will be on his case!"

"Michael, the guy only got what he deserved. Steve always could dish it out; now let's see if he can take it!"

◆ TAKE A LOOK / 2 Samuel 9:3-11

If kindness were something we earned, Gil might have a point. But remember what Ephesians 4:32 says? Kindness is something we are to give regardless of whether or not the other person deserves it.

In Old Testament times when a king died and a new family came to power, it was common for the new king to look for—and do away with—any remaining members of the previous king's family. In that way his throne would be secured.

After Saul died, David became king. And sure enough, he began to look for any surviving members of Saul's family. There was only one person left—a grandson named Mephibosheth. So he was summoned to David's palace. Imagine how fearful poor Mephibosheth must have felt! But David wasn't going to kill him; instead he wanted to show him kindness. Read 2 Samuel 9:3-11 right now to discover what that kindness included.

▲ TAKE A STEP

David's treatment of an undeserving member of Saul's family reminds us of how God treats us.

"With everlasting kindness I will have compassion on you" (Isaiah 54:8).

Why should we show kindness to others? For the same reason God shows kindness to us! Not because we deserve it, but because we need it.

Gil's reaction to Steve's dismissal from the basketball team is understandable. But if Gil had understood why God wants us to show kindness to others, he may have acted differently. Pretend that you are Gil and you've just heard the news about Steve. What are some ways you could show kindness to your teammate at a time when he really needs it most?

Q

Why should I be kind to those who aren't kind to me?

A

Kindness is something I give because others need it, not because they deserve it.

E rin, come quick. You've got to see this!"
"What is it, Debra?"
"Remember that new girl, Leslie? The one who looks like her clothes come from a secondhand shop? Well, she's coming down the hall right now. And she's wearing the same outfit for the third time this week! It must be her favorite hand-me-down."

"Debra, listen. I really felt bad about how we treated Leslie the other day. I think we hurt her feelings."

"Maybe we ought to nominate her for homecoming queen," Debra broke in. "C'mon, let's go to class before she sees us."

"No, Debra. You go. I've got something I need to do. Uh, Leslie? You don't know me, but my name is Erin. You're new here at Wilson, aren't you? It's kind of a big school—maybe I could help show you around . . ."

◆ TAKE A LOOK / Luke 10:25-37

Erin was reaching out to help where help was needed. And she was being gentle and encouraging without expecting anything in return.

In Luke 10:25-37 Jesus told the story (or parable) of the Good Samaritan to answer the question, "Who is my neighbor?" But the story also answers the question we are asking today: "To whom should I show kindness?"

As someone in your family reads the story aloud, listen carefully and count the number of ways the Samaritan showed kindness to the man who needed his help.

▲ TAKE A STEP

Do you think the Samaritan knew that two other people had already passed by the wounded man? The Bible doesn't say. But when the Samaritan saw a person in need—someone he could help —he didn't stop to ask! He simply obeyed one of the most important commands in the Bible:

"Love your neighbor as yourself" (Luke 10:27).

The Samaritan didn't wait until he got to the next town to send back an ambulance. He didn't wait until the man regained consciousness so he could ask if the man had insurance to cover the cost. He simply did for the wounded man what he would have wanted someone to do for him.

Think of Leslie as the wounded man, and Erin as the Good Samaritan. What are some ways Erin could show herself to be a friend and neighbor to Leslie?

Hey, neighbor, tell me where it hurts

To whom should I show kindness?

A

Kindness should be shown to my neighbor— anyone near me who needs my help.

PARENT:
Have each family member identify a "neighbor" in his or her life. Plan a Good Samaritan gesture toward that person.

Enemies I have plenty; would you be my friend?

*E*rin, I'm really glad you invited me to eat lunch with you. I've been so scared and lonely since my family moved here."

"There's no need to be scared, Leslie. We're not so bad! I think you'll like it here at Wilson. Besides, you and I have a lot in common. Do you realize we have five classes together?"

"Well, I don't think I could have made it without you, Erin. We moved here from a small town with only about 500 people in it. And now there are three times that many kids in my school! Thanks for being my friend, Erin. It means so much to me."

◆ TAKE A LOOK / Ruth 2:10-17

Kindness (tender treatment of others) means looking for hurting people and helping them feel wanted and needed. It means being sensitive to others when they are lonely or afraid.

The Old Testament book of Ruth describes a wonderful example of kindness. Ruth was from the land of Moab, just across the Jordan River from the land of Israel. She married a man from Israel; but after he died, Ruth and her mother-in-law, Naomi, moved to the town of Bethlehem—the place where Jesus would be born hundreds of years later.

Because Ruth and Naomi were very poor, Ruth went into the fields to glean the leftovers from the harvest, the portion of the crop which the harvesters missed. Without knowing it, Ruth had chosen the field belonging to one of her in-laws—a man named Boaz. Would he treat her harshly? Would he tell her to go elsewhere to find food? Read about his response in Ruth 2:10-17.

▲ TAKE A STEP

Boaz did more than leave Ruth alone to find food. He actually gave orders to his men to leave extra grain for her to find! Boaz went out of his way to be kind to Ruth. Boaz was practicing the truth of this proverb:

Whoever is kind to the needy honors God (Proverbs 14:31).

Erin too was sensitive to another's feelings. Rather than ignore Leslie or hope that someone else would spend time with her, Erin went out of her way to show kindness.

As a family, think of one person in your neighborhood or school with whom you can share a kind word or thoughtful deed today. Then do it!

Q

How can I show kindness to others?

A

Kindness means treating others as if their feelings are more important than my own.

*H*ey, Chuck, I know how we can make some quick money."

"Yeah? How, Ronny?"

"You know Mrs. Hightower, that old lady down the street—the one with the little poodle? Well, it just ran off into the woods behind my house. Mrs. Hightower's really upset. She can't run after it, and she's afraid the German shepherd next door will kill it. So if we find that old poodle, we can get her to give us a reward!"

"Ronny, that's a dumb idea. It's mean. We ought to catch her dog and take it back for nothing. She's an old lady and doesn't have a lot of money. C'mon, let's hurry before it gets dark."

"Naw, you go on. I'll just watch TV until you get back."

◆ TAKE A LOOK / Luke 18:35-43

Doing something nice for someone without expecting a reward—that's the type of kindness Jesus described:

"Love your enemies, do good to them . . . without expecting to get anything back" (Luke 6:35).

Close your eyes for a moment and imagine that you are blind. You can hear noises and smell smells, but all you can see is darkness. Luke 18 describes a man in that sad condition. But then something unexpected happened. He began to hear the sounds of a crowd approaching. It was Jesus! So the blind man began to cry out loudly, "Jesus, Son of David, have mercy on me!"

Jesus stopped right in front of him. The crowd fell silent. Jesus asked, "What do you want me to do for you?" He didn't have to wait long for an answer! "Lord, I want to see."

"All right," Jesus replied. "But first you'll have to pay me $200 for the 'doctor's visit.' "

Is that what the Bible says? Of course not! Turn to Luke 18:35-43 to learn what really happened to the blind man.

▲ TAKE A STEP

When you think about it, Jesus' entire life was marked by acts of kindness.

It's easy to be kind when the price is right. But how do you treat those who can't repay you . . . and maybe don't even appreciate what you've done? Treat them as Jesus would!

If you were Chuck and Ronny were your friend, how would you show him that God's brand of kindness isn't for sale at any price?

The reward for kindness is much more than money

Q

What do I get in return for showing kindness?

A

Kindness brings its own reward by making both God and me happy.

HABITS

A *fter his bath, six-year-old Bobby Benson carefully folded his*
towel and hung it on the rack. When he brushed his teeth, he
squeezed from the end of the toothpaste tube, then replaced the cap.
After he finished, he picked up his dirty clothes, put them in the hamper,
straightened the bath mat, and returned to his room. He chose a clean
shirt and slacks from the closet and hung them on the doorknob for
tomorrow.

Next door, twelve-year-old Jesse Smith was also getting into bed. But
in his bathroom, water dripped in the tub, a soggy towel lay heaped on
the counter, toothpaste oozed in the sink, and dirty clothes littered the
floor. When he woke up the next morning, he couldn't find the shirt he
wanted to wear, his best jeans were wadded up behind the door, and he
figured his tennis shoes must have been stolen during the night!

◆ THINKING ABOUT HABITS

Just like Bobby and Jesse, nearly every area of your life is
affected by habits. The habits you've developed for eating, sleeping,
and exercising largely determine how healthy you feel each day.
And your habits of study, TV viewing, and reading greatly affect
how well and how much you learn.

Habits are **personal actions repeated so often that they
become part of our lives**. If you put your mind to it, God will help
you build healthy new habits and break harmful old ones.

*"Don't tell Mom, but I kind of enjoy
a day off from TV now and then."*

● KEY VERSE ON HABITS

*Those who live in
accordance with the
Spirit have their
minds set on what
the Spirit desires
(Romans 8:5).*

▲ LOOKING AHEAD

Okay—confession
time! Go around the
family circle and tell
one habit you'd like to
break. Then read
Romans 8:9 to find out
whom you can depend
on for help in getting
rid of those bad habits!

*A*nother dull breakfast! This family is definitely in a rut," Melody accused her dad. "Every morning it's the same old thing. You and Mom never do anything interesting."

"Well, maybe every once in a while Mom could fix fried eggs instead of scrambled eggs," her dad chuckled.

"You know that's not what I mean!" Melody said.

The next morning when Melody's alarm sounded, she realized the house was quiet. No one had turned up the heat, started breakfast, or let the dog out. The newspaper still lay in the front yard. Then Melody spotted a note in the kitchen: "Mom and I are breaking our old habits by having breakfast at the Pancake House. Cereal is in the cabinet; milk's in the 'frig. Love, Dad."

That night, Melody left this note beside the coffee pot: "Dad, I learned today that your dull, routine habits are what keep us all comfortable. Sorry I complained. I love you!"

◆ **TAKE A LOOK / Colossians 3:1-2, 5-10, 12-17**

Like the morning routine of Melody's parents, some habits can be as comfortable as warm slippers and make life easier for everyone. Bad habits can be as irritating as fingernails scratching on a chalkboard. And some habits can even be harmful to your health. But whether healthy or harmful, habits affect every area of your life.

God wants to break sinful habits in His children's lives and replace them with holy habits which please Him and help us grow. That's what the Bible means when it says to put off the old self and put on the new. Read Colossians 3:1-2, 5-10, and 12-17 to learn what habits you should "put on."

▲ **TAKE A STEP**

Have each family member list on a sheet of paper as many of his or her personal habits as possible in three minutes, including harmful or irritating habits . . . cleanliness habits . . . exercise habits . . . study habits . . . and spiritual habits.

Then from those lists, have each person pick one bad habit to avoid and one good habit to cultivate. Plan how the whole family can help each member break that bad habit and strengthen that good one. As a family, work to build the habit of encouraging one another, because . . .

Each of us should please his neighbor for his good, to build him up (Romans 15:2).

Get into the habit of evaluating your habits!

Q

Does everyone have habits?

A

Habits— good and bad—can affect everyone in every area of life.

Today's a good day to begin a good habit

Q

What are some habits God wants me to develop?

A

Habits God wants to see in my life include studying and memorizing His Word.

PARENT: The Practice of Godliness by Jerry White will help you build holy habits.

"**O**h, Father," Mrs. Trench prayed silently as she hung up the phone, "I haven't seen Gloria for years—since she was in my afternoon Bible Club. I have no idea why she wants to see me. I hope nothing is wrong. Help me say and do what I should."

Later, Mrs. Trench listened with growing joy as Gloria told her story. At college she had gotten in with the wrong crowd. One night she lay in bed wondering what to do about the mess she had made of her life. Then some verses she had memorized years earlier in Bible Club came to her mind. She remembered what Mrs. Trench had said time and again—that the best habit she could ever develop was to read her Bible and pray every day. So Gloria determined to begin that simple habit again. Soon the girls on her dormitory floor noticed a difference in her life. And as a result, five girls had come to know Jesus personally.

"I just want to thank you," Gloria told Mrs. Trench happily, "because you were the one who got me started in the most wonderful habit I've ever had!"

◆ TAKE A LOOK / 1 Timothy 4:7-8

Because Gloria practiced the habit of spending time daily with God through prayer and Bible study, her friends noticed a difference in her life. In developing that habit, Gloria was obeying the command God gave through Paul to Timothy:

Train yourself to be godly. For physical training is of some value, but godliness has value for all things (1 Timothy 4:7-8).

Each of the six verses below describes a habit God wants His children to develop. After you read the verses, write the habits in the spaces provided.

God wants me to develop . . . the habit of:

Deuteronomy 17:19	_____
Colossians 3:16	_____
Psalm 119:11	_____
1 Thessalonians 5:16	_____
1 Thessalonians 5:17	_____
Hebrews 13:1	_____

▲ TAKE A STEP

Reading, studying, and memorizing God's Word . . . praying and rejoicing . . . loving one another. Those are habits that produce Christ-likeness in God's children. Are they your regular habits? What's the first step you need to take to build one of those habits into your life?

*A*rthur, I don't understand why you and your friends won't let Nick play with you," Mrs. Toombs said sharply. "His mother mentioned it to me again today. You know it's not right to treat anyone unfairly. I think you need to do some explaining."

"But Mom, you don't understand," ten-year-old Arthur answered. "We don't leave him out on purpose . . . he just doesn't fit in! He can't keep up with us. He's too fat because he doesn't get enough exercise, and he doesn't like to ride his bike, and he won't play soccer with us in the backyard. So I don't see what we can do about it, Mom. He's got to quit eating so much, and start exercising more. And he can only do that himself!"

◆ TAKE A LOOK / Romans 6:12-14

Exercising to stay fit has become a popular pastime today. But in Bible times few people ever had to get in shape to run a mile. If they were going somewhere, they walked . . . even for miles and miles. Labor-saving devices were unheard of, and nearly everyone had to work very hard. Even so, then—as now—the body's desires for pleasurable feelings (including eating and drinking) had to be controlled so they wouldn't lead to sin.

As you read Romans 6:12-14, you'll see that your body can be either "an instrument of wickedness" or an "instrument of righteousness." Which kind of "instrument" is your body?

▲ TAKE A STEP

Times have changed since the Bible was written. But it's as important now as it was then to have habits which keep your body under control, because . . .

You are not your own; you were bought at a price. Therefore honor God with your body (1 Corinthians 6:19-20).

Here are two suggestions to help you control your body's cravings: (1) Develop habits which help—not harm—your body. Eat properly, get adequate exercise and rest, and keep away from things which hurt your body, like cigarettes, alcohol, and drugs; (2) Decide now to avoid activities or places in which you know your body will be tempted to sin. For instance, if you're fighting the battle of the bulge, don't have your quiet time in an ice cream parlor or a pizza place!

If you were Arthur, how could you help Nick honor God with his body?

I know what I should do—my body just won't do it

Q

Why should I develop good physical habits?

A

Habits can help me keep my body strong so I can use it for God's glory.

PARENT: Do you have a harmful habit you wouldn't want your child to develop?

Some habits are good; others, good for nothing

Q

How can I keep from starting bad habits?

A

Habits that are sinful grow only when I plant and water them.

"This just can't be happening to me," Mr. Towne thought.

Though he had a hacking cough, he had rarely been ill. He'd just come in for a routine checkup. To his horror, the diagnosis was not good. "I'm sorry—it's lung cancer," the doctor said.

Slouched with his head in his hands, Mr. Towne thought about his family. Unless God worked a miracle, he had only six months to live; he wouldn't even see his daughter Jan graduate in June! "Why did I ever smoke that first cigarette?" he agonized. His mind went back to the night nearly 30 years ago when his friend Jack had offered him a "smoke" behind the school. His eyes, nose, and throat had burned, and he hated the smell. But he was so determined to be "cool" that he kept smoking. By age 16, he was hooked. And now, at age 45, he was paying a terrible price for his habit.

◆ **TAKE A LOOK / Proverbs 25:28**

Whenever the body is so used to something that it feels uncomfortable when it doesn't get it, a habit has been formed. Drugs, alcohol, tobacco, and even foods (like chocolate, caffeine, and sugar) can become habit-forming. So can sinful actions, like looking at magazines, reading books, or watching movies that make sin seem acceptable.

The best way to avoid these harmful habits is to recognize that they are sinful, and then determine not to begin them at all. Self-control enables us—with God's power—to say no to our body's desires and instead do what pleases Him. Without self-control our desires can deceive us and lead us into sin (read Proverbs 25:28). Read the following verses to discover three areas where self-control is needed:

God's Word says . . .	I need self-control in:
1 Peter 1:13	_____
1 Thessalonians 4:3-5	_____
Proverbs 16:32	_____

▲ **TAKE A STEP**

God wants His children to have control over their minds, their bodies, and their emotions. His Word gives this command to help us avoid bad habits:

Train yourself to be godly (1 Timothy 4:7).

By practicing the simple good habits of saying no every time you are tempted by a sinful desire, you can avoid starting bad habits. For each of the three areas above, think of one habit you should never start—and with God's help, never will.

GOD

*T*he first man to orbit the earth—a Russian cosmonaut looked out his window at the blackness of space and reported, "I see neither God nor angels." He decided there was no God.

Six years later, an American astronaut blasted off into space. As he sped thousands of miles in space toward the moon on Christmas Eve, he read these words: "In the beginning God created the heavens and the earth." He saw God everywhere he looked.

Both men cannot be right. Either God is there, or there is no God.

In our world today, people have many different beliefs about God. Some believe there is no God; others believe there are many gods; still others believe there is only one God. Not everyone can be right. And what you believe about God influences what you believe about the world you live in.

◆ THINKING ABOUT GOD
This verse puts that thought another way:

> People all around the world see God in different ways—
> Some see Him as an idol of wood or glass or stone;
> Some see Him as a power, the force of nature strong.
> Christians see Him as Creator, the One to whom we belong.
> We know He sent a Savior, to put right all the wrong.
>
> All these views are different, but only one is true.
> Your life shows forth the answer:
> What is God to you?

This week we'll be learning about the true and living God— **the Creator of all we see and know** the One who said . . .

● KEY VERSE ON GOD
"I am the first and I am the last; apart from me there is no God" (Isaiah 44:6).

▲ LOOKING AHEAD
This week we'll get to know God better. But for today, answer the question asked by the verse above: "What is God to you?"

"Bless this broccoli, Sir, even though it's not an example of Your best work."

I know you're there; your finger-prints are everywhere

Getting off to school on time was hard enough. But with their mother out of town, things were even more frantic for Heather and her sister, Meredith.

"I'll sure be glad when Mom gets back," sighed Heather.

"Yeah, it's a good thing Grandpa wasn't sick another week. We never would have survived any more of Dad's cooking!"

"Well, I'll be glad to see Mom, but if she comes home today we're in big trouble. Look at this mess—dishes in the sink, dirty clothes everywhere. And your room, Meredith! It's a disaster!"

"I know, Heather, but I just haven't had time to do all that stuff. I'll get at it tonight. Mom isn't due back till tomorrow morning."

Returning home that afternoon, the girls discovered dishes sparkling on the drainboard, neatly folded clothes, freshly made beds, and the aroma of something delicious cooking on the stove. Without saying a word, they knew: Mom was home!

◆ TAKE A LOOK / Romans 1:20

How did Heather and Meredith know their mother was there? They saw the evidence of her presence in her "handiwork": neatly folded clothes, washed dishes, homemade soup.

In the same way, God shows His presence in the world. How? By the design and order He has placed in His creation.

The universe we live in is orderly: 24-hour days, seasons and tides, sunrise and sunset. And order does not happen by chance. Someone is really there, and His name is God.

"It is I who made the earth and created mankind upon it. My own hands stretched out the heavens" (Isaiah 45:12).

In Romans 1:20 you'll discover the invisible qualities God reveals about Himself through His visible creation.

▲ TAKE A STEP

God wants you to know what He is like. And that's quite a challenge. After all, you can't see God, hear God, smell God, feel God, or taste God. So how can you know God? You can learn a lot about Him and His character in the things He has made.

Think of what you can learn about your *invisible* Creator by studying His *visible* creation. What lesson can you learn from a tree? a flower? Close by reading Psalm 24:1 together.

Q

How can I know there is a God?

A

God teaches me about Himself in the things He has made.

*I*f only Lewis had known his father, even a little. But that wasn't to be. And now, eight years after the plane crash, Lewis was old enough to ask the hard questions.

"Mom, what was Dad like? I've seen pictures of him, but sometimes it's hard to believe he even was my father."

"Oh, but he was, Lew. Every time I look at you, I see your father's smile. He loved the Lord, and I know he loved you."

Lewis's mother was quiet for a moment. Then she moved slowly toward the closet.

"Lew, your father loved to write letters, especially when he was away on trips. You're old enough now to understand what he wrote. Would you like me to read you some of his letters?"

"Oh, yeah! That would be great, Mom—kind of like Dad was right here in the room with me."

◆ TAKE A LOOK / 1 Samuel 26:5-12

There is more than one way to get to know a person. Face to face is best, but letters are a good way, too. David, the young shepherd boy, had never seen God in person. But he loved God with all his heart because he had spent many hours reading God's Law—God's "love letter" to him. And as David studied the things God had written, he discovered more and more about what God was like.

Years later, David was in a life-and-death chase with King Saul. David needed to know what to do—and fast! Should he kill Saul if he got the chance? His friends and advisors said yes, but what did God want David to do? Read 1 Samuel 26:5-12 to find out!

▲ TAKE A STEP

David was able to do what God wanted him to do because he knew what God wanted him to know. God didn't have to thunder from heaven, "Don't you kill the king!" God had already spoken clearly in His written Word.

David used God's Law the same way Lewis used his father's letters: to get to know a person he couldn't see. And that's important, because God has said:

"I have not spoken in secret. . . . I, the LORD, speak the truth" (Isaiah 45:19).

As a family, close your time together by thanking God for the Bible and promising to read it regularly in order to know Him better.

If you got a love letter, wouldn't you read it?

Q

Does God have something to say to me?

A

God has told me about Himself in the Bible.

PARENT:
By example, encourage your child to stay in touch with those people who have touched his or her life in a meaningful way. Why not write a letter today?

I can't see Him, but I know what He looks like!

Complimenting the artwork of each five-year-old as she walked around the classroom, Mrs. Baker, the kindergarten teacher, stopped beside Philip, who was bent intently over his picture.

"What beautiful colors, Philip. Can you tell me what you're drawing?"

"It's a picture of God," Philip responded matter-of-factly.

Surprised, Mrs. Baker said sweetly, "It's a lovely picture, Philip, but no one really knows what God looks like."

Philip looked up with a grin. "They will when I'm finished!"

◆ TAKE A LOOK / John 14:1-11

Not many people speak that confidently about what God is really like. And rightly so, for God is invisible. Although the Bible tells us much about His throne, His angels, and even heaven where He lives, it does not tell us what God looks like.

But it does tell us what God is like—what He has said and done, what He thinks and feels. In order for us to get to know the invisible God personally, He sent His Son, Jesus Christ. By looking at Jesus, we can discover what God is like, because

[Jesus] is the image of the invisible God (Colossians 1:15).

Just hours before His death, Jesus had a long talk with His disciples. And in the middle of that conversation, Jesus made a remarkable statement: "Anyone who has seen me has seen the Father" (John 14:9).

If God is invisible, then what did Jesus mean by that? Open your Bible to John 14:11 and find out right now!

▲ TAKE A STEP

When you see someone on television, you are really seeing only an image of that person. The real person is many miles away. But the image on TV shows you in detail what that person is like. In the same way, Jesus—God's Son—is God made visible, showing you what your heavenly Father is like.

Five-year-old Philip might have surprised his teacher by trying to draw a picture of God. But it really isn't that hard to know what God "looks" like. All you need to do is look at His Son, Jesus.

As a family, share some of the things you know about God. Then close your time together by reading again the words of John 14:1-3.

Q

What is God like?

A

God can be known by knowing His Son, Jesus.

L *eaving the mall, Shelly and her mom passed a group of people dressed in white robes and talking with passers-by.*

When they were in the car, Shelly turned to her mother and asked thoughtfully, "Mom, it's like those people are from another planet. They dress funny. They play different music. But you know, Mom, they are really sincere. Nobody would dress like that if they didn't think it was important. They seem to be just as sure about their beliefs as we are about ours. So how do we know that we're right and they're wrong?"

◆ **TAKE A LOOK / 1 Kings 18:21-40**

Shelly was asking a very important question: Is it enough to be sincere in what you believe?

If you sincerely believed that you were a cat, you would try to behave like a cat—climb trees, chase mice, and purr. But you would soon discover that believing you are a cat doesn't make you one! Misguided beliefs can never change facts.

The same is true about the God of the Bible. Wrong beliefs about this God do not change the facts about Him. And sincere beliefs in gods who do not exist cannot make them real either. This is seen in an Old Testament story. A group of 450 men sincerely believed in and prayed to a false god. The sincere beliefs of all 450 could not cause anything to happen because their god was not the real God. Elijah believed in and prayed to the one true and living God, the God of the Bible. Read 1 Kings 18:21-40 to see what his God did.

▲ **TAKE A STEP**

Only the God of the Bible—the invisible God who made Himself visible in His creation and knowable in His Son, Jesus Christ—has the right to say:

"I am the LORD, and there is no other" (Isaiah 45:18).

We know our God is the real God because He has done what no other "god" could do! He created the world (Genesis 1:1) . . . He sent fire from heaven to burn up Elijah's sacrifice (1 Kings 18:38) . . . He raised His Son, Jesus, from the dead (Romans 8:11).

Shelly was impressed with the sincerity of people who didn't believe in the God of the Bible. What is even more important than sincerity if you really want to know the one true God?

Are you sincere, or sincerely wrong?

Q

How do I know my God is the real one?

A

God has shown Himself to be real by what He has said and done.

PARENT: *Discuss with your child other events from the Bible and his or her own life which point to the existence of God.*

JUSTICE

*H*ave you ever been . . .
- *punished for something your brother or sister did?*
- *charged with a foul by a referee when you knew you didn't commit one?*
- *given an A on a paper that really deserved a C?*
- *stopped by the police for driving too fast?*
- *sent to your room for doing something you knew you shouldn't?*

If so, then you've experienced justice (or its opposite, injustice) first-hand. Hardly a day passes without justice touching your life in many ways.

◆ THINKING ABOUT JUSTICE

But what is justice? Simply put, it is **fair treatment**. Justice is a big concept, so let's divide it into four parts. Justice involves:

1. Rules: the laws you must obey.
2. Referees: the ones who make sure the laws are obeyed.
3. Rulings: decisions on whether the laws have been obeyed.
4. Rewards: the good things that happen when you keep the laws, and the bad things that happen when you break them.

Justice is not only important to referees, parents, policemen, and principals; it is important to you. Why? Because God has commanded you to practice it. Have someone read Micah 6:8 out loud:

"You wouldn't punish a guy for making a hole in one, would you Dad?"

● KEY VERSE ON JUSTICE

And what does the LORD require of you? To act justly and to love mercy and to walk humbly with your God (Micah 6:8).

▲ LOOKING AHEAD

This week we'll meet some Bible characters who wrestled with situations involving justice and injustice. We'll see that God has answers to questions you may be asking.

A famous statue that represents "justice" is a blindfolded woman holding measuring scales. Why do you suppose she has a blindfold? What do the scales tell you about justice?

*I*t's okay. Everyone does it. And besides, no one will ever find out. Go ahead, take it," Reg's friend urged.

"But it's wrong to steal, isn't it? I mean, they lock people up for shoplifting, don't they?" Reg said.

"Only if you're dumb enough to get caught. You want it, don't you? Then take it. They'll never miss one little thing."

Finally, convinced that it was all right because everyone did it . . . and no one would find out about it . . . and the store wouldn't miss it . . . young Reg slipped the item from the shelf to his pocket and walked quickly out of the store.

But the feeling of relief that it was all so simple was shattered by a matter-of-fact voice: "Stop right there, please, and empty your pockets. . . ."

◆ TAKE A LOOK / Exodus 20:1-17

Rules and laws tell us what is right and wrong, good and bad, acceptable and unacceptable behavior. Families need rules; schools need rules; games need rules; cities and nations need rules. They are an essential part of "justice for all."

Laws made by human beings are not perfect, because the people making the laws are not perfect. But laws made by God are perfectly fair because God is perfectly just.

God's laws are written in the Bible. When we read them, we discover what is just and how we should treat others.

The most famous list of rules ever given is found in Exodus 20:1-17. This list is often called the "Ten Commandments." Turn in your Bible and read them right now. Watch for the one that promises a reward for obeying it.

▲ TAKE A STEP

Can you say for sure, "This is right . . . and this is wrong"? You can if you are using God's unchanging rule book, the Bible. Styles will change, fads will change, but there are two things that never will: God and His Word.

The grass withers and the flowers fall, but the word of our God stands forever (Isaiah 40:8).

Not everyone agrees with or obeys God's rules (remember Reg's friend in the department store?). So it is important that you listen to the right voice when you ask, "Is this right . . . or wrong?" If you were Reg and your friend was urging you to shoplift, what would you have done? Which one of the Ten Commandments tells you the right thing to do?

God has the rule book to the game of life

Q

How can I know what is right and wrong?

A

Justice as explained in the Bible is God's standard of right and wrong.

If God loves me, why am I in the pits?

Working intently on her test paper, Rosa didn't see the look on her friend Sabrina's face.

It was a look of panic—the kind you have when you realize that you forgot there was going to be a test today!

Finally in desperation, Sabrina scrawled a note on a piece of paper, folded it up, and slipped it on Rosa's desk. Rosa frowned, shook her head no, and started to hand the paper back.

Just then the teacher's stern voice interrupted: "I'll take that." Unfolding the note, the teacher read, "What's the answer to #2?"

"I'm surprised at you, Rosa and Sabrina, cheating like that. Both of you get an F on the test, and will stay after school."

◆ TAKE A LOOK / Genesis 39:1-2, 6-21

How should I respond when I'm treated unfairly?

Poor Rosa. She tried to do what was right, and it turned out all wrong. Has that ever happened to you? Take it from a teenager named Joseph, Rosa's experience is not unique. In the very first book of the Bible you'll find his story.

Born into a family of twelve sons (he was number eleven), Joseph became his father's favorite, a fact that was a secret to no one. Do you remember why? His father gave him a beautiful, full-length, multicolored coat to wear as the sign that he was "number one" with Dad!

And on top of that, Joseph himself dreamed that his brothers bowed down to him! "Let's get rid of this dreamer once and for all," his brothers may have said as they threw Joseph into a pit. Then, seeing a passing caravan, they sold him into slavery, and Joseph became the slave of an Egyptian named Potiphar. But the worst injustice was yet to come! Find Genesis 39:1-2, 6-21, and read about it right now.

Justice demands that I trust God and not try to get even.

▲ TAKE A STEP

How did Joseph respond to such injustice? The same way God wants you to respond: by trusting that your heavenly Father knows best and then leaving revenge with Him. Years later, when Joseph had become the prime minister in Egypt and had power over his brothers, he still refused to even the score. He said:

"You intended to harm me, but God intended it for good" (Genesis 50:20).

What would your attitude be if you were Rosa staying after school? What would you tell Sabrina during those after-school hours together?

*F*urious at the player who kept running the plays wrong during the last practice before the biggest game of the year, the football coach called him over to the sidelines.

"I'll teach you a lesson you'll never forget," he bellowed. "Stand there and put your hands on your head. And don't move."

Then turning to his biggest lineman, he thundered an order: "Ram him right in the middle 10 times. That'll teach him to run the plays right!"

All the team members, including the lineman, knew this "lesson" was not only wrong but very dangerous. Their friend could really be hurt. What could they do? What should the lineman do?

◆ TAKE A LOOK / 1 Samuel 19:1-7

You won't find football in the Bible, but you will find examples of people who were called upon to take a stand for what they knew was right.

Jonathan, the son of Israel's first king, had a friend named David (the same young shepherd who killed the giant Goliath). Normally, Jonathan would have been next in line to become king. But God made it clear that David, not Jonathan, would be the next ruler of Israel. And for that reason, Jonathan's father, King Saul, became very angry— angry enough to want to kill David.

Jonathan knew that his father was being unfair. He knew David had done nothing wrong. But if Jonathan stood up for David, his father might become angry with him. To find out what Jonathan did, turn to 1 Samuel 19:1-7 and read about it right now.

▲ TAKE A STEP

Because of sin, we've all "missed plays" in the game of life. God's punishment for that sin is just and fair—not like the anger of King Saul or the football coach. And Jesus Christ, God's Son, experienced unjust treatment willingly, allowing His hands and feet to be nailed to a cross in order to give you the power to stand up for what's right.

"Stop doing wrong, learn to do right!
Seek justice, encourage the oppressed"
(Isaiah 1:16-17).

Think back to the story about the football player. His teammates faced a challenge much like Jonathan's. They could either do nothing and see their friend suffer unjustly, or do something and perhaps suffer unjustly themselves. If you were the lineman, what would you have done?

Life may not be fair, but God is always there

Q

What should I do when I see others treated unfairly?

A

Justice demands that I help those who are mistreated.

PARENT:
As you discuss this situation, lead your child to think of broader situations where injustice occurs and where your family might take a stand.

Don't confuse me with the facts; my mind is made up!

I'm so mad! Justin knew he would ruin my bicycle if he rode it before I got the gear fixed. And he didn't even tell me he broke it. Well, I'll fix him . . . "

Enraged, Jeff sprinted to his brother's room and dumped the contents of Justin's closet and dresser drawers in the middle of the bedroom floor.

A short time later, Jeff's mother called to him. "Jeff, I nearly forgot. I accidentally hit your bike with the car door this morning and something on it broke. I'm really sorry. I'll see that it gets fixed this weekend. Okay?"

Just then Justin came running into the kitchen. "Who's the turkey who messed up my room?"

◆ TAKE A LOOK / 1 Kings 3:23-28

Jeff thought he understood what had happened to his bicycle. He knew who the culprit was—at least he thought he did. And because he was wrong, his brother suffered unjustly.

What was Jeff's problem? He needed someone who knew all the circumstances and could tell him what really happened to his damaged bike.

King Solomon of Israel was a judge like that. He was loved by his countrymen "because they saw that he had wisdom from God to administer justice" (1 Kings 3:28).

Two mothers came to Solomon, both claiming that a certain baby was theirs. Clearly one was right; the other was lying. But how could Solomon tell which was which? Read about the king's wise decision in 1 Kings 3:23-28.

▲ TAKE A STEP

It's always easier to jump to conclusions than to dig for the facts, but you'll seldom do justice that way!

Appearance alone can be deceiving. Even Jesus commanded His followers:

"Stop judging by mere appearances, and make a right judgment" (John 7:24).

If Jeff had taken the time to ask his mother or brother instead of making up his mind ahead of time, the story probably would have had a far different ending.

How would it have ended? Let three members of your family pretend they are the members of Jeff's family: Jeff, Justin, and their mother. Retell the story, showing how Jeff should have reacted when he found his bicycle damaged.

WISDOM

"**C**ome on, make up your mind," Reid urged. "This is too good a deal to pass up!" Larry stared at the car Reid wanted to sell. He knew the price was fair, and he would need a car when he started working. But he was afraid that if he bought now he'd regret later. "Look, I'll give you until 8:00 to decide, okay?" Reid said as he walked away.

Larry had made a lot of decisions since he had started college, but so far this was the biggest . . . the most expensive. "I wish Dad was alive," he thought. "I wonder what he'd tell me to do."

As soon as those words came to mind, Larry knew what to do. His dad had always been a wise buyer. He compared prices and checked everything carefully. Larry had often heard him tell a salesman, "It doesn't pay to be too hasty. I'd like to sleep on it before I decide."

What do you think Larry should do? Why?

◆ LOOKING AT WISDOM

Over the years Larry had observed how his dad dealt with all kinds of family situations. So he knew how his father made decisions and what he based them on. Even though his father wasn't there, Larry could still see the situation through his father's eyes.

When you know God as Larry knew his father, your actions will be marked by God's wisdom. Wisdom is **responding to life's circumstances in God's way**.

Wisdom comes from knowing the difference between what's true and what's false . . . between good influences and bad . . . between God's ways and the world's ways.

Wisdom is a way of life. At every moment of every day you are acting either wisely or foolishly. Knowing how to act wisely is so important that God's Word says:

● KEY VERSE ON WISDOM:
Wisdom is supreme; therefore get wisdom (Proverbs 4:7).

▲ LOOKING AHEAD
To start your week on wisdom, have one person read Proverbs 30:24-28 aloud. What does each animal mentioned in that passage teach you about wisdom?

"And you thought I knew it all."

A fool follows his own nose to trouble!

Q

What's the difference between a wise person and a fool?

A

Wisdom is obeying God's Word; foolishness is doing things my own way.

*PARENT:
These verses will get you started:
Ephesians 5:22, 25; 6:4;
Colossians 3:18-21;
Matthew 5:44; 19:19;
Romans 13:9-10.*

"**Y**ou don't really have a reason for not letting me go to the game—you just don't want me to have any fun!" Abby shouted.

"Abby Wilson," her mother said sternly, "I don't want to hear one more word. I explained why your father and I will not let you go to the game tonight. We don't owe you any further explanation. So there's no need to say anything else about it."

"But Mother," Abby whined, "everyone else will be there. It's embarrassing to be treated like a little kid! You're just being mean!" With that outburst, Abby stomped to her room and slammed the door loudly— not once, but twice!

Her mother followed right behind her. "Abby, I told you not to say anything else. Because of the way you have just acted, you won't be going to the next game either."

◆ **TAKE A LOOK / Matthew 7:24-27**

Solomon described wise and foolish people this way:

The wise in heart accept commands, but a chattering fool comes to ruin (Proverbs 10:8).

As important as obeying your parents is, it is even more important to hear and obey the commands of God our Father. In the Sermon on the Mount, Jesus taught His disciples how to live wisely in the world. Jesus ended His message with a parable which clearly answers our question for today: What's the difference between a wise man and a fool? A big difference! Find out what it is by reading Matthew 7:24-27.

▲ **TAKE A STEP**

Building a house is serious business—you need to do it right. If the foundation isn't strong, the whole house might fall down! Building relationships is serious business, too. We need to know how to treat parents, neighbors, friends, spouses, children, and even enemies in the right way. And the most important relationship we have is with God.

If we treat others as Abby treated her mother, those relationships will fall apart. But God's Word gives us a sure foundation for building proper relationships. Using a concordance (or from memory), find a verse that can help you in each of the relationships listed above. Which verses might especially help Abby in her relationship with her mother?

"Caroline should have gotten home before now," Mrs. Crockett said. "I wonder what—" The telephone's ring interrupted her.

Mr. Crockett answered. After a moment he said, "Now calm down, honey, stop crying. You did the right thing. Wait right there for me. I'll come get you."

"She's okay," Mr. Crockett said as he hung up, "but she's really scared. When she started walking home from LeAnn's house, she noticed a man following her. She walked down different streets, but he kept getting closer. She said she was praying the whole time, trusting God to keep her safe and help her do the right thing. She knew she shouldn't try to walk all the way home with him following, so she ran to her piano teacher's house on the way. That's where she called from, so I'll go get her. There may be nothing to it, but you never know. She did the wise thing—it's better to be safe than sorry."

◆ TAKE A LOOK / 1 Kings 3:4-14

When Caroline realized a strange man was following her, she had to decide what to do instantly. You may sometimes find yourself in a situation you hadn't expected. But whether you are dealing with a life-threatening circumstance or just daily routine, you're constantly faced with decisions. And to know what to do every time, you need wisdom.

When Solomon became king, he wanted to be as great as his father David. But his top priority was not to enlarge his kingdom or even please the people. Find out what Solomon wanted more than anything by reading 1 Kings 3:4-14.

▲ TAKE A STEP

Solomon knew he would face some tough decisions as king. He pleased the Lord by asking for wisdom so that he could rule God's people in the best way possible.

You may never be a king, but you will need wisdom throughout your life, too. King Solomon—whom God did bless with wisdom—later said this:

Wisdom is more precious than rubies, and nothing you desire can compare with her (Proverbs 8:11).

Wisdom is the opposite of trusting yourself. It is making decisions and following through with complete trust in God. How did Caroline show wisdom in the decisions she made? Share a situation (though perhaps not as dramatic as Caroline's) in which you needed wisdom.

It's worth more than all the gold in Fort Knox

Q

Why do I need wisdom?

A

Wisdom helps me make decisions that please God and show that I am trusting Him.

PARENT:
Since the book of Proverbs has 31 chapters, read one per day for a month.

Ask God for wisdom —it's the wise thing to do!

"*T*his thing is driving me crazy! Why did we even buy it?*" 13-year-old Warner said in disgust. For several hours he had been reading instruction books trying to learn a few basics about the family's new home computer. But nothing he read made sense to him. And now he was tired, irritable, and ready to quit.*

"Hey," his father assured him, "you're the one who really wanted the computer, remember? Anyway, Uncle John is coming over tomorrow to help us out. Computers are his business, so he'll have it up and running in no time."

A few days later when Warner's dad returned home from a trip, Warner was bubbling over with excitement. "After Uncle John helped me, it all began to fall into place. I could even understand the instruction manual! Come see what I can do!"

Q

How do I get wisdom?

◆ **TAKE A LOOK / James 1:5-8**

Even though Warner's computer came with complete instructions, it was still difficult to run . . . until Uncle John explained the words and showed him what to do.

People need both explanation and demonstration in order to learn a skill. And the more we use a skill, the better we become at it. The same is true with wisdom: The more we apply God's Word to everyday situations, the more our wisdom grows.

But how do God's children get wisdom in the first place? You'll find out by reading James 1:5-8.

A

Wisdom comes when I ask God for it, believing He will keep His promise to give it.

▲ **TAKE A STEP**

If any of you lacks wisdom, he should ask God, who gives generously to all without finding fault, and it will be given to him (James 1:5).

Many people feel they can solve their problems by themselves. But true wisdom is not found in ourselves; it comes from God.

The first step in getting wisdom is to recognize that we need it. The second step is to ask God for it. And the third step is to believe that God will keep His promise to give it.

When we take those steps, James says, God promises to give us the gift of wisdom generously. Not that He'll just zap you with wisdom—instead He will likely bring you through situations where your wisdom will grow as you obey Him.

What situation in your life needs a good dose of wisdom? As a family, ask God for His wisdom to deal with it. Then make a note to ask yourself in one week how God is answering your prayer.

"**M**om, what's wrong with Ellie?" 12-year-old Chad asked as he was clearing the dinner table. "Is she in trouble?"

"I don't think so," his mother replied. "Why do you ask?"

"It's just that she's not the same old Ellie," Chad replied. "She doesn't talk to me much, and she's staying in her room a lot more."

The next few days, Mrs. Dawson observed Ellie closely. Soon she realized Chad was right.

About a week later, Mrs. Dawson found some tapes while she was cleaning Ellie's room. They were by a rock singer Ellie wasn't allowed to listen to, and belonged to a girl she wasn't allowed to visit. Right away Mrs. Dawson realized why Ellie had been feeling unhappy. What do you think the reason was?

◆ TAKE A LOOK / Colossians 1:9-14

Chad was sensitive to his sister's unhappiness. And Mrs. Dawson discovered why Ellie was unhappy: She felt guilty because of her disobedience.

Being aware of the problems of others is one result of wisdom. Another kind of sensitivity that wisdom produces is the ability to recognize evil. And when we do that, we can keep from falling into the traps Satan likes to set.

A wise man fears the LORD and shuns evil,
but a fool is hotheaded and reckless
(Proverbs 14:16).

The most wonderful result of wisdom is described by Paul in Colossians 1:9-14. Read the passage aloud, and after you hear the words "please him in every way," listen for four words ending in –ing which describe the life that does just that.

▲ TAKE A STEP

Paul teaches that when your life is full of wisdom, four things will happen:

• Your actions please God ("bearing fruit" in good works.)

• Your goals focus on God ("growing in the knowledge of God").

• Your strength comes from God ("being strengthened with all power . . . so that you may have great endurance").

• Your attitudes honor God ("giving thanks to the Father").

Think about your life in terms of your actions, goals, strength, and attitudes. Does wisdom fill your life? If not, why not talk to God about it right now!

When you're living unwisely —wise up!

Q

How will having wisdom affect my life?

A

Wisdom affects my actions, goals, strength, and attitudes.

PARENT:
Learn to respond to your child's requests by asking, "Is that a wise thing to do?" It opens discussions and helps your child learn wise decision making.

ORDERLINESS

*H*ere's a list of instructions from traffic signs you often see on streets and highways. What do you think each one means?
Slower Traffic Keep Right.
One Way. Do Not Enter.
Yield Right of Way.
4-Way Stop.
Now read these school rules. Do they sound familiar to you?
Raise your hand to be recognized.
No running in the halls.
Library—quiet, please.
No food or drink outside the cafeteria.
How are the traffic rules and the school rules alike?

◆ **THINKING ABOUT ORDERLINESS**
At first glance, traffic signs and school rules might not seem to have much in common. But both kinds of rules do the same thing: They help people act in a safe and orderly way.

You may be more concerned about safety than about orderliness . . . at least until Mom tells you to straighten your room! But orderliness—**doing things in a well-organized, systematic way**—affects every area of your life. When you wake up in the morning, you expect the sun to rise. School begins and ends at regular times. Your favorite TV show comes on at a certain hour. Obviously, your life follows a schedule whether you realize it or not.

Our God is a God of order. And He wants us to know that . . .

"None of the other things had instructions."

● **KEY VERSE ON ORDERLINESS**
Everything should be done in a fitting and orderly way (1 Corinthians 14:40).

▲ **LOOKING AHEAD**
Orderliness in our lives honors our orderly God. Proverbs 24:30-34 describes a disorderly vineyard. What words describe the man who owned the field? Would you want anyone to describe your life that way?

I know that chart I drew is here someplace," Cliff muttered as the pile of papers on his desk slid in all directions.

Storming over to his dresser, he rummaged through the drawers, showering clothes onto the floor.

Just then his older brother Shelby came to the door. "Hey Cliff, where's that knife I loaned you? I need it to finish my shop project. It's due tomorrow."

"I don't have time to look for it," Cliff exclaimed. But then he saw the look in Shelby's eyes. "Oh, all right!" he said, and began searching for the knife. Still he came up empty-handed.

"Well," Shelby said sarcastically, "if you want to live in a pigpen, that's okay. But you find that knife in 15 minutes or pay me for it so I can get another one before the hardware store closes."

Cliff slumped in his chair. "If I pay him today, I'll find his knife tomorrow. And if I draw my chart over, I'm sure to find the one I already did! Why do these things always happen to me?"

◆ **TAKE A LOOK / Exodus 18:12-19, 24-26**

Cliff's lack of orderliness caused him a lot of frustration. He couldn't keep up with his school-work, he misplaced items he needed, and his room was so untidy he didn't even like being in it! Worst of all, he wasted a lot of time (and sometimes money) looking for and replacing what he had mislaid.

As the leader of three million people, there were times when Moses, like Cliff, was the victim of his own disorder. With so many demands on his time, Moses needed to learn how to be efficient—to spend his time wisely. Read "The Simple Solution to a Million Problems" in Exodus 18:12-19 and 24-26 to find out what he did.

▲ **TAKE A STEP**

You may not be the leader of millions, but—like Moses—your life may sometimes seem like a whirlwind of activity. Unless your life is efficient, neat, and orderly in all areas, the same criticism might be made of you as was made of Moses:

"You and these people who come to you will only wear yourselves out. The work is too heavy for you; you cannot handle it alone" (Exodus 18:18).

Moses took the advice his father-in-law gave him and organized his work. In light of that, what advice would you give Cliff about making his life more orderly?

I'll straighten my room —as soon as I can find it!

Q

How does orderliness affect my life?

A

Orderliness helps me to spend my time wisely and not get frustrated.

PARENT:
Encourage your children to make time for devotions in their daily routines in addition to your devotional time together.

The longest journey begins with just one step

"*T*hose hours I spent in the library sure paid off,*" Wayne thought as he flipped through a thick stack of notecards. The topic of oceanography was so fascinating that he had actually enjoyed doing the research, making note cards, and writing his rough draft. Now Wayne knew he could easily finish typing the last four pages . . . and still get a good night's sleep!

Around the corner from Wayne's house, his friend Earl was working on the same assignment. He was feverishly scribbling notes on cards when he glanced anxiously at his watch. "They never give you enough time to do these papers," he muttered. "I'll try to finish going through these books by 10:00; then I can write the bibliography. I'll just skip the rough draft. But then . . . " Earl took a deep breath, "I'll have to type the final. Ohhh . . . it looks like another 'all-nighter'!"

◆ TAKE A LOOK / Matthew 28:18-20; Acts 1:8

While Wayne had an orderly method for finishing his assignment, Earl put it off until the last minute. As you might imagine, Wayne made an A on his term paper; Earl barely passed.

Whether you break a big job down into small steps, or combine several small jobs together, orderliness has a lot to do with how much you accomplish every day.

When Jesus was ready to return to heaven after His resurrection, He left His disciples with a major assignment. Read Matthew 28:18-20 to find out what it was. Then turn to Acts 1:8 and see if you can discover how that big job was to be broken down into small steps.

▲ TAKE A STEP

"You will be my witnesses in Jerusalem, and in all Judea and Samaria, and to the ends of the earth" (Acts 1:8).

The disciples had a big job. To accomplish it, they relied on the Holy Spirit's power, followed God's orderly plan, and did the work step by step. And the result? A changed world.

The job the disciples started continues today. Find Jerusalem, Judea, and Samaria on a map in the back of a Bible, and think about how they relate to each other. What would your Jerusalem, Judea, and Samaria be? What can you do to reach the "ends of the earth"? Close your time together by discussing how your family can have an impact for Christ on the world—all the way from your own backyard to the ends of the earth.

Q

Why is orderliness often so hard to achieve?

A

Orderliness requires careful planning and hard work in the strength God gives.

---

*A*s she did nearly every afternoon when the bell rang, Joanna shot out of the classroom, hurried to the locker room, and was soon whirling on the parallel bars in the gym. It wasn't until practice was halfway over that Joanna missed two other gymnasts. "Wonder where Margo and Emma are," she said to a girl nearby. "It's not like them to forget practice."

"Oh, they're in the Honor Society, and this is the afternoon they tutor younger kids in the school cafeteria," the other girl replied. "Hey, I thought you were in the Honor Society, Joanna. Why aren't you there?"

Joanna slapped her hand to her forehead. "Oh no! I forgot all about it! I didn't mark it on my calendar. Maybe my student didn't show up." But when she rushed into the cafeteria five minutes later, Joanna spotted her student instantly—a little girl sitting alone with tears in her eyes.

◆ TAKE A LOOK / 2 Timothy 4:9-22

It's easy to forget the little things, as Joanna discovered. But little things to us can be big things to others. Since our lives affect people around us, we should keep them in order.

The apostle Paul set an example for us in many areas of life. He was a powerful teacher and a dedicated missionary. Inspired by the Holy Spirit, Paul set forth God's truth in ways everyone could understand. How did he accomplish so much? One reason is that orderliness marked every aspect of his life and ministry.

Paul's New Testament letters contain many clues which reveal that he was an orderly man. As you read 2 Timothy 4:9-22—the closing verses of a letter to his young friend Timothy—think of some of the ways Paul's orderly life affected those around him.

▲ TAKE A STEP

Paul's orderliness helped him keep up with the people who were important to him. In your busy life, orderliness—or the lack of it—will also affect those you love.

Take time now to mark your family calendar for special times of enjoyment with people who are important to you. Record birthdays and other important dates. Be prompt in sending them cards and letters. Orderliness in those areas of your life tells others loud and clear:

My love to all of you in Christ Jesus
(1 Corinthians 16:24).

An orderly life says, "I care about you!"

Q

How does orderliness in my life affect others?

A

Orderliness helps me minister to others better.

PARENT:
Winter is a good time to help your child organize his or her closet and drawers. Clothes and shoes no longer worn could be given to a charity.

In order to please God, it helps to be in order

Mrs. Fields and her daughter were leafing through last year's calendar, recording birthdays and anniversaries on the new calendar. "One of the new year's resolutions I made last month was to get this family organized," Mrs. Fields chuckled, "and I'm only now getting around to it!"

"Oh, Mom, do you remember that day?" Carla exclaimed as she pointed to a date last April. "I got all dressed up and left early for the school play. But the only person there was the janitor—the play wasn't until the next week! I had written it on the wrong date. And look at all those orthodontist appointments I had. It was worth it, but I'm glad I don't have to go through that anymore! It seems like I spent weeks in that office." Carla grinned, revealing her straight teeth.

"Well, you spend every day doing something somewhere, that's for sure," her mother replied. "And this calendar lets me know when and where. Don't forget: Filling in the blanks is your job. And you know the rule—"

"I know—'If it doesn't show, I don't go!'"

Q

How can I make my life more orderly?

A

Orderliness comes when I commit myself to doing things God's way.

◆ **TAKE A LOOK / 1 Corinthians 14:26, 33, 40**

Mrs. Fields knew that orderliness helped her household run smoothly. Whether it was a recital or a camping trip, each child scheduled all of his or her activities on the large kitchen calendar.

God Himself gave instructions on orderliness to His "family," the children of Israel. For example, during their wilderness wanderings, the 12 tribes were to camp in specific places around the tabernacle. Each time they broke camp to wander some more, they were to do so in a certain way. (If you have time, glance through Numbers 1 and 2 to find out how this worked.)

In New Testament times, God also gave the church instructions for orderly worship. Find out why by reading 1 Corinthians 14:26, 33 and 40.

▲ **TAKE A STEP**

The week's key verse teaches an important principle:

Everything should be done in a fitting and orderly way (1 Corinthians 14:40).

Orderliness benefits not only our worship but all of life. As you close this week's study, tell one another an area of your life in which you would like to become more orderly. Then let each person suggest one way that can happen—beginning today!

CREATION

Mom, could you please wash these clothes today? I need this yellow blouse tonight." Renee pointed to the garments piled on her bedroom floor.

"Sure will," Mrs. Palmer said casually, scooping the clothes into her arms. Suddenly the house echoed with her piercing scream. Renee turned and saw what caused the uproar—and she screamed too! "Daddy, Daddy, come here! Hurry!"

Mr. Palmer found his wide-eyed wife and daughter pointing excitedly at the pile of clothes Mrs. Palmer had dropped.

"There's an enormous spider in there!" Mrs. Palmer gasped. "I've never seen one like it. It's as big as a tarantula!"

Renee was horrified. "Where did it come from, Daddy? How did it get in my clothes? Oh, Mother, let's move out of this house!"

◆THINKING ABOUT CREATION

Where did the spider come from? Renee will never know because no one had seen it crawl into the pile of clothes. And it was an event that would never be repeated . . . she hoped!

From the beginning of time people have wondered where life came from and how the universe was made. The Creation of the universe is also an unrepeatable event; scientists simply can't recreate it in a laboratory for study. But unlike the mystery of the spider, the mystery of creation can be solved if we trust the one eye-witness to it—God Himself. He tells us about it in Genesis 1 and 2.

● KEY VERSE ON CREATION

In the beginning God created the heavens and the earth (Genesis 1:1).

▲ LOOKING AHEAD

The Bible is clear: The Creation was that **supernatural act by which God caused everything (except Himself) to exist.**

In Job 38:1-2 and 18 God asked Job some questions about creation. With all the modern scientific knowledge available today, do you think you could answer God better than Job did?

"I thought love made the whole world go round."

The original "once-in-a-lifetime event"

Who created the universe?

Creation of the universe and everything in it was done by our all-powerful God.

PARENT: *As you watch science programs on TV with your child, help him or her recognize the evolutionary basis many of these programs assume.*

How would you like to take a trip through space? Even if you never get to travel on a space shuttle, you're already on a most fantastic space flight—you're a passenger on Spaceship Earth!

Though we may not realize it, our planet is constantly moving through space. Each year it makes one complete journey around the sun. While it revolves around the sun, it also rotates one complete turn every 24 hours, giving us night and day, and keeping the temperature fairly constant. Our planet is always tipped 23 1/2 degrees on its axis toward the North Star, causing the seasons in each hemisphere. And year after year, this spaceship stays 93 million miles away from the sun, allowing just the right amount of energy for our planet to produce the food we need. If Spaceship Earth went closer to the sun, we would be scorched; if it moved further away, we would freeze!

◆**TAKE A LOOK / Psalm 94:8-11; Romans 1:20-22, 25**

Did all these perfect arrangements for our "spaceship" just happen? Or did someone intelligently plan them? Throughout history scientists have thought of many theories about how the universe began. But only recently have some claimed that the great design had no designer. Some scientists now claim that the universe just accidentally happened. But the design had a designer. God was there.

God says He is the Creator. Psalm 94:8-11 tells us what He thinks of those who deny that fact. After you've read those four verses, turn to Romans 1:20-22 and 25 for a New Testament description of those who refuse to believe that God is the Creator.

▲ **TAKE A STEP**

From time to time you may read books or magazine articles supporting the theory that the universe happened by chance. You may watch TV programs or films in school which present this idea as if it were true. But God says this about those who make such theories:

They exchanged the truth of God for a lie (Romans 1:25).

The beautiful design of the universe itself shows us that an all-powerful God created it, rules it, and guides it. Discuss as a family ways to support that truth in your reports for science classes at school. Reading books about science and creation from your church library or Christian bookstore will help to prepare you.

P eople have always been fascinated by the stars. Observatories have been built to keep track of them. Wise men have studied them. Astronomers have even tried to count them. In the second century the Greek astronomer Ptolemy figured there were 1,056 stars. In the sixteenth century (before the telescope was invented), Tycho Brahe counted 777, and Johannes Kepler found 1,005. They were all wrong!

Today astronomers still study the stars, but they no longer try to count them. Scientists now know that there are over 100 billion stars in our own galaxy alone—and there are probably millions of other galaxies like ours! So even in our computerized age, it is humanly impossible to count the stars.

◆ TAKE A LOOK / Isaiah 55:8-9; 40:21-26

Before telescopes were invented, astronomers counted only the stars they could see. They would have been astounded if someone had told them about the billions of stars our modern telescopes have discovered. Similarly, if the Bible had been filled with charts and graphs like those in science books, it wouldn't have made sense to the people who read it before those discoveries were made.

The Bible isn't a science book. Instead, it is God's message of His love for people of all ages. But when it includes a fact of history or science, we can count on it to be true.

Over the centuries many ideas have been thought up to explain creation. In ancient times people believed gods and goddesses helped in creation. More recently scientists have suggested other theories such as the big bang theory.

But not one fact has ever been discovered which contradicts God's statement that He created the universe. Find out why by reading Isaiah 55:8-9 and 40:21-26.

▲ TAKE A STEP

A scientist who did not believe in God once said: "I conjectured that our universe had its physical origin as a quantum fluctuation of some pre-existing true vacuum, or state of nothingness." Does that make much sense? Of course not. But the Bible clearly says:

The universe was formed at God's command, so that what is seen was not made out of what was visible (Hebrews 11:3).

Pretend that you meet a scientist who tells you that the universe began all by itself. What question would you most like to ask him?

Twinkle, twinkle little star, how I wonder ...

Q

Does the biblical account of the Creation agree with science?

A

Creation as presented in the Bible is supported by scientific facts but not by every scientific theory.

Rocks reveal the record of a really ravaging rain

Rod studied the rock-like object that looked like a large clam shell. "This isn't really a fossil," he said with a sneer.

"It is too," 10-year-old Hugh protested. "My dad took me to dig for fossils when we went to see Grandma in Mississippi."

"See, that proves it," Rod said loudly. "Your grandmother lives on a farm. How could a fossil seashell be so far from the ocean?"

"Well, my dad says after Noah's flood all that area was covered with water," Hugh replied. "These fossils were made before it finally drained out into the Gulf of Mexico."

"Now I know you're crazy," Rod mocked. "It rained 20-some days straight last summer, and it didn't come close to flooding the whole world. That Bible story about a flood can't be true . . . and I'll bet that's not a fossil either!"

Q

How has the world changed since the time of the Creation?

A

Creation was affected by the flood that God sent during the time of Noah.

◆**TAKE A LOOK / Genesis 7:11-12, 17-24**

Rod was surprised the next day when the teacher displayed Hugh's fossil and asked him to explain where he had found it. Fossils are the remains of plant and animal life found in coal and rock. They show that life on earth used to be very different. What caused the change? Some scientists say the change took millions and millions of years to complete. But the Bible tells of a catastrophe which could have caused the world to change quickly, even within a single year. Read Genesis 7:11-12 and 17-24 for a description of that catastrophe.

▲ **TAKE A STEP**

Rod was right—40 days of normal rain wouldn't come close to covering the whole earth. So where did all the water come from?

Genesis 1:6 tells us that when God created the world, the earth's atmosphere ("the expanse") separated water that was above it from water under it, on the surface. The earth may have been like a huge terrarium, encircled by a layer of water which no one could see. When God judged the earth,

All the springs of the great deep burst forth,
and the floodgates of the heavens were opened
(Genesis 7:11).

Books about the Flood are available at Christian bookstores and libraries. For adults and older children we recommend *The Early Earth* and *The World that Perished,* both by John C. Whitcomb. How would you explain the Genesis flood to Rod? Do a little research of your own!

I said no and I meant it," Edith stated firmly. "I didn't take all that time and trouble to risk having my project thrown in a dusty old closet somewhere after the scholastic fair is over. I want to make sure I get it back, and the best way to do that is not to send it in the first place."

"But Edie," her friend Miriam protested, "Mrs. Wilson said part of our grade depended on sending the projects to the fair. You'll get a lower grade in Latin if you take yours home now."

"I don't care. I'd rather have my grade lowered than lose it. I spent a lot of time making this Roman lamp, and I don't want anything to happen to it. I want to give it to my dad so he can keep it on his desk in the den. So if I can't get an A on it, a B+ will do just fine!"

◆ TAKE A LOOK / Matthew 6:25-34

Like Edith, you've probably been pretty proud of projects you've made for school or youth groups. You'd like everyone to be enthusiastic about the result. But usually you discover that your excitement is greater than theirs because you have a personal interest in your own creation.

In a far greater way, God has a personal interest in the universe He made. He has never stopped caring for His creation. The Bible tells us that . . .

All things were created by him and for him. He is before all things, and in him all things hold together (Colossians 1:16-17).

Knowing that God created all things and is even now holding them together gives us confidence that He loves and cares for us. You'll see this even more clearly as you read the words of Jesus in Matthew 6:25-34.

▲ TAKE A STEP

Scientists make new discoveries all the time. And the facts they're learning agree more and more with what the Bible says. That would be unlikely . . . unless the God who created the world and rules the universe also guided the writers of the Bible long ago.

The passage you just read shows God's care for His whole creation—from the flowers and the birds to you! Share something you've seen in nature which shows God's design and care. Can anyone think of a Bible verse or passage about God's care over His creation? (Try Psalm 104; Psalm 145:9; Matthew 5:45; and Acts 14:17).

He's got the whole world in His hands

Q

Why does it matter how the world was made?

A

Creation tells me that God loves and cares for me personally.

PARENT:
Encourage your child to praise God by calling attention to the designs of ordinary objects— snowflakes, apple cores, spider webs, even the human body.

LEADERSHIP

What we need to do now," Della said thoughtfully, "is to outline what we want to say tomorrow."

Della and some of her classmates had been working to improve the food in their school cafeteria. They felt the students would benefit if a salad bar were added. Two weeks ago Della had given each girl a task. One researched nutrition in the library; two others took a poll to find out how many students would use a salad bar; another found out how much a salad bar would cost; and Della had presented their findings to the principal. Their hard work had paid off. The principal asked them to present their plan to the school board.

"What if they won't agree?" one girl asked.

"I wouldn't worry," Della replied excitedly. "This is a good idea, and it can be done. But if they don't accept it, we'll just try again!"

◆ THINKING ABOUT LEADERSHIP

When more than two people work together on a project, one of them—like Della—usually emerges as the leader. Leadership is **the process of guiding people toward a common goal**. If the leadership is good, people work together enthusiastically to meet goals. But if the leadership is poor, people feel unhappy and the work suffers.

In one way or another, just about everyone is a leader—whether you're a parent, a big brother or sister, a student, or a member of a youth group. And God wants you to be the best leader you can—which takes godly obedience and hard work.

● KEY VERSE ON LEADERSHIP

If a man's gift is . . . leadership, let him govern diligently (Romans 12:8).

▲ LOOKING AHEAD

Leadership does not mean making others serve you. Instead, it is giving yourself in service to others.

Begin your study of leadership by following the instruction Paul gives in 1 Timothy 2:1-2.

"And in citizenship I got a C . . . for catalyst."

During the French and Indian War, an aide advised British General Braddock to let his soldiers hide behind trees and bushes as they fired on the enemy. Instead General Braddock chose to face the enemy in the open—only to see all but 30 of his soldiers shot when sharpshooters fired on them from the woods!

After that disastrous battle, the aide wrote his brother. He didn't criticize General Braddock, nor did he take credit for giving good advice that wasn't followed. Instead, he generously praised the courage of the troops. But later that aide—George Washington— followed his own advice, resulting again in the defeat of the British army during the American Revolution.

When the Continental Congress nominated Washington to be commander-in-chief of the American forces, he tried to talk his friends out of voting for him, and even left the room during the balloting. He accepted his election humbly, admitting he didn't feel equal to the command he'd been given. George Washington was truly a great leader and a humble man.

◆ **TAKE A LOOK / 1 Peter 5:1-7**
The Continental Congress recognized leadership qualities in George Washington which he did not see in himself. We know from the Bible that God has made great leaders of men who were murderers and cowards, young and old—people we would never consider to be leaders. But God sees beyond human strengths and weaknesses to the leadership potential in each person.

Peter, who had been trained under Jesus' leadership, listed qualities God seeks to develop in individuals who want to be leaders (or elders) in the church. As you read 1 Peter 5:1-7, find three qualities any leader should have.

▲ **TAKE A STEP**
A leader doesn't act like a dictator, ordering people around. Instead he sets an example of humility. His example to others comes when he follows the example of Jesus, whose words and actions taught that . . .

"Whoever wants to become great among you must be your servant; and whoever wants to be first must be slave of all" (Mark 10:43-44).

Whom would you like to lead? Think of a friend, relative, or fellow student in whose life you'd like to have an impact for God. Test your leadership potential by answering this question honestly: "Am I willing to be _____'s servant?"

To serve them all my days is what a leader prays

Q

What kind of leadership pleases God?

A

Leadership that pleases God involves being a humble servant to others.

Win or lose, I'll follow in His shoes

Facing a hail of deadly bullets, the Confederate troops were retreating—even running—from the Union army at Spotsylvania during the Civil War. But General Robert E. Lee, the Confederate commander, was determined to defend the position. Turning his horse Traveller toward the fierce conflict, he urged the men on. A captain blocked the way with his own horse. "You can't lead my men into battle," he protested. "Nobody can."

But Lee started forward again. The rain of bullets was so strong that even trees were toppled! "You'll be killed!" his men shouted as they held Traveller's bridle and turned him back.

"We must defend!" Lee replied.

Inspired by Lee's own determination and courage, the soldiers plunged once more into battle. Many were killed or wounded, but they successfully defended their position.

◆ TAKE A LOOK / John 13:3-5, 12-17; 1 Peter 5:5; 1 John 3:16, 18

General Lee's courageous leadership in victory and defeat made an impact in the lives of all who knew him. He motivated others through his strong character and personality. The men who served under his command felt privileged to have known him—even though they lost the war.

Only one person fills all the qualifications for a *perfect* leader: Jesus Christ. While on earth He trained His disciples to be the leaders of His church after His return to heaven.

Yesterday we learned that one mark of leadership is being a servant. Peter and John were present when Jesus demonstrated this truth by washing the disciples' feet. After you read John 13:3-5 and 12-17, read what those two men wrote later in 1 Peter 5:5 and 1 John 3:16 and 18. Do you think they learned the lesson of leadership?

▲ TAKE A STEP

The leadership of a courageous yet humble person in your life can benefit you as you learn from his or her example. Think of a leader you know, and describe that person in three words. Do words like *forceful, dynamic, creative,* and *courageous* come to mind? What about the important characteristic in 1 Peter 5:5:

Clothe yourselves with humility toward one another (1 Peter 5:5).

Talk about ways God might develop a humble spirit in your life.

Q

How does good leadership affect my life?

A

Leadership exercised by godly people benefits my life as I follow their example.

PARENT: How do the standards of your governmental leaders measure up to God's standards?

---

*A*fter escaping from slavery at age 29, Harriet Tubman could simply have stayed safely in Philadelphia. Instead, she rescued her entire family: her aging parents, six brothers, one sister—and her sister's family!

In 10 years, this modern Moses made 19 trips to the South to free other slaves. She dodged night patrols and man-hunting dogs to lead more than 300 slaves to freedom on the secret trails and unmarked roads which came to be known as the "Underground Railroad." As a result, she was wanted dead or alive, with a $12,000 reward offered for her capture.

Late in life Harriet declared: "On my underground railroad I never ran my train off the track and I never lost a passenger." And that took vision, courage, and a deep concern for others.

◆ **TAKE A LOOK** / Matthew 24:4-5; 1 Timothy 4:1-2; 1 John 4:1-6

A leader has a vision of something which must be done despite danger or hardships. Like Harriet Tubman, a leader must persuade people to accept the risks they may face as they follow. But not all causes are worthy, not all risks should be taken, and not all leaders are good.

God's Word warns us of leaders we shouldn't follow. As the time of Jesus' own return to earth draws closer, Satan will raise up leaders under his evil influence. You'll read three of these warnings in Matthew 24:4-5; 1 Timothy 4:1-2; and 1 John 4:1-6.

▲ **TAKE A STEP**

Jesus warned His disciples that some evil people will claim to be Christ. Paul cautioned Timothy about lying demons. John alerted believers about the spirit of antichrist opposing the true Christ.

Today, those who promote new religions, philosophies, scientific theories, and political views clamor for followers. We must be careful to find out who is behind these new ideas. Is it God or Satan?

This is how you can recognize the Spirit of God: Every spirit that acknowledges that Jesus Christ has come in the flesh is from God (1 John 4:2).

One way to test the spirits is to find out what kind of ideas are presented in the books you read, the music you hear, and the movies you see. Listen to a song or two on a rock radio station. What does their music say . . . and what would Jesus, Paul, and John urge you to do in response?

Before you follow, stop, look, and listen

How do I recognize a leader I should follow?

Leadership must be tested according to God's standard in the Bible.

You don't have to look like a leader to be one

Small and sickly, the orphaned son of slave parents spent his childhood in the lonely woods and fields of the Carver farm. Though he was slow to talk and received little early education, his one wish was to study growing things.

He had no desire to be a leader . . . and yet people follow in his footsteps even today.

George Washington Carver became one of the most honored scientists in America. The advanced degrees he earned could have brought huge payments for his work. Instead, he lived and worked at the small, struggling Tuskegee Institute in Alabama.

There, under his guidance, the peanut became a multimillion dollar crop which brought prosperity to the South. In his creative research he discovered how to make roads out of cotton, insulation from corn stalks, and paint from clay. The entire country profited from his work, yet he rarely cashed a salary check.

By inspiring others and giving glory to God, George Washington Carver was a true leader.

Q

Should I try to become a leader?

◆ **TAKE A LOOK / Nehemiah 1:4; 2:8; 6:11; 8:10**

George Washington Carver never commanded an army nor staged a protest. He didn't even make many speeches. But by his work and his life, he led his entire race to great heights of achievement. His vision of what people can do when they use the talents and gifts God has given them has inspired generations of people.

Like Carver, Nehemiah was an ex-slave. He too had qualities which inspired people to follow him to accomplish a great task. What leadership qualities do you find in these verses from the book of Nehemiah: 1:4; 2:8; 6:11; 8:10?

A

Leadership qualities should be developed in my life, even if I am never in a leadership position.

PARENT:
Your child might enjoy reading the fascinating and inspirational story of George Washington Carver.

▲ **TAKE A STEP**

Nehemiah was first of all a man of prayer. He made good plans, and he had great courage. He also knew how to inspire his followers; he was genuinely concerned about their welfare, and when they were discouraged or weary, he worked hard to raise their spirits. Nehemiah's own faith was so strong they could not help but believe him when he told them:

"The joy of the LORD is your strength"
(Nehemiah 8:10).

You might not pursue a leader's position, but you should develop a leader's character. Close your family time by having each person tell the quality in Nehemiah's life he or she would like most to develop. How can the whole family help that happen?

BEATITUDES

As he lay dying, the American millionaire Jay Gould said, "I suppose I am the most miserable man on earth."

Lord Beaconsfield, who enjoyed the privilege of a high position, wrote: "Youth is a mistake; manhood, a struggle; old age, a regret."

Having conquered the entire known world, Alexander the Great grieved because "there are no more worlds to conquer."

Voltaire, the French philosopher who did not believe in God, wrote: "I wish I had never been born."

A teenager who committed suicide left this note: "I don't have anything to live for. I know I will never be happy."

◆ THINKING ABOUT THE BEATITUDES

As these examples indicate, the world is full of people who search for happiness without finding it. They seek it through money, success, and fame . . . through pleasure, excitement, and power. "If only the hard times and the sad times would go away, I'd be happy"—or so some think. But time and again, people come to the end of their lives with empty hearts. Nothing gave them lasting joy.

This week we'll be reading from what is known as the Sermon on the Mount (Matthew 5–7). In that sermon Jesus presents life principles He wants His disciples to follow. Jesus began with nine sayings we call the Beatitudes (which means "blessings"). The Beatitudes are **truths which show how to find real happiness in life**. A verse at the end of Jesus' sermon summarizes the Beatitudes:

● KEY VERSE ON THE BEATITUDES

"Everyone who hears these words of mine and puts them into practice is like a wise man who built his house on the rock" *(Matthew 7:24).*

▲ LOOKING AHEAD

God-given happiness is based on the truths of the Beatitudes.

We won't study all of the Beatitudes this week, but if you read Matthew 5:3-12 aloud together each day, you should have them memorized by the weekend. Why not start now!

". . . and give us this day our daily bread, excluding the knuckle sandwich Eddie Whitcomb promised me . . ."

Does anybody practice what Jesus preached?

Q

Why did Jesus give the Beatitudes?

A

The Beatitudes tell me what to expect and how to act as a follower of Jesus.

PARENT:
Write each Beatitude on a sheet of paper. On the back, have family members draw a picture which reminds them of that verse. Put the sheets in order and let each "artist" explain his or her picture.

*I*t was unusual to have a new teacher take over in the middle of a semester, but Mr. Ellis's accident left no choice. Now the students sat wondering what their new teacher would be like. Would his teaching style be different? Would he use Mr. Ellis's lesson plans or make his own? Would his tests be hard or easy?

Then the door opened, and the new teacher entered with a big smile. He walked to the front of the room, opened his briefcase, and handed a stack of papers to the first person in each row.

"I'm Mr. Scott. This handout explains how our class will be conducted," he said as the papers were passed around. "When everyone has a copy, we'll read through it. I want you to know exactly what I expect from you and what you can expect from me. When we've gotten that straight, we'll get started on today's lesson. Okay? Okay!"

◆ TAKE A LOOK / Matthew 5:3-12

New situations are easier to handle once you know who's in charge and what to expect.

Early in His ministry Jesus chose a small band of disciples—12 men He would train in a special way. Many others listened to what He had to say. Like the teacher with his class, Jesus wanted His followers to know what was expected of them.

Imagine for a moment that you are sitting on that hillside as Jesus speaks. You feel proud to be a Jew—even though you are persecuted, mistreated, and severely taxed by the Romans who rule your country. You are sure that this Jesus is the Messiah, the promised Savior who will overthrow the Romans and set up God's kingdom. At last your nation will get even with those hated Romans, and everyone will be happy!

Eagerly you wait for Jesus to explain His plan of action, to make His "declaration of independence." Instead, you hear Jesus speak the words found in Matthew 5:3-12. (Read them now.) If you were that person listening, how would you feel?

▲ TAKE A STEP

"Any of you who does not give up everything he has cannot be my disciple" (Luke 14:33).

Jesus clearly explained the hardships His followers would face. Poverty, sadness, hunger, thirst, persecution—they're all experiences we try to avoid. But He said they would bring blessings. Now that you know these hardships can come into your life, plan together as a family how you will react when they do.

We can't let them get away with this, Anita," Glen said forcefully to his friend. "We've got to fight back."

"Don't worry, Glen," Anita replied calmly. "I know some of the girls are spreading lies about the Thursday-night Bible study we're having. But saying unkind things about them isn't the way to solve the problem."

"But what if the other kids actually believe their stories?" Glen protested. "They could ruin everything!"

Anita chewed her lip thoughtfully for a moment. "Glen, there's a song that says, 'Happiness is to know the Savior,/Living a life within His favor,/Having a change in my behavior,/Happiness is the Lord.' My behavior is supposed to be different because I'm living for the Lord and for His kingdom. That's why I won't let those girls upset me."

Glen shook his head. "Sounds to me like you're living in a dreamworld!"

◆ TAKE A LOOK
Matthew 5:3, 10; 13:24-30, 36-43
From the land of Narnia to the planet Tatooine, fantasy worlds abound in today's culture. Video games, books, movies, and television present imaginary worlds where life is not at all like reality. But when Anita said she was living for the Lord and for His kingdom, she wasn't talking about an imaginary world, but a spiritual reality— God ruling in the lives of His children on earth.

The word *kingdom* can refer to three things: (1) the land area a certain king rules; (2) the people under that king; and (3) the period of time that king rules. Read what Jesus said about the kingdom of heaven in Matthew 5:3, and 10 and Matthew 13:24-30 and 36-43. How do those three things relate to His kingdom?

▲ TAKE A STEP
"Blessed are the poor in spirit, for theirs is the kingdom of heaven" (Matthew 5:3).

Jesus the King cannot be seen yet with human eyes. Nor can His kingdom be found on a map. Even so, the kingdom of heaven is a real kingdom. It is made up of all who let Christ rule in their hearts and lives, all who know they can do nothing except trust God—for their salvation, their daily needs, and even life itself.

Now that you know what Anita meant when she said she was living for the Lord and for His kingdom of heaven, how do you think she could explain this idea to Glen?

The kingdom not found on any map

What is life like in the kingdom of heaven?

The Beatitudes teach me that living in the kingdom of heaven means letting God rule in my life.

PARENT: *Agree as a family on a reward for each one who can repeat the Beatitudes from memory this weekend.*

Are you living on full meals or just snacks?

I *'m starving!"* 10-year-old Darla announced, sniffing the spaghetti sauce simmering on the stove. *"When's supper?"*

"Not for another hour or so," Mrs. Sawyer replied. *"But you can have a snack. Would you like an apple, chesse and crackers, or a cup of boullion?"*

"Oh, yuck," Darla grimaced. *"I'd rather be hungry!"*

Half a world away, another 10-year-old stood quietly with the other children of her village, waiting for a dipper of mush to be poured into her wooden bowl. Her arms and legs looked like brittle sticks. Her belly was swollen, and her eyes seemed sunken in her head. The famine in her country had made food and water scarce. She would have eaten anything.

◆ TAKE A LOOK / Matthew 5:6; John 6:30-35

Most people in our country are like Darla. We have so much food that it's sometimes hard to choose what to eat. Few of us ever go to bed hungry—unless we're on a diet! And hardly anyone has suffered real thirst.

But during the time Jesus lived, the situation was different. People often didn't have enough food. Because they lived in a dry climate, they also knew what it was like to crave water.

Satisfying physical hunger and thirst is basic to life. Jesus used this idea to teach that true happiness comes only when you hunger and thirst for *righteousness*—when you want more than anything to be like Jesus. Read Matthew 5:6. Then read John 6:30-35 to help you understand what Jesus meant.

▲ TAKE A STEP

Righteousness means "rightness"—living in a godly way. When you accept Jesus as Savior, He forgives your sins and gives you His own righteousness so that you can stand clean and pure before a holy God. But as members of His kingdom, we are to hunger and thirst for righteousness daily. Living by His power and becoming more like Him bring true happiness. We must be . . .

Filled with the fruit of righteousness that comes through Jesus Christ—to the glory and praise of God (Philippians 1:11).

Calculate how many hours each day your family spends shopping for food, planning and preparing meals, eating, and cleaning the kitchen. Then figure how much time you spend daily preparing and "eating" spiritual food. How do the figures compare? Should you find more time for spiritual nourishment?

Q

What happens when I hunger and thirst after righteousness?

A

The Beatitudes teach me that when I seek after righteousness I become more like Jesus.

"**I** think I know who did this, Dad," Byron said as he and his father looked at his bent bicycle. "Lou and Ozzie got suspended from school for setting off the fire alarm, and they know I'm the one who turned them in. The principal said if anyone knew who did it, they should tell him—and I did. But if I'd known this would happen, I probably would have kept my mouth shut. Now I'll have to buy a new bike!"

"No, you did the right thing, son," his father assured him. "Pulling that one alarm disrupted the entire school. And if someone had really needed the fire department during that time, they might not have been able to respond quickly enough."

"Maybe so. But I bet Lou and Ozzie will still try to get even with me when they come back. I don't know if one little fire alarm is worth getting beat up over. What should I do?"

◆ TAKE A LOOK / Matthew 5:10-12

No one wants to suffer; we'd all rather be happy. But the Beatitudes tell us that the path of happiness sometimes leads in the direction of suffering for doing what's right. That's what Jesus meant when He said:

"Blessed are those who are persecuted because of righteousness, for theirs is the kingdom of heaven" (Matthew 5:10).

Like Lou and Ozzie, we may sometimes be punished because we've done wrong. But on other occasions, we—like Byron—suffer because we are persecuted for doing what's right. If that's the case, then we are promised God's blessing.

What does Matthew 5:10-12 tell us to do when we are persecuted for doing right?

▲ TAKE A STEP

Jesus never asks us to do anything that will be bad for us. But when somebody attacks us because we're obeying God, we need to remember that we're in good company—because the same thing happened to Isaiah, John the Baptist, Stephen, Peter, and many others in the Bible. Like them, we can stand firm in God's power, looking forward to the wonderful future we will have in heaven with Jesus. Because of that promise, we can rejoice and be happy!

Share a time when you were attacked for doing what was right. How did you feel? How did that experience strengthen your faith? After talking about it, close your family walk today by reciting the Beatitudes together.

I may be hurting, but I'm still happy!

How can I be happy when people mistreat me?

The Beatitudes teach that God will bless me if I suffer for doing right.

PARENT:
Look in your church library or local Christian bookstore for biographies of people who have been persecuted for their faith.

MEEKNESS

I don't understand why you're being so nice to her," Bridget
whispered to Hilary as they passed Jeannette in the hall. "Not after
what she said about you. If you'd tell your side of the story, everybody
would see that she's just being mean!"

"No, Bridget, I can't do that. I think everybody knows me well enough
to realize that Jeannette exaggerated about what happened."

"But Hilary, don't you want to get even for the trouble she's caused?
She lied about what happened that Saturday night, and her parents
believed every word she said. They wouldn't even listen to you."

"I know. But my parents believe me. That's the important thing. Really,
I feel sorry for Jeannette. The only person she's hurting by saying all those
things is herself—not me. So getting even just isn't the thing to do."

◆ THINKING ABOUT MEEKNESS

It's easy to think that someone who won't take revenge is a
weakling. But what kept Hilary from getting even with Jeannette
wasn't weakness; it was the little-known and often-misunderstood
character quality called meekness.

We don't often use the word *meekness*. But when the Bible was
written, it was well known that meekness meant **acting calmly
and gently with strength under control**. The King James Version
of the Bible says:

"If the meek are going to inherit this earth,
they're going to have to toughen up."

● KEY VERSE ON MEEKNESS
*Walk worthy of the
vocation wherewith
ye are called,
with all lowliness
and meekness
(Ephesians 4:1-2).*

▲ LOOKING AHEAD
Look up Ephesians
4:1-2 in a Bible trans-
lation other than the
King James Version.
What word do you find
that means the same as
meekness? Does that
word describe Hilary?
Does it describe you?

Warren looked at his handiwork and smiled. The stores, houses, and office buildings he had made were well designed, and he was proud. Yes—these building blocks were fun! Bounding downstairs, he called, "Mom, come see my city!"

"Let me turn this meat and I'll be right there!" she answered.

They climbed the steps together. Warren began to open the door to his room. "Okay, Mom. Close your eyes and—" He gasped sharply. Warren's magnificent city was now a huge pile of blocks! His two-year-old sister stood right in the middle of the rubble. Before his mother could stop him, Warren lunged at his sister. As she tried to run away, she tripped. Suddenly blood was streaming from a long gash on her forehead, and her screams filled the room.

◆ TAKE A LOOK / Genesis 13:1-2, 5-18

"Stand up for your rights . . . Go for all you can get . . . Don't take anything from anybody!"

That's what the world says. And that's how Warren felt.

Without stopping to think how he might hurt her, he was determined to make his little sister pay for what she had done. After all, it was his room and his building blocks, and he had spent his whole afternoon building his city!

All of us sometimes feel as Warren did. It's at moments like that when meekness shows up the most or doesn't show up at all! After you read about Abraham and Lot in Genesis 13:1-2 and 5-18, can you tell who was meek and who was selfish and aggressive?

▲ TAKE A STEP

Abraham had risked everything to leave his home in the city of Ur and move his family to an unknown area. And God had promised him the very land that his nephew Lot had chosen. Abraham had every "right" to be angry. He could have forced Lot to move. Instead, Abraham chose to be meek. And God chose to bless Abraham—not Lot.

The world seldom rewards meekness. But God always does! And God's reward is greater than anything this world can offer. Jesus taught this truth when He said:

"Blessed are the meek, for they will inherit the earth" (Matthew 5:5).

Maybe you've been in a situation like Warren's or Abraham's. Did you react like Warren or like Abraham? What will you do next time?

It's tough to be meek when your sister's a sneak

Why should I be meek?

Meekness is commanded and rewarded by God.

Meekness is easy when God's in control

Q

How do I know when I'm meek?

Meekness becomes part of my character when I let God control my life.

PARENT:
Are you meek while driving or standing in lines? Do your actions teach your child to be first in line, or first in serving others?

"Two bits, four bits, six bits, a dollar; all for Eastside stand up and holler!" Kitty bounced enthusiastically through the cheer, finishing with splits that brought applause and shouts.

She knew she had done her best. The air felt electric as the judges marked their ballots.

The winners were announced the next day in a school assembly. One by one, each girl chosen walked forward. Now the cheerleading squad was nearly complete. Kitty prayed silently, "Lord, I'll be so disappointed if I don't make it, but give me the strength to accept it. Help me to be truly glad for the others."

Then the principal took the microphone one last time.

"Now—the captain of our cheerleading squad—Kitty Douglas!"

Filled with joyful excitement, Kitty breathed another prayer: "Thank You, Father! I'll do my best cheer—this time for You."

◆ **TAKE A LOOK / Galatians 5:22-23; 1 Peter 3:4**

Did Kitty know she was being meek? Before we can answer, we need to understand more about meekness.

Meekness is one of the qualities God produces in the lives of people who put Him in control. Galatians 5:22-23 (in the King James Version) puts it this way:

The fruit of the Spirit is love, joy, peace, longsuffering [patience], gentleness, goodness, faith, meekness, temperance [self-control] (Galatians 5:22-23).

To find out what meekness means, read the same verses in another translation. Then look up 1 Peter 3:4 and see if you can find the word that means "meekness."

▲ **TAKE A STEP**

The basic meaning of meek is "gentle, tender, mild." In Bible times the word was used to describe soothing medicines, mild breezes, and gentle horses. Since medicines can be poisonous, breezes can become hurricanes, and horses can be dangerous, meekness really means being under control.

God wants you to put Him in control of your life, to trust Him in every circumstance, and to become more like Jesus.

Kitty might not have realized she was behaving meekly, but she was. Can you tell why? By the way, who's in control of your life?

"*L* ooks like I've got this election in the bag!" Harold boasted as he slapped Kurt on the back.

Both boys were running for class president. Kurt had carefully thought out his proposals and had offered creative ideas to help his class. But Harold was running mostly to boost himself.

Finally the results were in: Kurt lost by only a few votes. Later that day as Kurt was talking with a friend, Harold walked by and said with a smirk, "Looks like the best man won!"

Kurt smiled sincerely. "Congratulations, Mr. President."

After Harold walked off, Kurt's friend just looked at him. "How could you act like that? I felt like slugging him!"

"Well, Someone else's honor was at stake, not just my own. Besides, it seemed like the right thing to do."

◆ TAKE A LOOK / Matthew 26:36-44

Deep down, Harold knew that Kurt would have made a great class president. He was simply trying to provoke Kurt—who he knew was a Christian—to behave badly.

But as a Christian, Kurt wanted to please God. He didn't go around complaining about the election, charging that the voters were stupid for electing Harold. He accepted the outcome and sincerely congratulated the winner. That's meekness.

Jesus Himself is our example of meekness. When He was arrested, He could have called legions of angels to help Him. Instead He was willing to die in order that God's plan of salvation could be carried out. Matthew 26:36-44 records the prayer Jesus prayed before He was arrested. As you read it, see if you can find words that reveal the meekness of Jesus Christ.

▲ TAKE A STEP

"*Yet not as I will, but as you will*" (Matthew 26:39).

Jesus knew that only an attitude of submission to God's will would bring glory to His Father.

Meekness does not mean weakness. It means that, like Jesus, you are willing to be a peacemaker, forgiving others even if it costs you something. When you act in meekness, God can work through you in the lives of others. And that brings Him glory.

Do you know anybody like Harold? How did you respond to that person the last time you were together? With God's help, how will you respond the next time?

God can work through me to bring Him glory!

Q

What happens when I act meekly toward others?

Meekness on my part allows God to work through me to bring Him glory.

It's right to stand for what's right—right?

Why in the world would anyone ever name their kid 'Melba'?" Layne whispered loudly to Jacqueline. Their teacher had just introduced the new student, who stood up shyly. "I bet her middle name's 'Toast'! Isn't that a crummy name?" Both girls kept whispering, giggling, and staring at Melba.

That afternoon, Grace found Layne and Jacqueline in the locker room. "I think what you did this morning was awful. Melba may not have heard what you said, but she knew you were making fun of her. How would you feel if you were her? If you ever do anything like that again, you'll wish you hadn't!"

Both girls just stood there speechless. Grace was always so calm and quiet! And when anyone made fun of her, she never stood up for herself. What had gotten into her?

Q

Should I always be meek?

A

Meekness involves standing up for the rights of others— and that always pleases God.

PARENT:
If you know someone who models meekness, discuss that person's character and deeds with your child.

◆ **TAKE A LOOK / Exodus 32:19-20, 25-35**

Meekness was indeed one of Grace's character qualities. But meekness does not mean being a coward or letting other people get hurt. Instead, those who are meek will stand up for what's right —even though they might not fight for their own rights.

When you think of courageous Bible characters, perhaps Moses comes to mind. Moses challenged Pharaoh and the magicians of Egypt. He led the Israelites across the Red Sea.

No one has ever shown the mighty power or performed the awesome deeds that Moses did in the sight of all Israel (Deuteronomy 34:12).

But the Bible says that Moses was meek. In fact, he was the most humble man on earth (Numbers 12:3)! After Moses led the Israelites out of Egypt, he climbed Mount Sinai where God gave him the Ten Commandments. But he was gone so long that the people thought he was dead. They began to worship a golden calf instead of God. What do you think mild-mannered Moses did when he returned to find them disobeying God? Find out by reading Exodus 32:19-20 and 25-35.

▲ **TAKE A STEP**

Even in his anger, Moses was meek. He stood up for what was right, condemning the disobedient Israelites for worshiping idols.

God wants His children always to be meek but never to be weak. To do that, we must stand up for what His Word says is right. Moses did; Grace did; and so can you! Have you ever stood up for what's right? Was it easy? Will it be easier next time?

STRESS

• • • • • • *• • • • • • • •*

H *ave you ever told yourself (or heard someone else say):*
"I feel like I'm hanging by a thread."
"My nerves are frazzled."
"I think I've reached the breaking point."
"I need a way to let off steam."
"I'm so tired I could sleep for a week."
"Give me a break!"
"I'm burned out."
"I just can't take this anymore!"

◆ THINKING ABOUT STRESS

We may express it in different ways, but each of us—from the oldest to the youngest—experiences stress, **the mental and physical strain caused by the pressures of life**. Sometimes we hardly notice it; other times we really feel "under the pile." But in today's fast-paced world, stress is a part of everyone's life.

Different people handle stress in different ways. Some people cry; others scream. Some stuff themselves with food; others starve. Some take medication; others try meditation. Some run marathons; others run away. Some talk with friends; others talk to themselves. Some people seem to avoid the harmful effects of stress; others die from it.

But there is one way to deal with stress that's available for everyone. It's an invitation from God Himself to . . .

● KEY VERSE ON STRESS

Cast all your anxiety [stress] on him because he cares for you (1 Peter 5:7).

▲ LOOKING AHEAD

People have hundreds of ways to deal with stress. This week we'll learn God's way.

In Proverbs 17:22 you'll find one remedy for stress. What is it? This could happen in your family by laughing together at old family photo albums or watching some old home movies!

"Mother has nerves of steel, but even that's not strong enough."

Q

What
causes
stress?

A

Stress can
be caused
by circum-
stances,
people, sin,
or my own
feelings
about
myself.

PARENT:
Stress in a
child's life
may come
from the
parent's
expectations
for a child's
achievement.
Your child
might appre-
ciate an
opportunity
to discuss
the stress felt
at home.

Adam and Alaina Parsons sat alone on the sofa,
stunned by what had just happened. Their parents
had called them in to tell them that the company
Mr. Parsons worked for was going out of business. After
19 years their dad was out of work. When they got over
their initial shock, the family cried, hugged, and prayed
together.

"I can't believe it," Alaina said, wiping her eyes.
"Dad would have retired in a few years. What if he
can't get another job?"

"That's what worries me," Adam replied. "He's not
young anymore and he has diabetes. And besides that,
his job was so technical it might not be easy to find
another one like it."

"It scares me to death. My chest feels like
somebody's sitting on it. But think how Dad must feel!
And Adam, I know it sounds selfish, but what if we
can't go to college like we'd planned?"

◆ **TAKE A LOOK / Psalm 38:4-7, 9-12, 17-22**
Stress is easier to handle when we know its
cause. In Psalm 38:4-7, 9-12 and 17-22, David
mentions three causes of stress in life: circumstances, people, and sin.

According to these verses, what effects can
those three sources of stress have on us?

▲ **TAKE A STEP**
Like David, the Parsons family suffered from
stress caused by circumstances they couldn't
control. Job loss or transfer, deadlines, illness, and
exams are just a few of the stressful circumstances
you may experience. Thinking about fearful things
—like nuclear war or death—can also cause stress.

Other people can bring stress. Job disputes,
family squabbles, teasing playmates, and disagree-
able neighbors can cause strain in your life.

Another source of stress is your own uncon-
fessed sin. The wise writer of Proverbs knew that . . .
He who conceals his sins does not prosper, but
whoever confesses and renounces them finds
mercy (Proverbs 28:13).

A fourth source of stress, not mentioned in
Psalm 38, is inner concern about yourself. You
may worry about your looks, your intelligence,
your ability to succeed. When you put too much
pressure on yourself, stress results.

Can you think of a stressful situation in your
life caused by one or more of these four sources?
What are you doing about that stress?

*A*dam dropped his fork onto his plate with a loud clatter. "I refuse to eat one more bean! I'm sick of 'em."

"Just go hungry then," Mrs. Parsons snapped. "On our budget, you can't have steak every night." ("Not even once a month," she thought as she served herself a spoonful of mashed potatoes.)

Then she nervously cleared her throat and turned to her husband. "Well, Joe, how did your interviews go?"

Mr. Parsons shook his head. "One man said I was overqualified. The second said my skills were too specialized—"

"That's just what we need to hear," Alaina interrupted rudely. "More bad news!" Pushing her plate away, she left the table. In a moment her stereo was blaring loudly.

Mrs. Parsons sighed. "I'm worried about her. Lately she's been leaving more food than she's eating."

"Well, you're eating enough for you and her both, Mom," Adam blurted, pointing to his mother's full plate.

"Quiet, Adam," Mr. Parsons said as he slowly rose from his seat. "I can't eat; my stomach's upset." Mrs. Parsons looked at her husband, and a pang of anxiety shot through her. He seemed to have aged 10 years in the past few weeks.

◆ TAKE A LOOK / Psalm 102:1, 3-12, 17

Stress was taking its toll on the Parsons family. Mom, Dad, and Alaina were affected physically; Adam was grouchy.

Though the Bible uses words like *anxiety, distress,* and *trouble* to describe what we call "stress," the writers still recognized that it can cause physical harm. For example, Psalm 102 is the prayer of a man under great stress. As you read verses 1, 3-12 and 17, see if you can find descriptions of five ways stress can affect the body.

▲ TAKE A STEP

Stress lowers the body's defenses against illness. Stress-related problems account for two-thirds of all office visits to doctors. But the psalmist David knew the best way to deal with life's pressures.

In my distress I called to the LORD; I cried to my God for help. . . . My cry came before him, into his ears (Psalm 18:6).

What specific effects of stress did you see in each member of the Parsons family? When you're under a lot of stress, what usually happens to you? What "remedy" for stress would you suggest the Parsons family try?

I can't get sick— I've got too much to do!

Q

What happens to me when I'm under stress?

A

Stress can make me sick or grouchy if I try to handle it alone.

Safety valves for your pressure-cooker life

I didn't help matters at all last night," Alaina confessed to her family. "Please forgive me for the way I acted."

"I was pretty awful, too," Adam admitted. "I'm really sorry."

Mr. Parsons smiled as he rubbed Adam's back. "You know, we've got to build each other up, not attack one another. Remember, God is our main source of strength. He knows exactly what we're going through. Why don't we pray together?"

After each family member prayed, Mrs. Parsons spoke up: "I've got an idea! Let's have a picnic Saturday. You kids enjoyed the zoo when you were little, but we haven't been there for years."

"That'll be a kick!" Adam said. "The monkeys always did remind me of someone I know." He grinned at his sister.

Mr. Parsons leaned back in his chair. "I think I'll be inspired by the giraffes—they're always looking up!"

◆ TAKE A LOOK / Proverbs 4:20-27

Stress can result from tough trials. But most stress comes from everyday hassles. The kind of stress we experience is not nearly as important as the way we respond to it.

Hundreds of techniques can be used to deal with stress. Some may help, others may hurt. But for God's children, one of the most important ways to cope with stress is this:

Above all else, guard your heart, for it is the wellspring of life (Proverbs 4:23).

In stressful situations, you must be especially careful to guard against sin in your relationships with others. You'll learn more specifically how to do this when you read Proverbs 4:20-27.

▲ TAKE A STEP

Learn to recognize stress in your life. If your body tells you it's being pushed too hard, loosen up and pace yourself. Remember to sleep well, relax, exercise, and eat right. Don't become absorbed by the fantasy worlds of television, movies, or books. Instead, share your feelings honestly with people who will pray with you and encourage you.

Change what you can in your life to reduce stress; accept what you can't change. Cry a little; laugh a lot. But always "guard your heart"—be careful about your attitudes and your actions.

Compare the difference 24 hours made in the Parsons family's attitudes. How did they ease their stress by guarding their hearts?

Q

How can I reduce stress in my life?

A

Stress can be reduced if I guard my heart from sin in my attitudes and actions.

O *God, our help in ages past, / Our hope for years to come, / Our shelter from the stormy blast, / And our eternal home."*

Mr. Parsons felt his tense shoulders relax as he sang the familiar hymn. "God is in control," he reminded himself.

Beside him Mrs. Parsons prayed silently, thanking God for the food co-op she had been invited to join. What a help it would be in reducing food costs. Maybe she could even afford steak soon!

As Alaina turned to the Scripture reading for the day, a verse seemed to leap off the page: "Confess your sins to each other and pray for each other so that you may be healed" (James 5:16).

Silently she confessed feeling resentful that she could not buy a new dress for Easter. Last year's dress was perfectly good.

Adam basked in the sunshine filtering through the stained-glass windows. "God has made a beautiful world," he thought. "And it's so much fun, too; we had a blast at the zoo!"

◆ TAKE A LOOK
1 Corinthians 10:13; Romans 8:35-39

We have learned a lot about stress this week: what causes it, how to recognize it, and how to cope with it. We've also learned how to guard against sin in both our attitudes and our actions.

Now we're ready to learn two more important facts about stress, courtesy of Paul (an expert on stress management). So go on a fact-finding mission right now by reading 1 Corinthians 10:13 and Romans 8:35-39.

▲ TAKE A STEP

Did you find the two stress-busting facts Paul shared? (1) God will not bring anything into your life that He will not give you strength to bear. (2) Nothing can ever separate you from His love.

God is in control. Everything that comes into our lives is filtered through His hands with love. You may have some anxious moments or sorrowful tears, but if you look at life knowing God is working His purposes out, then . . .

The peace of God, which transcends all understanding, will guard your hearts and minds in Christ Jesus (Philippians 4:7).

As the Parsons family members sat in church, how do you think they showed that they believed these two crucial facts? Do you believe them? Could someone who knows you see that you do?

Let the peace of God stand guard over you

How can God help me handle stress?

A

If I rely on God's promised strength, stress will not overcome me or keep me from His love.

PARENT:
One way to reduce stress is to declare a "quiet hour" each night. Turn off all TVs, radios, and stereos. Use the time to talk or read.

PASSOVER

*W*hat would you think if you received this dinner invitation:
You are cordially invited to celebrate
Hag-ha-Pesach
with our family on the 14th day of Nisan.
Hametz will be cleared from our house
and the Seder prepared.
On that day we will fill ourselves with history
as we remember it with symbols.
Maror, haroset, zroah, beitzah, and karpas
will fill the plate.

◆ THINKING ABOUT PASSOVER

If you received an invitation like that, you might think you were in a foreign country! But if you were Jewish, you would know this is an invitation to celebrate Passover at a Seder (SAY-der) meal.

Passover is **an eight-day festival celebrated by Jewish people each spring**. They consider it their most important holiday because it reminds them of how God freed them from slavery in Egypt. For nearly 3,000 years, during times of joy and sorrow, the Jewish people have celebrated Passover in obedience to this command:

"I'll bet it was quite a media event when Moses parted the Red Sea."

● KEY VERSE ON PASSOVER

"On that day tell your son, 'I do this because of what the LORD did for me when I came out of Egypt'" (Exodus 13:8).

▲ LOOKING AHEAD

The highlight of the eight days of Passover is the Seder, an evening meal full of unusual foods and symbolic customs. This week we'll find out what Passover means to Jewish people and to Christians.

You'll understand Passover better when you see how it can remind Jews and Christians alike of the bitterness of slavery and the joy of freedom. To begin your study, read Exodus 1:6-16. How would you feel if you were set free from a situation like that? How would you celebrate?

We can't play our soccer game next Saturday," Clark told his dad after practice. "Three of our guys said it's the first day of Passover and they have to stay home. I know they're Jewish, but they've always played before on Saturdays."

"Well, you don't understand how important Passover is to Jewish families," Mr. Hodges explained. "For them, it's the most important holiday of the year. Some Jewish families spend quite a bit of time getting ready for the holiday, cleaning the house from top to bottom, planning the Seder, giving to the poor, and studying about the holiday. And you know what? For a Jewish person to miss the Seder would be like you missing Christmas!"

◆ TAKE A LOOK
Exodus 12:1, 3, 6-8, 11-15, 24-27
Passover is so important that preparing for it is as much a part of the celebration as the holiday itself. Some Jewish families do a thorough spring-cleaning, even changing shelf paper and cleaning closets. Their everyday dishes, silverware, and cooking utensils are put away and replaced by others used only during the eight days of Passover.

This thorough cleaning is important because, during Passover, Jews are not to eat—or even possess—a single crumb of hametz, or yeast. The evening before Passover begins, a final search for hametz is made. Find out how this search began by reading Exodus 12:1, 3, 6-8, 11-15, and 24-27.

▲ TAKE A STEP
While the angel of death killed the firstborn in every Egyptian home, he passed over the Israelite homes because lamb's blood was spread on their doorposts. This is what Passover means, and why it is so important to Jewish people. But Passover is important to Christians as well. Paul urged the Corinthians to . . .

Get rid of the old yeast that you may be a new batch without yeast—as you really are. For Christ, our Passover lamb, has been sacrificed (1 Corinthians 5:7).

Only the blood of Jesus Christ can permanently cleanse the "yeast" of sin from human lives. If He is your Savior, His blood is on the "doorposts" of your life; death cannot touch you. But is there any "yeast" in your life? Search your attitudes and actions now for sins to confess. Then pray together.

Hunt through your house for hametz!

Q

How do Jewish families prepare for Passover?

A

Passover—preceded by thorough cleansing—pictures Jesus as the Lamb who cleanses me from sin.

These natural foods tell a super-natural story

Clark followed his mother up and down the super-market aisles. Around one corner he spotted a special display.

"Hey, Mom—look!" Clark gestured. "See? The sign says 'Food for Passover.' " As they stopped at the display of kosher foods (foods prepared according to Jewish laws), Clark gazed with interest at the matzo meal, crushed almonds, matzo bread, and more. The packages were labeled in both English and Hebrew.

"David, a Jewish boy on my soccer team, was telling me about Passover at practice yesterday," Clark explained. "He told me about the great things his mom fixes for dinner. They eat things like matzo-ball soup. But he said the main meal isn't served until after the Seder plate is explained. It sounds really weird to me! What is a Seder plate anyway, Mom?"

◆ **TAKE A LOOK / Matthew 26:26-29**

Clark's Jewish friend had described his family's Seder meal, but it still seemed strange to Clark.

The first part of the meal is ceremonial. A decorated plate beside the leader's place holds five symbolic foods that are explained, tasted, or touched before the actual meal begins.

Maror, or bitter herbs, suggests the bitterness of slavery. Horseradish is often used for this. The mixture called haroset—made of chopped apples, nuts, cinnamon, and wine—represents the mortar used with bricks to build cities for Pharaoh. Karpas—fresh greens such as parsley, celery, or lettuce—are dipped in a bowl of salt water as a reminder of the tears shed by the Israelites. A roasted egg, the beitzah, symbolizes hope for new life or resurrection. Jewish people no longer kill a Passover lamb, but the shankbone of a lamb, the zroah, symbolizes the lamb whose blood was spread on the doorposts in Egypt.

Read Matthew 26:26-29 to find out how those who have been freed from sin's slavery can remember Christ, our Passover Lamb. What do we call this ceremony today?

▲ **TAKE A STEP**

When Jesus celebrated the Passover with His disciples, He explained how His body would be broken and His blood shed for the forgiveness of sins. If you have a Jewish friend, ask him how his family celebrates Passover. Then you can tell him about the Lord's Supper (also called Communion)!

Q

What do the foods eaten during a Seder mean?

A

Passover foods picture Israel's deliverance from slavery, just as the Lord's Supper pictures Christ's death for my sins.

M om, can we buy some?" Clark pointed to the box of matzo bread in the supermarket. "I want to know what it's really like."

That evening the Hodges family opened the box of matzo. What they found inside were square, flat wafers pierced with rows of tiny holes. The baking process had left brown stripes on them. They looked like crackers because there was no yeast in them.

"Yuk," Clark said after he ate one. "They're so tasteless! Why would anybody want to eat this stuff?"

◆ TAKE A LOOK / John 6:51

During the time of the Israelites' escape from Egypt, God commanded them to eat only unleavened bread:

"For seven days no yeast is to be found in your houses. . . . Wherever you live, you must eat unleavened bread" (Exodus 12:19-20).

The unleavened bread Jewish people eat today is called matzo. It's made by quickly mixing flour and water and then baking the mixture at a high temperature before any natural rising can begin.

Though it is eaten during the entire Passover period, matzo plays an important part in the Seder. Three pieces of matzo are wrapped in a special cloth that lies beside the Seder plate. At the beginning of the meal, the middle piece is broken, and half of it is hidden. At the end of the evening the children search for the hidden half, which represents the Passover lamb. The other half represents the bread of the poor that was eaten in Egypt. The leader begins the Seder ritual by holding this second half up and saying, "Let all who are hungry come and eat."

Though they continue to follow their customs, many Jewish people today do not really under-stand what the broken piece of matzo represents. Who is the "living bread"? Find out by reading John 6:51.

▲ TAKE A STEP

The broken matzo reminds us of Jesus, the Passover Lamb, the Bread of Life. He died (was broken) for humanity's sins, was buried (hidden), and rose again (was found).

Reread the description of matzo above. Then read Isaiah 53:5 and Zechariah 12:10 (in both the New International and King James versions if possible). How do the stripes and holes of matzo bread remind you of Jesus?

There's a lot of meaning packed into that cracker!

Q

Why is matzo bread used during this season?

A

Passover's broken piece of unleavened bread pictures Jesus, the Lamb of God who died and rose again.

You're invited to a super supper!

Q

Why is Passover important to Christians?

A

Passover looks back to Christ's death and looks ahead to His marriage supper in heaven.

PARENT: *During this season, many churches offer Passover meals, explaining how each part points to Christ.*

By now, Clark had learned a lot about the way his Jewish friends celebrated Passover. By reading library books about Passover, he learned that the whole celebration told the story of how God freed the Jewish people from slavery in Egypt. Every detail of the ritual seemed important. For instance, the leader sat on a cushion, because only a free person can be that relaxed.

Clark also liked the fact that the Seder ritual was begun each year not by an adult but by the youngest child in the family, who asked these questions: (1) Why is this night different from all other nights? (2) Why is matzo eaten rather than bread? (3) Why do we eat bitter herbs? (4) Why do we dip the parsley in salt water? (5) Why do we recline at the table instead of sitting straight in chairs? Clark learned the answers to those questions, but he also learned something about the Passover Lamb that his Jewish friends had not. He hoped he could someday tell them.

◆ TAKE A LOOK / Revelation 19:6-9

For Clark's Jewish friends, the Passover celebration was a reminder that they were once slaves to Pharaoh, but are now free by God's power. For Clark, it is a reminder that all people were once slaves to sin, and that it is only through the power of Jesus that they can be made free.

For Jewish people, the Passover Lamb reminds them of the blood that was shed so they could be rescued from slavery and death. For Christians, Jesus Christ is the perfect Lamb of God, who gave His blood to rescue us from the slavery of sin.

The Jews celebrate Passover in obedience to God's command and look back to a time when God freed them from slavery. But the Passover season reminds Christians to look forward to another wonderful supper with the Lamb of God. You can read a description of it in Revelation 19:6-9.

▲ TAKE A STEP

"Blessed are those who are invited to the wedding supper of the Lamb!" (Revelation 19:9).

Just as the Passover meal begins with the words, "Let all who are hungry come and eat," so too all are invited to the marriage supper of the Lamb. But you must accept that invitation before you can come! You can do that by trusting in Jesus, who died for you, confessing that He is the Lamb of God who takes away the sins of the world.

If you have never done so, tell God right now in a simple prayer that you believe Jesus died for your sins, and that you want to follow Him.

EASTER

*R*achel shivered as she heard the husky voices of the two strangers in the next room. Why were they here, in her house, talking to Father about that man Jesus—the one who was put to death on a cross yesterday?

Rumors had been flying for weeks. Some said Jesus had healed the sick; others reported that He had brought the dead back to life. A few were sure He was the Messiah that God had promised.

Everyone had an opinion about this Jesus . . . and about what would happen to Him. Even Grandmother Miriam, wagging her finger at Rachel's mother, had said, "You mark my words. No good will come of it. Those big-shot Pharisees always side with the Romans. And nobody can stand up to that crowd."

Grandmother was right. In the past few hours Jesus had been arrested, quickly tried, and then crucified. Yet Jesus had promised He would come to life on the third day. "I wonder if it's true?" Rachel thought. "Can anyone really come back from the dead?"

◆ THINKING ABOUT EASTER

About 2,000 years ago in a medium-sized city ruled by the mighty Romans, something happened that changed the world. And without TV newscasts or front-page headlines, nearly everyone heard the news that's summed up in these words:

● KEY VERSE ON EASTER

"He is not here; he has risen, just as he said" (Matthew 28:6).

▲ LOOKING AHEAD

The word *Easter* is **the name given to the celebration of Jesus' resurrection**. Through the eyes of Rachel and her family we'll think about that event.

Doctor Luke, who wrote about Jesus, wanted to get the story straight. After reading Luke 1:1-4, can you suggest ways he may have gathered the facts with the Holy Spirit's help?

"I'm playing a crowd member in the Easter pageant. I was going to play Pilate 'til I found out I'd have to wash my hands."

Dead men don't move great big boulders

*T*he chief priest asked Pilate to put guards at the tomb," Rachel heard her father say in the next room. "They're afraid somebody will steal the body, I guess."

"That sounds like something they'd do," Rachel's mother remarked sharply. "But don't they realize that Jesus' followers are all in hiding? The two you just talked with couldn't wait to get out of town for fear they'd be crucified next."

"Well, you can't deny that strange things have been happening," Father replied. "Jesus did perform miracles. And both the Jews and the Romans know He promised He would rise from the dead. If He does, it would prove that He is who He claimed to be. So they'll do anything to keep Him in that tomb!"

Rachel pulled her cloak around her ears. "This is scary," she thought. "Will He really come back to life?"

Q

Did Jesus really die?

A

Easter recalls the time when Jesus, God's Son, actually died on the cross.

PARENT:
A concise examination of the evidence for the Resurrection is found in The Ressurection Factor *by Josh McDowell.*

◆ **TAKE A LOOK / John 19:28-42**

Some scholars have claimed that Jesus didn't really die on the cross. They say He was only unconscious and revived when He was in the cool tomb. Even though He was seriously wounded, according to this theory, He moved the huge stone blocking the tomb's entrance and escaped.

But those who were there when it happened knew the truth. They knew a victim of Roman crucifixion could never escape with his life. They knew the mourners preparing the body for burial would notice any sign of life. They knew someone who had suffered as Jesus did would be too weak to unwrap the graveclothes, heavy with spices, much less move the stone weighing as much as two tons! Yes, they knew the truth: Jesus was *really* dead.

As you read John 19:28-42, see how many clues you can find that prove Jesus really died. Why is John's account worth believing?

▲ **TAKE A STEP**

If anyone knew how to put a condemned man to death—and to make sure he was dead—the Romans soldiers did. John, an eyewitness, tells us what they saw:

When they came to Jesus and found that he was already dead, they did not break his legs. Instead, one of the soldiers pierced Jesus' side with a spear (John 19:33-34).

Have one member of your family pretend to believe Jesus didn't really die. Use the evidence you've learned today to explain to that person that Jesus did die—for everyone's sins!

By now everyone in Jerusalem was talking about Jesus. Even Rachel's father, who always said that seeing is believing, was convinced Jesus had risen from the dead.

"But how do you know it's true, Father?" Rachel asked at supper. "Have you seen Him?"

"No, I haven't. But all the evidence tells me He's alive."

"What evidence, Father?"

"Well, think about it, Rachel. Both our Jewish leaders and the Romans knew Jesus said He would rise from the dead after three days. So they took special precautions to keep that from happening. They put a Roman seal on the tomb, and anyone caught breaking it would be put to death. Then they stationed a Roman guard unit at the tomb—16 specially trained soldiers who could lose their lives if they failed.

"But something happened. Everyone in Jerusalem knows that tomb is empty now. The graveclothes were found just lying there. I saw them myself. The Jewish leaders are saying the disciples stole the body, but nobody could have gotten by the guards—much less moved that stone—without being caught. And if the Jews had His body, they could show it to stop these rumors. But the best evidence is Jesus' followers. Three days ago they were in hiding. Now they're boldly telling everyone Jesus is risen. Only His resurrection could have caused that!"

◆ TAKE A LOOK
Matthew 27:62-66; 28:2-6, 11-15

It's a fact of history! Roman soldiers were guarding the tomb; an enormous stone was blocking its entrance; and yet the tomb was found empty! If the women had gone to the wrong tomb, the Jewish leaders could have found His body in the right tomb, and the uproar would have soon settled down. But even the Jewish leaders knew the tomb was empty. Read their version of "The Mystery of the Empty Tomb" in Matthew 27:62-66 and 28:2-6 and 11-15.

▲ TAKE A STEP

With great power, God raised Jesus from death. As proof, the angel invited the women to . . .

"*Come and see the place where he lay*" (Matthew 28:6).

Anyone in Jerusalem could have taken a short walk to see the empty tomb. Pretend you were a friend of Rachel's living in Jerusalem. Would you have wanted to see the empty tomb? What would it have meant to you?

The empty tomb opens the door to life

Q

Why is the empty tomb so important?

A

Easter celebrates the fact that Jesus' tomb is empty because He rose from the dead.

The evidence calls for a verdict of "Alive!"

Father! What they're saying about Jesus is true!" Rachel yelled as she ran into the house. "My friend Rebekah told me her uncle saw Jesus alive!"

"You're right, Rachel," her father replied. "One of my closest friends has seen Jesus. It seems everyone knows someone who has seen Him alive again. It's clear to me: Jesus is the Messiah that God promised His people."

"I believe it too, Father. Mother said Jesus' resurrection is the greatest miracle ever."

"Yes, it is. And no one, Jew or Roman, can prove otherwise. Even the leaders know something unique has happened. Reports are coming from everywhere of people seeing Jesus alive. Who could deny the testimony of so many witnesses?"

How do we know the Resurrection really happened?

A

Easter celebrates the resurrection of Jesus because it is a fact of history.

PARENT:
In Acts 12:4 in the King James Version the word "Easter" refers to the Passover celebration.

◆ **TAKE A LOOK / 1 Corinthians 15:3-8**
Criminals are caught and sent to jail because of evidence, not merely opinion. Physical evidence collected at the scene of the crime, along with the testimony of witnesses, is used at the trial to prove what really happened.

The resurrection of Jesus Christ can also be proved on the basis of evidence. The empty tomb, the graveclothes no longer wrapped around a body, the large stone rolled away in spite of the Roman guards, the broken Roman seal—all of that evidence and more points to the truth of Jesus' resurrection.

But in addition to the physical evidence for the Resurrection, there is also the testimony of eyewitnesses. Jesus appeared first to Mary Magdalene and her companions. Then He appeared to His 11 disciples. But that's not all! There were literally hundreds of eyewitnesses, as you'll discover by reading 1 Corinthians 15:3-8.

▲ **TAKE A STEP**
He appeared to more than five hundred of the brothers at the same time (1 Corinthians 15:6).
Because of these many eyewitnesses, there probably wasn't anyone in Jerusalem who didn't hear the news: "Jesus is risen from the dead! He is the Messiah."

Fold a piece of paper in half lengthwise. On the left side, write all the evidence you've learned this week that proves Jesus' resurrection. On the right side, write all the evidence you can think of that indicates Jesus is still dead. How do the two sides compare? What is your family's verdict about Jesus of Nazareth: Is He dead or alive?

*F*ather," Rachel asked, "if Rabbi Ezra finds out we've decided to join those who follow Jesus, will he be angry?"

"Perhaps," Rachel's father answered thoughtfully. "Many who are now following the way of Christ have been forbidden to come back to the synagogue. But let's not worry about what Rabbi Ezra thinks. Today is a special day! More new believers are being baptized this afternoon. So you and your mother better hurry— you don't want to miss it, do you?"

"Oh, Father, of course not!" Rachel laughed as she hugged him.

"You know, things seem so different now. Just a few days ago I was scared and worried. Now the future looks so bright."

"I know what you mean," her father said. "Knowing that Jesus is alive makes us feel even more alive, doesn't it?"

◆ TAKE A LOOK
Titus 2:13; 1 Corinthians 15:20-23

After Jesus' resurrection, many believed He was who He had claimed to be—God's Son, the Savior.

His followers began to meet on Sunday, in honor of the day of His resurrection, instead of on Saturday, the Sabbath. They learned that Jesus had died on the cross to pay the penalty for their sins, and that all who put their trust in Him would be freed from the power of death. These truths give us the hope and encouragement to live for the Lord— even in difficult circumstances!

Praise be to the God and Father of our Lord Jesus Christ! In his great mercy he has given us new birth into a living hope through the resurrection of Jesus Christ from the dead (1 Peter 1:3).

As it did then, Jesus' resurrection can give believers today a great hope for the future. Find out what that great hope is by reading Titus 2:13 and 1 Corinthians 15:20-23.

▲ TAKE A STEP

The resurrected Jesus changed lives long ago, and He's still changing lives today! Someday, those who belong to Him will be resurrected as He was.

Go through some old magazines together and cut out pictures of butterflies (or draw your own). Butterflies symbolize resurrection—life (the caterpillar), death (the cocoon), and life again (the butterfly). Glue the pictures on a sheet of paper, and write the words of 2 Corinthians 5:17 across the top.

What a difference that day can make!

Q

What difference can Easter make in my life?

A

Easter celebrates Jesus' resurrection, which gives me hope for today and the future.

HOPE

I *f I could make your wishes come true," said Mrs. Tolbert to her second-grade class, waving her pointer like a wand, "what would you wish for? Amy, you start."*

Amy slid down in her seat a little and giggled behind her hand. "I wish I didn't have to go to school!"

"I wish I could eat all the ice cream in the world!" Louise chimed in.

A small boy with black curly hair raised his hand. "Yes, Mason," Mrs. Tolbert pointed to him, "what's your wish?"

"I wish my daddy could find a job," Mason said softly, "and that Mommy would be happy like she used to be."

"Those are good wishes, Mason," Mrs. Tolbert said. "Maybe someday they will come true." Then she thought to herself, "I wish I did have a magic wand to make them come true."

◆ THINKING ABOUT HOPE

Like some of Mrs. Tolbert's second-graders, we sometimes make wishes which can't possibly come true. And that's usually a good thing, for we might be sorry if they did. But as in Mason's case, true hope is more than just wishful thinking.

Hope for a cure gives someone who is seriously ill the strength to keep on taking difficult treatments. Hope for a better grade spurs a student to study harder. Hope that a runaway child may return leads his parents to leave the porch light on each night. Hope is **believing with confidence that God's perfect plan for us will eventually happen**. Hope is an essential ingredient of life.

"And we were just hoping for twins."

● KEY VERSE ON HOPE

*The L*ORD *delights in those who fear him, who put their hope in his unfailing love (Psalm 147:11).*

▲ LOOKING AHEAD

We could live without a lot of things. But take away hope, and we might give up!

What are you looking forward to next week . . . next year? After each family member shares something he or she is hoping for in those time periods, turn to Titus 2:13 for a look at the one event all Christians hope for!

*R*alph walked home slowly, his head hanging, his shoulders sagging. Why did the rest of the class seem to catch on quickly to equations while he couldn't seem to make any sense of them? If he didn't pull his grades up soon, he might have to repeat algebra next year. Ralph hated the thought.

Walking in the front door, he slumped on the sofa and sighed. "Something go wrong today?" his mom asked.

"It's the same old thing!" Ralph exploded, pounding his fist into a cushion. "I can't do that math. I hate being stupid."

"I'm sure you're not the only one having trouble," his mother reassured him. "But I do think it's time we got some help. I'll call Mr. Greer and arrange for some tutoring."

Ralph shrugged. "That's not a fun way to spend an afternoon . . . but at this point I'll try anything."

◆ **TAKE A LOOK / Romans 4:18-21**

Tutoring was no guarantee that Ralph would pass algebra, but it did offer him hope. It gave him a reason to keep trying. Like Ralph, sometimes you may feel there's no way out of a tough situation. Maybe it's a problem at school or work, or guilt over not spending enough time with your family, or not showing proper respect to your parents. Maybe it's a concern about your health or your wealth—or not having enough of either. In all these situations discouragement comes easily . . . unless hope opens a door.

Abraham went through the "door of hope." The facts of his story are found in Genesis 15–21. But Romans 4:18-21 shows us why Abraham had hope even when things looked bleak. Read those verses to see if you can find the reason.

▲ **TAKE A STEP**

Some people are so discouraged with life they become depressed, doubting that God is still in control. Others, like Abraham, have hope even in hard times because they are

. . . fully persuaded that God [has] power to do what he [has] promised (Romans 4:21).

What's got you down? Discouraged about a lack of wisdom? Check out God's promise in James 1:5. Depressed over tight finances? Look up Hebrews 13:5. Defeated by difficulties? Read God's promise in 1 Peter 1:6-8. Choose a concern that's troubling you and write a promise from God's Word on a 3 x 5 card to carry with you.

Q

Why is hope important?

A

Hope gives me a reason to keep trusting and to keep trying.

PARENT:
When your family goes through tough times, verbalize your hope (confidence) in God's control both through prayer and in everyday conversation.

I'm sick and tired of being sick and tired!

Mrs. Beatty slowly opened the hospital room door and went in. Her daughter Mitzi lay there looking as white as the sheets on the bed. "Look at that sunshine pouring in the window, honey," Mom said with a smile. "Looks like spring has sprung!"

Mitzi winced and rolled over slowly. "Mom, would you raise the bed, please? I'd like to see out the window."

Gently, Mrs. Beatty raised Mitzi's bed and smoothed her hair. She still could hardly believe that her daughter had cancer. Cancer was supposed to happen to other families, not hers. Why must Mitzi suffer so? After all, she had such high hopes for life. She'd graduated from high school and had just taken a job when the disease was discovered. Now her life seemed to be a blur of pain, sickness, and chemotherapy.

"Mom," Mitzi said softly as she gazed at the late afternoon sky, "it's been a tough day, and I need some encouragement. Will you read the Twenty-third Psalm to me?"

Q

What causes me to lose hope?

A

Hope is tested when circumstances in my life seem out of control.

◆ TAKE A LOOK / Hebrews 6:13-19

In the dark days of personal tragedy, some people begin to lose confidence in God's love. They want Him to say yes, but instead He says no or wait. How can we have hope even when our circumstances seem as hopeless as Mitzi's?

Hope—for a better life, for a cure, for perfect justice—can be hard to hold onto. But even in tough times, a Christian can have hope in the unchanging love and care of our sovereign God. As you read Hebrews 6:13-19, listen for the words the writer uses to describe hope.

▲ TAKE A STEP

It is impossible for God to lie. . . . We have this hope as an anchor for the soul, firm and secure (Hebrews 6:18-19).

It's easy to praise God in the good times. But even in hard times, God's love for us never changes. He guarantees it. When you accept the fact that God is in control in good times and bad, your hope is focused on the right object.

When you praise God for the "what" even though you can't understand the "why," He will give you peace in the storm. Your soul will be anchored to an immovable Rock.

Mitzi's life was certainly stormy. Why do you think she asked her mother to read the Bible to her? Describe a stormy time in your life when God's Word strengthened your hope.

Mrs. Beatty finished reading Psalm 23 and closed the Bible.

"I really like that last part: 'I will dwell in the house of the Lord forever,' " Mitzi said. "These treatments make me so sick, I almost think if the cancer doesn't kill me, the cure will."

Then Mitzi noticed a flicker of fear cross her mother's face. "Mom," she said softly, "we all know there's no guarantee this treatment will work. I sure hope it will, because I have a lot of living left to do. But if it doesn't—well, don't worry. I have an even greater hope than that."

Mrs. Beatty gripped her daughter's hand. "I know. But it's hard for Dad and me to think about—let alone talk about."

"But Mom," Mitzi said. "I need you and Dad to understand how I'm feeling. I haven't given up yet, but I know my chances. It helps me to hear God's promises to me for the future. It's a hope that really gives me peace."

◆ **TAKE A LOOK / 1 Peter 1:3; Titus 1:2**

While she was growing up Mitzi had discovered that God is in control of the bad times as well as the good. Now her faith is being tested. She doesn't know if her cancer will be cured, but she is absolutely sure that everything will be all right in the end. That is her confident hope.

Though the human hopes we have are possible —like recovering from cancer, getting a better job, or succeeding in school—there is no guarantee they will happen. But the hope we have as Christians is different. It is guaranteed by God Himself—and He cannot lie. Our hope is based on a fact. You'll find the fact that gives us hope for the future in 1 Peter 1:3 and Titus 1:2.

▲ **TAKE A STEP**

Our hope for the future—that Christ will return and we will live forever with Him—is based firmly on the fact of His resurrection and on the promises of God. And that hope can make every day meaningful, even if our circumstances are bad.

For as in Adam all die, so in Christ all will be made alive. But each in his own turn: Christ, the firstfruits; then, when he comes, those who belong to him (1 Corinthians 15:22-23).

God promises that all who belong to Him will be resurrected just as Jesus was. Close your family time today with a prayer of praise that God is in control of your lives, both now and in the future. Thank Him for the hope that truth brings.

A steady hope in a rocky world

Q

What is my ultimate, unchanging hope?

A

Hope is knowing for sure that I have a wonderful future with Jesus.

A touch of love gives a taste of hope

How can I help this poor girl?" Mrs. Allen, the English teacher, thought as she took the paper from Vangie. "She's been so unhappy since her parents were divorced. There must be something I can do."

Later Mrs. Allen called Vangie aside. "I think you have real potential as a writer, Vangie. If you will work as my student aide next semester, I'll help you improve your writing skills."

Though reluctant at first, Vangie started working with her teacher. As Vangie gained confidence and experience, Mrs. Allen encouraged her to enter some of her work in student writing competitions. No one was more excited than Mrs. Allen when one of Vangie's short stories won first place in a state contest.

Two years later, Vangie graduated with honors. "I owe it to you, Mrs. Allen," she smiled as she showed the teacher her diploma. "Your encouragement kept me going when my world was falling apart. You gave me hope. You'll always be my friend."

◆ TAKE A LOOK / Psalm 33:18-22; 1 Corinthians 13:6-7, 13; Hebrews 11:1

Mrs. Allen was a friend to Vangie and helped her during some hard times. Vangie's confidence and hope grew as a result of that friendship.

You may know someone like Vangie, someone who feels hopeless and lost in difficult circumstances. It's not enough just to tell that person to have hope. You may not even be able to show how things will get better. What you can do though is offer love and care. And when someone knows he or she is loved, hope can grow in his or her life.

The writer of Psalm 33 understood that the only love we can ever really count on is the unchanging love of God, which He gives freely. Read Psalm 33:18-22 aloud slowly, emphasizing the words love and hope. Then read 1 Corinthians 13:6-7 and 13 and Hebrews 11:1 to see how hope and love fit together.

▲ TAKE A STEP

And now these three remain: faith, hope and love. But the greatest of these is love (1 Corinthians 13:13).

Love is the greatest—but it stands side by side with faith and hope. Think of someone you know who, like Vangie, needs hope about a job, a grade, an illness, a family situation. From Mrs. Allen's example, and from the verses you just read, what could you do to help that person rekindle hope?

Q

How can I help others to have hope?

A

Hope can be sparked by my love for and encouragement of others.

GOD'S WILL

*A*s he climbed the steps to Harriet's house, Kirby felt tense. At first he hadn't thought much about using his electronics skills with a mission organization to broadcast the gospel into Asia. But as time passed it seemed that every Scripture, every thought, and every conversation pointed him in that direction.

But what should he do about Harriet? After all, plans were well under way for their wedding!

An hour later, Kirby and Harriet were excitedly talking to Harriet's parents. "Here I was all set to tell Kirby that God was leading me to Asia," Harriet laughed, "and all the while he was trying to tell me God was calling him there! We knew we were in love, but we both wanted to do God's will. And now we will—together!"

"Y'know," Kirby added, "I think God had this planned all along."

◆ THINKING ABOUT GOD'S WILL

We face big decisions throughout life. We wish we could hear God say, "Do this, not that." But as important as the big decisions are, it's just as important to know—and do—God's will in the little things of life, moment by moment. The Bible gives us this command about **doing what pleases God.**

● KEY VERSE ON GOD'S WILL

Do not be foolish, but understand what the Lord's will is (Ephesians 5:17).

▲ LOOKING AHEAD

God's will isn't always like a well-marked highway. More often it's like hiking in a forest with a guide who has gone ahead to mark a trail. This week we'll discover some "trail markers" for knowing God's will.

Begin by reading Proverbs 3:5-7. What "trail markers" do you think Kirby and Harriet followed in making their decisions?

"If God had meant for me to eat brussels sprouts, he would've put me in Belgium!"

Doing what you know is the only way to go!

"**L**ook at that, Dad!" Kent pointed to the uprooted trees, overturned cars, and ruined houses. "How could all this happen in just a few seconds?"

Mr. Harris stood with his son as they studied the path of destruction the tornado had taken through their small town the day before. Seven houses were completely demolished. But one man's broken leg was the only serious injury.

As Kent and his dad watched the work crews, Kent said softly, "Dad, people are saying it's God's will that no one was killed. But why did it have to happen at all? Couldn't God have stopped the tornado from even coming through town?

◆ TAKE A LOOK
Romans 8:19-23; 2 Peter 3:7, 10-13

Like Kent, you too may have wondered why God allows natural disasters. Are tornados, famines, and accidents that destroy lives and property really part of God's will?

When God gave human beings the choice of whether or not to obey Him, they chose to sin. That sin caused a big change: Adam and Eve, as well as the world they lived in, were no longer perfect. Nature now includes harmful things like earthquakes, floods, and tornados as well as beneficial things like rain, sunlight, and the seasons.

In Romans 8:19-23, Paul explains how the created world has suffered. After you've read those verses, turn to 2 Peter 3:7 and 10-13 to find out what will eventually happen to the earth.

▲ TAKE A STEP

God permits events to happen even though we might not understand them. But there is a part of God's will we can understand and do something about.

The part of God's will involving your attitudes and actions is revealed in the Bible, so you don't have to wonder about it. All you have to do is obey it. And you can know that you are able to do God's will, because . . .

The God of peace . . . [will] equip you with every-thing good for doing his will (Hebrews 13:21).

Pretend that you, instead of Kent, were thinking about the tornado's aftermath. From the verses you read today, can you find one that tells you what God would want you to do in a situation like that, and one that explains God's will for the people whose homes were destroyed by the tornado?

Q

What do we mean when we talk about "God's will"?

A

God's will for me is whatever He wants to happen in my life.

PARENT:
Other verses you might find helpful are James 1:27; 2:15-16; Matthew 6:25-34.

Kerri was excited about the interview. If she got this job, she'd be able to save even more for college than she'd planned.

After Kerri completed the typing test, Mrs. Cranston explained the job. "As a specialized placement agency, our duty is to find the best people for the job openings we've been hired to fill. We call successful firms and pretend we're a prospective client. Soon we find out who their top employees are. Then we pass that information on to our clients. Your job would be to type the reports our agents send in."

As Kerri listened, she began to have doubts. She wouldn't be lying, but if she took the job she would be typing for agents who did tell lies for a living. As Mrs. Cranston offered her the job, Kerri also heard an inner voice telling her,

Hold on to the good. Avoid every kind of evil (1 Thessalonians 5:21-22).

Kerri quietly told Mrs. Cranston, "I appreciate your offer, but I can't take the job. Thank you for your time."

◆ **TAKE A LOOK**
Romans 12:2; 2 Corinthians 10:4-5
Kerri was faced with an important decision, and she needed to know God's will right then. But she couldn't just open her Bible and look for guidance: There was no time to pray, and there were no Christian friends around to ask for advice. But Kerri was able to do what pleased God in this situation because she already knew His will.

Sometimes it's not easy to know God's will in a certain situation. He doesn't always give a flash of insight as He gave Kerri. We may have to go through a process of reading the Word, praying, and listening to the advice of other believers before we make a decision. But unless your mind is filled with God's Word, you won't learn God's will either quickly or over a period of time, as you'll discover in Romans 12:2 and 2 Corinthians 10:4-5.

▲ **TAKE A STEP**
You can't just say to God, "Show me Your will, Lord, and then I'll decide if I want to do it." If you are committed to doing His will, He will show it to you—one step at a time. God wants His children to say, "I'll do Your will—no matter what!"

Kerri's mind was "programmed" with Scripture, which helped her decide not to take that job. What has programmed your mind: television . . . music . . . the world? How important is God's Word in your life?

God's Word shows the way to live day by day

Q

Why is it important for me to know God's Word?

A

God's will is always consistent with God's Word, so that's where I should look first.

Where there's a will (of God), there's a way!

Q

How can I recognize God's will?

A

God's will for me can be known through His Word, prayer, circumstances, and wise counsel.

Why couldn't they just leave it the way it was?" Boyd grumbled. He was reading the church bulletin announcing a new time for the youth meeting. "I go to Scouts on Tuesdays and youth group is on Thursdays. Now they've switched the youth meeting to Tuesdays too. I sure can't do both."

"You're right, son," his dad replied. "You have a tough decision to make."

"But Dad, how can I decide? I'm so close to becoming an Eagle Scout, I don't want to quit now. But I like the youth group, and I know it's important too. Do you think it would be wrong if I decided to stay in Scouts and finish what I've started?"

"Not necessarily. Staying in Scouts may be what God wants you to do. Why not do this: For the rest of the week, let God speak to you through His Word. Pray about it, and ask Him to show you His will. Then talk to the youth director. By then you should have a pretty good idea of what you should do. But whatever you decide, Mom and I will support you."

◆ **TAKE A LOOK / Psalm 119:24; James 1:5**

You don't need to wonder what God's will is if you are tempted to steal. He's already said, *"Do not steal" (Exodus 20:15).*

Nor do you have to ask God if you should obey your parents. His will is clear: *"Children, obey your parents" (Ephesians 6:1).*

But, as Boyd discovered, finding God's will is not always that easy.

The following verses describe some things that will help you discover God's will. On the line at the right, jot down what you think each verse suggests that you do when you have a decision to make.

The Bible says . . .	I can find God's will (how?):
Psalm 119:24	
James 1:5	
Romans 8:28	
Proverbs 15:22	
Psalm 37:4	

▲ **TAKE A STEP**

When God's Word, prayer, circumstances, the counsel of Christian friends, and your own desires about something work together, God's will becomes clear.

If you were Boyd, what specific steps would you take to make your decision? What do you think you would decide?

We were positive it was God's will for us to go to the mission field," a young man lamented. "Now the mission board won't accept us because our child has a heart defect."

"I prayed hard about taking this job," a man told his pastor. "It seemed so right. But now the company is declaring bankruptcy, and I'm out of a job. Did I miss God's will?"

"I'm homesick and unhappy," a student said. "Maybe I should have gone to a school closer to home and given up this scholarship. But I was sure this was God's way of providing for my education."

"My husband and I decided I should stop working and stay home with the children," a young mother told a friend. "But now we barely have enough money to pay our bills and all we do is argue. I must be out of God's will."

◆ TAKE A LOOK
Acts 19:21; 25:10-12; Philippians 1:12-14

Like the people in those situations, you may sometimes wonder if a decision you made was really God's will because of what happened as a result. The apostle Paul may have wondered too—especially when doing God's will landed him in a Roman jail! Paul knew it was God's will that he should preach the gospel in Rome. Read Acts 19:21 and see how the idea first came about; then read Acts 25:10-12 to see how Paul got to Rome. Finally, in Philippians 1:12-14 (which Paul wrote from a Roman jail), find out how Paul felt about the way it all worked out.

▲ TAKE A STEP

If we sincerely seek God's will, and then do it, we must also trust God with whatever happens. Even if things don't work out as we'd hoped, we know that what Paul wrote is true:

But one thing I do: Forgetting what is behind and straining toward what is ahead, I press on toward the goal to win the prize for which God has called me (Philippians 3:13-14).

Trust God to give you opportunities and pray that He'll block the wrong way and keep you from making a mistake. Then, like the apostle Paul, believe that what happens in your life is God's will.

Romans 8:28 assures us that God doesn't make mistakes. Pick one (or more) of the situations above and try to answer this question: "What might God be trying to teach that person through his or her difficult situation?"

Did I miss a turn on the road of life?

If things go wrong, have I missed God's will?

God's will may bring surprises or difficulties, but it is still what's best for me.

PARENT:
If you'd like to learn more about God's will, you'll enjoy Knowing God's Will and Doing It *by J. Grant Howard.*

DEATH

F *rom the obituary page of the* Clarkston Observer:
*"Mrs. Iris Greenwood, age 81, of 1022 Rosewood Lane, died April 14,
1991. Funeral services will be held at 2:00 P.M. Thursday at Clarkston
Bible Chapel, with the Rev. Frank Ellis officiating.*

*"Interment will be at Westview Cemetery. Mrs. Greenwood is survived
by her children, Mr. Robert Greenwood of Clarkston, Mr. Daniel
Greenwood of Fort Smith, and Mrs. Gerald Tandy of Providence; sister,
Mrs. Pearl Owens; grandchildren, Brian and Natalie Greenwood, and
Angela and Amy Tandy. The family will receive friends at the Clarkston
Funeral Home from 3:00-5:00 P.M. and 7:00-9:30 P.M. Wednesday.
Contributions may be made in her name to the National Bible Society."*

◆ THINKING ABOUT DEATH

No one likes to think about death. But the statistics are
impressive: Out of every hundred people, one hundred die.

Death is **the absence of physical life** and its physical signs:
heartbeat, breathing, and brainwaves. It sometimes seems more
"natural" when death comes to those who are very old. But even
babies, children, teenagers, and young adults can die from
accidents or illnesses.

Death has been a fact of life almost since the beginning of time.
But death was not part of God's
original creation; it came as the
result of sin. And the Bible is very
clear that there is no escape from
death.

● KEY VERSE ON DEATH

*Man is destined to die once,
and after that to face
judgment (Hebrews 9:27).*

▲ LOOKING AHEAD

In 1 Corinthians 15:26, the
apostle Paul calls death "the last
enemy" to be defeated by Christ.

One way to prepare yourself to
face death is to talk about it. This
week, try to visit a cemetery where
a friend or family member is
buried. Take a moment to pray for
the survivors . . . and to thank
God for the life your family
enjoys.

*"My whole life passed before my
eyes, except the part where I
learned the multiplication tables."*

*T*he Greenwood family had been in the hospital room as Memaw Iris had grown weaker and weaker . . . until she had finally stopped breathing.

"I sure will miss her, Dad," Natalie said, wiping her tears.

"I will too, Natalie," Mr. Greenwood said. "But Memaw lived a long, full life. We have lots of happy memories to treasure."

"Yes, we do," Mrs. Greenwood agreed. "You know, I think she was ready to leave us. She'd talked a lot lately about how her body was wearing out, and how Papaw was waiting for her."

"But Mom, it's still awful for us," Natalie cried. "Why do people have to die anyway? Why can't we all live forever?"

◆ TAKE A LOOK / Genesis 2:15-17; 3:17-19

You, like Natalie, may wonder why people have to die at all. We can find the answer to that difficult question in the Bible. There we learn that death was not part of God's original creation. Instead, death came as the result of humanity's sin and rebellion against God.

Read about Adam's disobedience to God in Genesis 2:15-17 and 3:17-19. What did Adam do that was so bad?

▲ TAKE A STEP

Sin entered the world because Adam disobeyed God. God punished that sin by causing Adam to work hard for his food and by allowing death into the world. You can think of Adam's sin like a hereditary disease, passed on to everyone who came after him. Nobody can avoid the result of sin, which is death. Paul explains it this way:

Sin entered the world through one man [Adam], and death through sin, and in this way death came to all men, because all sinned (Romans 5:12).

Because Adam was the father of all mankind, his sin was passed on to you. Only Jesus—who was born in a miraculous way—ever avoided that sin and lived a perfect life. He paid the penalty for your sin with His own death on the cross.

Many families plant a garden this time of year. Is it easy to raise a garden? No! It takes long, hard work. And that's part of the result of Adam's sin. Because of his rebellion long ago, we still must constantly face the toil of life and eventual death. Think about that when you eat your vegetables tonight!

It's hard to say goodbye to someone you love

Q

Why do people have to die?

A

Death will come to every human being— including me—as the result of Adam's sin.

PARENT: Explain to your children how they will be cared for if something should happen to you. If you haven't made a will and appointed a guardian, please don't put it off.

Death is a time to reach out and touch

I t's good to be home," Mr. Greenwood sighed as he took off his coat. "Let's see . . . I'll call the funeral director and ask him to take Mother to the funeral home. Then I'll call the rest of the family and let someone at church know. In the morning I need to choose a casket and fill out the obituary notice."

Mrs. Greenwood filled a coffeepot with water. "Honey, about a month ago, Memaw gave me a whole page of instructions to give you. She wanted to make things easier for you."

"That's just like her, isn't it? Thoughtful, organized . . . "

Mrs. Greenwood nodded as she pulled the paper from the desk drawer. "She left detailed instructions for her funeral. She doesn't want it to be a sad time—she wants everyone to know that she's with Jesus now. She even asked Mrs. Bowen to sing 'We Shall Behold Him.' It was one of her favorites."

Q

What happens when a Christian dies?

◆TAKE A LOOK / 1 Thessalonians 4:13-18

The death of a loved one is never easy. Making all the arrangements can be emotionally draining for those who are left, especially if the death is unexpected.

Making funeral arrangements involves setting a time for the service and choosing a casket. Sometimes it's necessary to visit the cemetery to choose a burial site. Pallbearers (who carry the casket in the service) must be chosen. Friends must be notified, usually through a notice in the paper called an *obituary*. The pastor and funeral director will help the family during this difficult time, but friends can show how much they care just by being with the family, listening, grieving, crying together. Paul suggests we do just that.

A

Death takes believers to be with Jesus in heaven.

Rejoice with those who rejoice; mourn with those who mourn (Romans 12:15).

Those who mourn can also rejoice if their loved one knew Jesus as Savior. Find out why by reading 1 Thessalonians 4:13-18. What will someday happen to them—and to you?

▲ TAKE A STEP

For the first few days after a funeral, many people help a grieving family by running errands, providing meals, or baby-sitting. Think of someone you know who recently lost a loved one. On slips of paper, have each member write down two ways your family could help that person. Share your ideas; then pick the best one, and call your friend. Now is the time to reach out and touch!

*T*hree days had passed since Memaw Iris died. Her other two children, Mr. Greenwood's brother and sister, had flown in for the funeral. Now the whole family stood beside the casket. The funeral director closed the casket lid so the body could be taken to the church.

"It's strange," Brian thought. "That looks like my Memaw, but she isn't really in that body. She's in heaven with Jesus."

Just then Brian heard his mother's gentle sob, and tears came to his own eyes. "But Mom," he whispered, "why are you crying? Memaw Iris is in heaven, isn't she?"

"Oh, yes, Brian, she is. My tears are for all the good memories and happy times we had together. She wasn't just my mother-in-law; she was my very good friend. We'll all miss her so much. God understands . . . it's all right to cry."

◆ TAKE A LOOK / John 11:25-26

He [Jesus] too shared in [our] humanity so that by his death he might destroy him who holds the power of death—that is, the devil—and free those who all their lives were held in slavery by their fear of death (Hebrews 2:14-15).

We may feel sad because death is an ending. We may cry because it is painful. We may even be afraid because it is an unknown experience. But Jesus' resurrection shows us that death is not just an ending; it is a beginning too. You'll see why when you read John 11:25-26.

▲ TAKE A STEP

When someone you love dies, you will usually feel sad. And when you think about your own death, you may be afraid. But there's nothing wrong with that. You can find comfort and courage by thinking about heaven and by knowing that you, like everyone else who believes in Jesus, will finally win over death when Jesus comes again.

Can you remember what life was like before you were born? You had everything you needed inside your mother's womb. It would have been hard to imagine a more wonderful place outside your comfortable little "home." It took the painful, unknown experience of birth to bring you into an exciting new life on earth. Experiencing death may well be a little bit like that.

Close your time together with a brain-stretching session. Have each family member tell why he or she thinks heaven will be a wonderful place to spend eternity.

Never fear to shed a tear—God understands

Q

Why do I feel sad when someone I love dies?

A

Death makes me sad because I am separated from one I love.

PARENT:
You might want to discuss Hebrews 12:22-24; Revelation 7:15-17; 14:13; 19:1; 21:1–22:5.

God comforts us so we can comfort others

Q

How can I help when someone has died?

A

Death is easier to face when friends are a source of comfort.

*T*hree months had passed since Memaw Iris died. Brian and Natalie found they missed her at the most unexpected times. Natalie felt an empty spot when her grandmother wasn't there in the afternoon to listen as she talked about her day at school. And Brian missed the special Saturday morning breakfasts he and Memaw made together when everyone else slept late.

One evening over dessert, Dad reminisced with the family about Memaw. "Her strong faith in God saw her through some really tough times—like when Papaw died and left her with three young children and a farm to run." He recalled when the farmhouse burned down, forcing Memaw to move to the city and take a factory job. "One thing she taught me has always stayed with me," Dad said. "And that's how important it is to trust God for everything in life—the little things as well as the big."

It took time, but gradually the Greenwoods replaced the pain of Memaw's death with thankfulness for her life and shining faith.

◆**TAKE A LOOK / Psalm 23; John 14:1-3**

The Bible doesn't give specific instructions for comforting a family when someone has died. But it does tell us that . . .

[God] comforts us in all our troubles, so that we can comfort those in any trouble with the comfort we ourselves have received from God (2 Corinthians 1:4).

When Memaw died, the Greenwoods were comforted by the Scriptures their pastor read with them. After you read Psalm 23 and John 14:1-3, tell why you think those words can bring comfort when a loved one dies.

▲ **TAKE A STEP**

God brings comfort in difficult times. So can friends. Many people send cards; some send flowers; others bring food to help out during the hectic days before the funeral. A few send memorial contributions to charities or mission organizations to honor the loved one. But perhaps the most comfort comes from the many friends who drop by the home during those difficult days to share the family's grief with a hug or listening ear.

It can take a long time for the hurt to go away. Even months after Memaw died, the Greenwood family still had times of sadness. During those later times, few people make an effort to help. If you knew the Greenwoods, what could you do to comfort them in the months after Memaw's death?

MIRACLES

"**G** uess what! I was so busy trying to finish my geography project that I didn't get to study much for this test . . . and I still got a B on it! It's a miracle!"

• "That old junk heap usually can't make it across town, and you took it on a 300-mile trip? It must be a miracle!"

• "Oh, no! It's 11:00—I was supposed to be home an hour ago, and Mom and Dad will be furious. Only a miracle could keep me from getting grounded for this!"

• "It was amazing. Bowzer was chasing a car, and it looked like he got hit. But he got up and ran back here. It's got to be a miracle!"

◆ THINKING ABOUT MIRACLES

When something unexpected or unusual happens to us, we're quick to call it a miracle. But the miracles in the Bible are different.

Some people think they are just made-up stories. But we know that God has the power to do anything He wants. Real miracles happen **when our almighty God does something out of the ordinary for a purpose**. The Bible also calls these special acts mighty works, signs, and wonders.

God performs miracles for specific purposes, not just to show off. They always reveal His power and love for His people and confirm His message—or His messenger. When Jesus walked the earth, His miracles proved that He is who He claimed to be.

● KEY VERSE ON MIRACLES

Many people saw the miraculous signs [Jesus] was doing and believed in his name (John 2:23).

▲ LOOKING AHEAD

Studying miracles can be exciting but it can also raise many questions.

Have each family member write on a piece of paper as many Bible miracles as he or she can think of in three minutes. Then share the results. The Bible records dozens and dozens of miracles—and that's only for starters (read John 20:30-31).

"I made an A on the math test. It was obviously a miracle, and now I'll probably be accused of praying in school."

I'll believe it when I see it— maybe!

"**H**ey, R.J.!" Tim yelled at his friend as they walked home after school. "Are you ready for summer? I sure am!"

"Yeah," R.J. replied. His mind seemed to be somewhere else. "I can't wait till June. I'm going to a church camp and —"

"Aw, more church stuff! That's all you're into!"

"Hey, Jesus is important to me, Tim. What would it take for you to believe in Jesus?"

"Maybe I'd believe it if a 50-foot angel stood right there and pointed to your Bible and said, 'It's all true, Tim!' "

"Yeah? Well, what if an angel really did that?"

"I still wouldn't believe it!" Tim blurted. "I'd think I was dreaming!"

◆ **TAKE A LOOK / Exodus 14:5-6, 10, 13-16, 21-28**

People who believe in miracles must believe in a "Miracle-Maker." If you know God exists, you know He can perform miracles.

The children of Israel learned this . . . the hard way. They had labored as slaves in Egypt for hundreds of years. Then God chose Moses to challenge Pharaoh to free His people. After suffering through 10 plagues, Pharaoh gave up, and the Israelites marched from Egypt. But all seemed lost when they found themselves stuck between the Red Sea and the approaching Egyptian army. Read Exodus 14:5-6, 10, 13-16, and 21-28 to find out what happened.

▲ **TAKE A STEP**

Even though God performed miracle after miracle, Pharaoh refused to free God's people (Exodus 7–12). It took the death of all the firstborn of Egypt—including Pharaoh's own son—to change his mind. But still his heart was hard.

Miracles don't make people believe in God. That's not their purpose. The Bible shows us that if someone is willing to believe, a miracle may help him or her take the final step of faith. But if that person is determined not to believe, nothing but God's grace can change it. As Jesus said,

"If they do not listen to Moses and the Prophets, they will not be convinced even if someone rises from the dead" (Luke 16:31).

Do you know someone who seems determined not to believe in God? How can you help that person know the truth?

Q

Why do some people not believe in miracles?

A

Miracles are only believable when I believe in an all-powerful God.

PARENT:
Listen for everyday uses of the word "miracle." Take time to remind your family what a real miracle is.

H ey, Bethany—look!" Brett pointed out his sister's bedroom window. "That man is getting out of a taxi in front of our house. Who is he?"

"I don't know. I don't recognize him." The twin third-graders huddled at the window and watched as the cabdriver unloaded the stranger's luggage.

"Who do we know with a big red beard?" Bethany asked.

"I can't think of anyone. Look, he's got a guitar," Brett noted.

"Wait a minute, Brett. He's wearing a cowboy hat . . . hey, he's limping a little! I bet I know who it is!"

"Sure—it's Uncle Ray!" Brett shouted. "Who else could it be?" Together the twins ran down the stairs to meet the uncle they'd never seen before.

◆ TAKE A LOOK
Matthew 8:23-27; 14:15-21, 25-33
Brett and Bethany had never met their Uncle Ray, but over the years they had heard their dad mention that he lived in Texas, had a big red beard, had been injured in the war, and played the guitar. So when they saw the unknown man who fit that description, they knew immediately who he was.

Jesus came to earth as the Messiah—the Son of God, the Savior of humankind. Those who were expecting Him knew that Jesus was their long-awaited Messiah because of the mighty miracles He performed. He turned water into wine, fed thousands of hungry people with just a few fish and loaves of bread, and calmed raging storms with a word. Read about three of His miracles in Matthew 8:23-27; 14:15-21, and 25-33. After Jesus' disciples witnessed all that, what did they conclude?

Those who were in the boat worshiped him, saying, "Truly you are the Son of God" (Matthew 14:33).

▲ TAKE A STEP
The Jewish religious leaders who opposed Jesus never denied the miracles He performed. Instead they claimed His power came from Satan—not God. But Jesus explained that He couldn't possibly be controlled by Satan and perform the kind of miracles He did (Matthew 12:24-28). No, His power came from the Spirit of God.

As exciting as those miracles are, there's one that's even more thrilling to think about. (Find out what it is in 1 Corinthians 15:3-7.) Why is that miracle so important to you . . . and to all Christians?

Q

How do Jesus' miracles show me that He is God's Son?

A

Only God's Son can perform true miracles.

The loving touch that means so much

I just can't believe it," Teddy muttered. "Here I am lying in this hospital bed with my leg in a cast while the swim team is facing our arch rival without me. I just can't believe it!"

"Teddy, these things happen," his dad assured him.

"Yeah, but it was such a stupid accident. I should've seen that drop-off, but no! I had to take my bike over it!"

"Hey, be thankful it wasn't worse." Teddy's dad sat on the edge of the bed. "Look, son, I know how you feel. It's frustrating. But you'll get over it. It will take time, but you'll be back on the swim team next year. If I could, I'd give you a new leg right now. But all we can do is wait."

◆TAKE A LOOK / John 11:21-27, 32-44

Q

How do Jesus' miracles show that He loves me?

Teddy's dad loved him deeply. But Jesus' love for people was far deeper . . . and He had the power to heal them. The miracles He performed not only proved He was God's Son, but also showed His compassion for people. He healed the sick, gave sight to the blind, and raised the dead. Those miracles revealed His power and love working together.

One time Jesus learned that His friend Lazarus was sick in another town. Jesus knew that God's glory would be seen in this situation, so He waited. When He arrived in Bethany, Lazarus had been dead for four days. Find out what happened next by reading aloud John 11:21-27 and 32-44. If you had been there when that miracle occurred, what would you have thought about Jesus?

A

Jesus' miracles show me that He loves and cares for people with needs— and that includes me.

▲ TAKE A STEP

Martha knew that Jesus could perform miracles because she knew that He is the Son of God (John 11:27). But even she wondered if it was too late for Jesus to help. Martha soon learned, though, that His love and power are without limits.

This awesome miracle clearly revealed Jesus' power and His love. But what happened afterwards?

Many of the Jews who had . . . seen what Jesus did, put their faith in him. But some of them went to the Pharisees and told them what Jesus had done (John 11:45-46).

As a result, the Jewish religious leaders plotted to kill Him.

We've seen that our loving Lord is able to heal. So why doesn't He heal everyone today? Why do you think so many people—like Teddy—have to suffer? Talk through those questions now to prepare for tomorrow's devotional.

B ut Mom, I don't understand it," Tamara blurted. "We prayed for Grandma to be healed. Why didn't God answer our prayers?"

"Calm down, honey," her mother answered softly. "We're all sad that Grandma died. I don't know why God didn't heal her, but she did live a good, long life."

The next evening, Uncle Frank stopped by the house. He seemed unusually quiet at first, but then turned to Tamara's mom. "Sis, I've got something on my mind. The day before Mom died, she talked to me about how I needed Christ. Seeing the way she lived, how she loved God—even in her last days—really made an impact on me. Can you help me? How do I become a Christian?"

◆ **TAKE A LOOK**
Deuteronomy 32:39; Romans 8:18-28
Grandma's death freed her from pain and brought her into God's presence. And God used her death to bring Uncle Frank to faith.

God is all-powerful. When you read of His miracles in the Bible, that's obvious. And it's still true today. Some people are miraculously healed. But other times God knows that something better will grow out of suffering—or even death.

Miracles occurred most often during those times when God was confirming the ministry of His messengers, such as Moses, the prophets, Jesus Christ, and the apostles. Today, Jesus doesn't have to prove who He is; His resurrection settled that. Even so, miracles can—and do—sometimes happen in the lives of God's children. Ultimately, God controls life and death, sickness and health (Deuteronomy 32:39).

The apostle Paul knew that Christians sometimes suffer. What does he tell us in Romans 8:18-28 about suffering?

▲ **TAKE A STEP**
God is still working today. Sometimes He may use miracles; other times He brings growth or change through difficulties. We should take our concerns to God in prayer, but leave the results up to Him. As David prayed:

In you our fathers put their trust . . . and [they] were not disappointed (Psalm 22:4-5).

Think of a time when you prayed for something or someone and God answered your prayer. Think of another prayer to which God answered no. In both cases, what did you learn about yourself . . . and about your God?

A miracle a day would keep my troubles away!

Why don't we see more miracles today like those in the Bible?

Miracles are no longer necessary to confirm God's message.

PARENT:
Lead your child in a study of a miracle promised to all believers: John 6:39-40 and 1 Corinthians 15:51-55.

DILIGENCE

I've just got to do better in Spanish," Cynthia thought as she looked at the C on her first test. "Knowing a second language is practically required to get a job overseas."

Right then, Cynthia made a plan. From now on, she would study Spanish every day—whether or not homework was assigned. She would review vocabulary cards on the bus, before classes, in homeroom. She would listen to Spanish records. She would try reading a Spanish Bible, and ask her friend Angela to speak Spanish with her. All that effort, along with prayer for the strength to do it, surely would make a difference.

Ten weeks later, final grades were given for the quarter. "¡El trabajo arduo trae su recompensa!" Cynthia said, grinning as she looked at the A on her report card.

◆ THINKING ABOUT DILIGENCE

Cynthia earned a good grade in Spanish because, with God's help, she planned her work and then worked her plan. She reached her goal by working toward it carefully and regularly. Instead of waiting until she felt like studying, Cynthia was diligent in her efforts to learn Spanish.

She was **working hard to do a job well**. And diligence doesn't give up until the job is finished.

● KEY VERSE ON DILIGENCE

God . . . will not forget your work and the love you have shown him as you have helped his people and continue to help them. We want each of you to show this same diligence to the very end (Hebrews 6:10-11).

▲ LOOKING AHEAD

This week we'll study the life of Nehemiah, who accomplished an "impossible" job by working diligently. Discover the big job Nehemiah faced by reading Nehemiah 2:2-6 and 11-18. How did he motivate others to work with him? How can you encourage other people to work with you on important projects?

"They never quit, do they?"

Don't forget: You must give Fluffy this medicine every day with his food," Mrs. Shuster reminded Marylou. "Make sure he has plenty of water, and always close the gate when you leave."

Since her husband died, Mrs. Shuster had rarely been away from her poodle, Fluffy. But now she had to go to St. Louis, where her daughter needed help with newborn twins.

As the days passed, Marylou became good friends with Fluffy. But one stormy day she decided to put off his feeding until after the rain. Soon she forgot completely. That night before she fell asleep, she remembered Fluffy. Two thoughts went through her mind: "I must feed Fluffy now. He has to have his medicine every day," and "Aw, I can do it in the morning; one night won't hurt him."

What do you think she did?

◆ **TAKE A LOOK / Nehemiah 3:1-12**

Marylou got out of bed, went downstairs, and told her dad what had happened. "I've got to go feed Fluffy," she said. "That medicine keeps his sickness under control. I'm glad I remembered!" Even though she had forgotten for a while, Marylou's determination to feed Fluffy that very night demonstrated her diligence. And diligence means that we do something because it's important—even if it's not convenient.

Most of the people in Jerusalem had been taken away as prisoners to Babylon in 606 B.C. But a large group of their descendants returned in 537 B.C. About a hundred years later the city walls were not yet rebuilt. When Nehemiah—who still lived in Babylon—heard about this, he asked the king's permission to return to Jerusalem and rebuild the walls. Read Nehemiah 3:1-12. When Nehemiah reminded the workers that they were servants of God and that He would honor their work, how did they react?

▲ **TAKE A STEP**

You read of the rebuilding of three city gates— and there were many more. Nehemiah had convinced people from every trade and every family that . . .

The God of heaven will give us success. We his servants will start rebuilding (Nehemiah 2:20).

Think of a task you do—not because you enjoy it, but because it's important to God and to someone you love. Now answer this question: "Do I do that task diligently and wholeheartedly?"

Work as you'd want others to work for you

Q

Why is diligence so important?

A

Diligence shows that I value what is important to God.

10,080 minutes make one week— or one weak!

Q

What should I be diligent in doing?

A

Diligence means using my time to please God in every area of my life.

PARENT: Teach your child diligence by giving a regular responsibility —such as making beds, feeding pets, or taking out the trash.

If you memorize a few measures each day, you'll soon learn this entire sonata," the music teacher encouraged Frances.

"There's real potential here," the sales manager said. "If you handle this account well, you could get a big bonus."

"Just stick to this diet," the doctor told Mrs. Casey, "and you'll lose two or three pounds a week—and that adds up."

"Class, we'll learn two new letters a week," the kindergarten teacher announced. "Soon you'll be able to write the entire alphabet—and you'll know the sound each letter makes."

"Lifting weights and running two miles a day will put you in top shape for the fall football season," Coach told his team. "I expect all of you to come back stronger than you are now."

"Reading God's Word daily is an important part of your spiritual growth," the church school teacher told the class. "And no one can do it for you. It takes diligence on your part."

◆ TAKE A LOOK / Nehemiah 4:10-21

Whatever our tasks or goals are, we all have the same amount of time each day to do them.

As God's children we should be diligent about whatever we do—whether it's learning a subject in school, practicing a musical instrument, exercising, or reading God's Word.

When Nehemiah faced his "impossible" job, he didn't have enough workers or the right materials. He also had to deal with enemies who didn't like what he was doing. Yet he was determined to rebuild the wall. You'll see how diligently he and his workers used their time when you read Nehemiah 4:10-21.

▲ TAKE A STEP

Hundreds of years later, the apostle Paul encouraged Christians with these words, which also describe the kind of diligence Nehemiah and his coworkers had.

Stand firm. Let nothing move you. Always give yourselves fully to the work of the Lord, because you know that your labor in the Lord is not in vain (1 Corinthians 15:58).

You have exactly 1,440 minutes to use each day. Sometime today, set a timer or an alarm watch to go off in a half hour. When it does, ask yourself: "Have I spent the past 30 minutes in a way that pleases God?"

C_'mon, Andy," Phil urged his brother. "We really only have to chop enough wood for today and tomorrow. We can do some more this weekend. Besides, it's cold out here."_

"You go on in, Phil. I want to finish splitting this pile of logs first. I don't want to chop wood on Saturday. And I'm also going to try to get the garage swept and the shed cleaned out. That way I'll have all my chores done. Then I'll have time to spend with my friends this weekend. You know, Phil, if you'd get a head start on your chores, you could have some free time on Saturday, too."

"Aw, Andy, nobody works unless they have to. There's plenty of time between now and Friday to chop wood. Let's go to the basement and play ping-pong," Phil challenged. "Or are you afraid I'll beat you?"

◆ TAKE A LOOK
Nehemiah 9:38; 10:29, 32, 36-39

Andy was diligent in the way he did his chores. Phil put things off. Like many people, he waited until the last possible minute to do what he had to do. He wasted his time because he was too lazy to make plans for the future.

After the Jerusalem wall was completed, the people assembled to hear Ezra the scribe read God's Law to them. Their nation had suffered because the people hadn't kept God's Law in the past. Now they wanted to obey it diligently, for God honors obedient hearts. They spent days confessing their sins and worshiping God. Read Nehemiah 9:38; 10:29, 32, and 36-39 to see what they agreed to do.

▲ TAKE A STEP

Years before the time of Nehemiah, the people of Israel had been taken captive by Babylon because they had disobeyed God's Law. Now the descendants of those captives planned to be diligent about keeping God's Law in the future. And their reward? God's blessings in their lives.

The apostle Peter encouraged believers to live holy lives as they looked forward to their reward when Jesus returns:

Since you are looking forward to this, make every effort to be found spotless, blameless and at peace with him (2 Peter 3:14).

If you believe your hard work will be rewarded in the future, you will probably be diligent. What was Andy's reward for his hard work? How does thinking about your future rewards affect the work you do right now?

The rewards of laziness aren't worth having

Q

How can I become more diligent?

A

Diligence increases when I think about the rewards it will bring in the future.

Ready or not, Jesus is coming soon!

*I*t was rainy and cold when Andy and Phil got off the school bus on Friday afternoon. "Oh, boy!" Phil exclaimed. "I won't have to do my chores this afternoon! Maybe it'll be raining tomorrow, too. See, Andy, if you'd waited, you would have had an excuse not to cut all that wood yesterday!"

The rain continued on through the night and Saturday morning. The boys did their homework and watched TV. When the rain stopped, Dad reminded them of their chores.

"But Dad," Phil whined, "it rained too long. Now we'll never be finished in time to go out with the youth group tonight. Can't we just wait until next week?"

"Phil," his father replied sternly, "you know the rule: You can't go out until your chores are done. The rain didn't keep Andy from doing his chores. Let's put the blame where it belongs—on you, not the raindrops."

◆ **TAKE A LOOK / Matthew 25:1-13**

Andy's diligence was rewarded. So was Phil's laziness. But the rewards were not the same!

In the life of Nehemiah we've seen that diligence applies to every area of life. It involves planning your work, and then doing whatever it takes to finish the task.

Diligence also means being spiritually alert. It means using time wisely while we wait for Jesus to return. Jesus told a parable in Matthew 25:1-13 about being diligent in your spiritual life. Why were the "wise virgins" wise?

▲ **TAKE A STEP**

A businessman works long hours for a high salary. A Scout learns many new skills to earn a higher rank. A gymnast exercises hard for the chance of winning a medal. A musician practices each day so she will perform well. Such diligence, as we learned yesterday, is often easier when we think about the rewards.

Some of Jesus' last words that are recorded in the Bible remind us that God rewards faithfulness and diligence.

"Behold, I am coming soon! My reward is with me, and I will give to everyone according to what he has done" (Revelation 22:12).

If Jesus had returned this morning at 7:30, what would He have found you doing? What if He had come last night at 8:00? Would you rather be found doing something else?

Q

What will happen if I am diligent?

A

Diligence will finally be rewarded when Jesus returns.

PARENT: Diligence in spiritual matters is most important. Help your child develop diligence to have personal devotions by both your example and encouragement.

MOTHERS

*S he gets up while it is still dark; she provides food for her family. . . .
She sets about her work vigorously; her arms are strong for her tasks.
She sees that her trading is profitable, and her lamp does not go out at
night. . . . When it snows, she has no fear for her household; for all of
them are clothed in scarlet. She makes coverings for her bed; she is clothed
in fine linen and purple. Her husband is respected at the city gate, where
he takes his seat among the elders of the land. She makes linen garments
and sells them, and supplies the merchants with sashes. She is clothed
with strength and dignity; she can laugh at the days to come. She speaks
with wisdom, and faithful instruction is on her tongue. She watches over
the affairs of her household and does not eat the bread of idleness.*

Do these statements bring to mind anyone you know?

◆ THINKING ABOUT MOTHERS

Maybe you wouldn't describe *your* mother in exactly that way,
but did you see glimpses of her in those verses from Proverbs 31?

When Proverbs 31 was written almost 3,000 years ago, mothers
worked hard to care for their husbands and children. And you know
what? They still do!

The Bible makes it clear that the father is to be the "head of the
house." But the mother sets the atmosphere of the home. Her
personality, character, love, and warmth continually affect her
home. Through her love and discipline, **a mother has the privilege
of training her children to bring glory to God.**

● KEY VERSE ON MOTHERS

*"Honor your . . . mother
. . . that it may go well
with you and that you may
enjoy long life on the
earth" (Ephesians 6:2-3).*

▲ LOOKING AHEAD

God has a big job—and
great blessings—in store for
mothers. And we should honor
them for that! This week we'll
learn about the important role
your mother plays in *your* life.

Before we start, share one way
your mother is a blessing to you.
Your answers will make
Proverbs 31:28 come true in
your home!

*"Mom's tough. She didn't wave the white
flag 'til halfway through the eggs."*

Who can measure a mother's love?

How many children are in your family—one . . . two . . . four . . . nineteen? What would it be like if you had eighteen brothers and sisters? Impossible, you say?

Susannah Wesley had 19 children, including John (the famous preacher) and Charles (the famous hymn writer). To manage her large family successfully, she followed these rules:

1. Eating between meals not allowed.
2. Children are to be in bed by 8 P.M.
3. They must take medicine without complaining.
4. Teach a child to pray as soon as he can speak.
5. Require all to be still during a family worship.
6. Give them nothing they cry for, and only that which they ask for politely.
7. To prevent lying, punish no fault which is first confessed and repented.
8. Never allow a sinful act to go unpunished.
9. Never punish a child twice for a single offense.
10. Commend and reward good behavior.
11. Any attempt to please, even if poorly performed, should be commended.
12. Preserve property rights, even in the smallest matters.
13. Strictly observe all promises.
14. Require no daughter to work before she can read well.
15. Teach children to fear the Lord.

◆**TAKE A LOOK / 1 Samuel 1:21-28; 2:18-21**

Like most mothers, Mrs. Wesley was concerned with the physical, mental, emotional, and spiritual growth of her children. Not even today's experts on child rearing could improve very much on the rules she used nearly 300 years ago to reach those goals! First Samuel 1:21-28 and 2:18-21 tells of another unusual mother. How did she show love for her child?

▲ **TAKE A STEP**

Hannah knew what was best for her son Samuel:

"For his whole life he will be given over to the LORD" (1 Samuel 1:28).

Both Hannah and Mrs. Wesley wanted their children to know and serve the Lord. How do you think Mrs. Wesley's rules helped her children learn to love God? Why not tape them to your refrigerator and try to follow them this month!

Q

Why is my mother important in God's eyes?

A

Mothers are responsible to teach their children to know and serve the Lord.

I f a child lives with criticism, he learns to condemn.
  If a child lives with hostility, he learns to fight.
If a child lives with ridicule, he learns to be shy.
  If a child lives with shame, he learns to feel guilty.
If a child lives with tolerance, he learns to be patient.
  If a child lives with encouragement, he learns
  confidence.
If a child lives with praise, he learns to appreciate.
  If a child lives with fairness, he learns justice.
If a child lives with security, he learns to have faith.
  If a child lives with approval, he learns to like
  himself.
If a child lives with acceptance and friendship, he
  learns to find love in the world.
                                   —Dorothy Law Nolte

◆ **TAKE A LOOK / Ephesians 5:22**
    An important part of God's plan for families is
that the mother and father teach their children to
know and obey Him. How? One way is by having
family devotions. But even more important is the
way the parents live their lives. The poem you just
read lists both good and bad ways a parent can
influence a child.
    In particular, a mother influences her child
when she obeys God's special commands to her as
a wife. As you read the verses listed below, fill in
the specific instructions given to wives in the blank
spaces at the right.

In this verse . . .   God tells a wife:
Ephesians 5:22   to be submissive to her _____ ;
1 Peter 3:4   to have a quiet and _____ spirit;
1 Cor. 7:10-11   not to _____ from her husband;
1 Tim. 2:9-10   to dress _____ and _____ ,
                  and to do good _____ .
Titus 2:4-5   to _____ her husband, to be
                  self-controlled and _____ , to be
                  busy at _____ , to be kind, and
                  to be _____ to her husband.

▲ **TAKE A STEP**
    The wife must respect her husband
    (Ephesians 5:33).
    Most mothers want to develop in their homes
the good qualities listed in the poem above. But
first and foremost, God wants the wife to honor
and respect her husband. Why do you think that's
so important to God?

Children are mirrors of their mothers

Q

How can a mother please God?

A

Mothers please God by being the examples God intends them to be.

Love doesn't divide, it multiplies!

I thought the children would be more excited about our news," Mrs. Swanson said to her husband.

"Well, I'm excited," Mr. Swanson said as he hugged his wife. "I can't wait to have another baby in the family!"

"I feel the same way. With Melinda in third grade and Joey in the fifth, it will be wonderful to have a baby at home. I just don't understand why they didn't seem very happy about it."

"You know, honey," Mr. Swanson replied, "Joey and Melinda may think we'll love them less when the baby comes. I was seven years old when my sister was born, and I still remember thinking that Mom and Dad would have to take some love away from me to give to the new baby. It took me a while to realize they had more than enough love to go around. I think maybe I'd better talk to the kids again."

How can a mother love more than one child?

◆ **TAKE A LOOK / Psalm 127:3-5**

Joey and Melinda aren't the first children to wonder whether a new baby might mean less love for them. When Mr. Swanson remembered his own feelings as a child, he was able to reassure Melinda and Joey that family love doesn't have to be divided—it can be multiplied.

In Old Testament times, some parents were not as wise as Mr. Swanson. Back then, a man might have more than one wife. The children of his favorite wife would be his favorite children. Big problems were the usual result. Jacob had this problem. He favored his son Joseph. This caused Joseph's nine older brothers to hate him so much they sold him as a slave (Genesis 37)!

Parents can avoid playing favorites if they see their children as the writer of Psalm 127 did. As you read verses 3-5, look for three ways the psalmist pictures children.

A

Mothers demonstrate God's love by treating their children as unique individuals.

▲ **TAKE A STEP**

Sons are a heritage from the LORD, *children a reward from him (Psalm 127:3).*

When each child is thought of as a unique gift from God, jealousy disappears. Wise parents will try to (1) treat each child as the special individual he or she is; (2) enforce rules fairly; and (3) never let one child make fun of another in a destructive way.

Jot down those three rules and post them with your copy of Mrs. Wesley's rules. Which of those rules would you like to see practiced in your family?

*H*ow well do you know your own mother? Can you fill in the blanks below? If not, try to find out the answers. (By the way, they might give you some good ideas for Mother's Day!)

Mother's favorite color is _____ .
Mother's hobbies are _____ :
Mother was born in the state of _____ :
Mother's last name before she married was _____ :
Mother's middle name is _____ .
Mother and Dad were married (where?) _____ .
When Mother has time to herself she likes to _____ .
Mother is _____ years old.
Mother's favorite perfume is _____ .
Mother's favorite food is _____ :
Mother's favorite kind of book is _____ .

◆ TAKE A LOOK / Proverbs 31:10-29

Mothers are people, too! They get tired, make mistakes (once in a while), and sometimes suffer from on-the-job frustration. Your mother may not be "Superwoman," but she is someone very special. She has an extra portion of patience, a large measure of wisdom, and an overflow of love—all just for you!

Make a mental list of (1) something your mother does for you that no one else would; (2) something you've learned from her; and (3) something about you, such as a habit or attitude you know doesn't please her. Perhaps the list will help you realize that your mother serves you, teaches you, and loves you as no one else could!

Think about your own mother—and how you can show your love for her on Sunday—as you read Proverbs 31:10-29 aloud again.

▲ TAKE A STEP

Her children arise and call her blessed; her husband also, and he praises her (Proverbs 31:28).

Do that right now by personalizing a few verses from Proverbs 31 for your mother. For example, "Who can find a mother like mine? . . . Dad loves her and she loves him (verse 11) . . . She gets up early and makes a wonderful breakfast for us all" (verse 15).

Now you try verses 17-18, 20-21, and 25-27. Write your personalized "verses" neatly on pretty paper, draw a colorful border around the words, and give it to your mom on Sunday!

My mother is like no other mother!

Q

How can I honor my mother?

A

Mother is honored when I show my apprecia-tion for her by what I say and do.

PARENT: Your attitudes toward your own parents influence how your child relates to you. Exodus 20:12 still applies, even if you've already fulfilled Genesis 2:24!

RESOURCES

*T*his is my Father's world, and to my listening ears
   All nature sings and 'round me rings the music of the spheres.
This is my Father's world, I rest me in the thought
   Of rocks and trees, of skies and seas; His hand the wonders wrought.
This is my Father's world, the birds their carols raise,
   The morning light, the lily white, declare their Maker's praise.
This is my Father's world: He shines in all that's fair;
   In the rustling grass I hear Him pass, He speaks to me every where."*

*"This Is My Father's World" by Maltbie D. Babcock. From A Child's Treasury of Verse, compiled by Eleanor Doan, Zondervan Publishing House.

◆ THINKING ABOUT RESOURCES

This is our Father's world. And He has filled it with resources that give us **all we need to do the things He has put us here to do.**

Each day we eat food . . . ride around in cars and buses . . . watch television or read books . . . and may never realize what raw materials were used to make all those things. We drink water and breathe air without giving them so much as a thought. But even though we use earth's resources every day, they still belong to God the Creator.

● KEY VERSE ON RESOURCES

The earth is the LORD'S, *and everything in it, the world, and all who live in it (Psalm 24:1).*

▲ LOOKING AHEAD

It's easy to take our planet's resources for granted, but we need them for survival. This week we'll explore how we can use this planet's precious resources wisely.

Look around the room at the furniture, decorations, and plants. What raw materials were they made from? Close your family time by reading Psalm 148 aloud and then thanking God in prayer for the "resource-full" world He made for everyone to enjoy—including you!

"Today we learned about acid rain, the destruction of the rain forests, and the hole in the ozone. But don't worry! I denied it all!"

I really want to do a good job on this project," Curtis told his mother as they climbed the steps to the public library. "It might mean I can make an A in geography."

"Well, I'll help you all I can," Mrs. Hudson whispered as they walked through the door. "What's your project on?"

"It's on the country of Zambia," Curtis whispered back. "I have to find out what agriculture and industry it has. Then I have to make two maps—one showing the natural features and the major cities, and the other showing the natural resources."

"Why don't you start by looking in the encyclopedia," Mrs. Hudson suggested. "I'll see if I can find some books in the card catalog, and then—"

"I know an easier way, Mom," Curtis smiled. "Let's just hop on an airplane and go to Zambia to see it for ourselves!"

◆ **TAKE A LOOK / Psalm 50:10-12;**
1 Chronicles 29:12; 1 Timothy 6:9, 17

Like Curtis, you've probably learned from your reports for history, geography, or social studies that a nation's wealth often depends on its natural resources—minerals, fish, timber, farmland, and energy sources, to name a few.

A natural resource is something found in the earth, not made by people. Many countries have oil, gold, or other valuable raw materials. When a nation has abundant natural resources, it can make money selling them to countries that need them.

The Bible can help us understand that God Himself owns the world—including its resources. Read the following verses; then match the phrase at the right with the verse it summarizes.

This verse shows me . . .	that resources are:
1. Psalm 50:10-12	a. to be used wisely
2. 1 Chronicles 29:12	b. God's possessions
3. 1 Timothy 6:9	c. given by God to human beings
4. 1 Timothy 6:17	d. for our enjoyment

▲ **TAKE A STEP**

Long ago, God warned the Israelites:
"When your . . . silver and gold increase and all you have is multiplied, then your heart will become proud and you will forget the LORD your God" (Deuteronomy 8:13-14).

Do you think the problem the Israelites faced long ago could be a problem today? How can you avoid it?

Praise the Maker for all He has made

Why does God give us natural resources?

A

Resources are given to us by God to enjoy and use wisely.

Let's give nature a helping hand

Have you ever read headlines like these in your newspaper?
- Acid Rain Problem Worries Northeast
- Smog Index Reaches Record High in Metro Area
- Industrial Pollution Killing Fish in the Bay
- Government Spends Millions to Clean Up Toxic Waste
- Environmental Issues Raised in Senate Campaign
- Flooding Caused by Improper Construction Methods
- Massive Oil Spill Kills Wildlife on Western Beaches
- Lack of Fresh Water Plagues Urban Areas
- Strip Mine Causes Danger of Mud Slides

Q

Why are our natural resources in danger?

◆ **TAKE A LOOK / Leviticus 25:1-7, 10-12**

Headlines like those show us how easily earth's natural resources can be harmed. It's not hard to see why we need to take better care of the resources God has given us!

In the beginning, God honored man by making him ruler over creation. But Adam's sin affected not only people, but the entire created world. As the centuries passed, people often used earth's resources greedily without caring how other people—or even the land itself—might be harmed.

God has such a special concern for His creation that He told the nation of Israel (which was to be an example to all other nations) specifically how to care for it. Read God's commands about using the land in Leviticus 25:1-7, and 10-12.

A

Resources are in danger when people do not properly care for God's creation.

PARENT:
Make sure your family practices conservation in your use of food, water, paper products, electricity, and fuel.

▲ **TAKE A STEP**

The command to let the land itself have a "sabbath"—or a period of rest—was only one of many commands God gave His people. But when the Israelites kept disobeying God and were taken into captivity, this command determined how long their punishment would last (read 2 Chronicles 36:20-21).

As God's children, we too should have a special concern for the world He has made. And we should look forward to the time when . . .

The creation itself will be liberated [set free] from its bondage to decay and brought into the glorious freedom of the children of God (Romans 8:21).

Look for stories in your local newspaper about our environment and resources. Are any natural resources in danger in your community? If so, what can your family do to help?

Mom—look!" Twelve-year-old Tim pointed excitedly as he and his mother walked to their car in the mall parking lot.

Mrs. Morgan glanced to where Tim was gesturing—and promptly jumped back. Beside their car lay a large black snake!

"How in the world did that thing get here?" she blurted.

"We can't worry about that now, Mom," Tim replied. "We've got to figure out how to save him!"

"What do you mean, 'how to save him'? We're going to walk slowly around to the other side of the car, get in, and drive away. The snake will move when I start the car."

"But Mom, if he stays here, he'll get run over for sure. Can't we put him in that box in the trunk and take him to the nature center? He's not poisonous. I'll keep him in the box and you won't have to do anything but drive. C'mon, Mom—please?"

◆ **TAKE A LOOK / Isaiah 65:17-25**

Though they lived in the city, Mr. and Mrs. Morgan had taught Tim to appreciate the world he lived in. They watched the squirrels gather nuts. They identified the birds that came to their feeder. They planted a small garden and didn't worry about the rabbit that ate the lettuce or the turtle that nibbled a cucumber now and then. The whole family enjoyed their pets: a cat, two dogs, six goldfish, and two gerbils. But Mrs. Morgan wasn't quite ready for a snake!

Looking after animals is one way to protect the resources God has given us. God's Word says:

A righteous man cares for the needs of his animal (Proverbs 12:10).

You can see how important God's entire creation is when you read the description of His new heavens and new earth in Isaiah 65:17-25. Even animals will have a place there!

▲ **TAKE A STEP**

The beautiful world we live in now cannot compare to the one God will create after Jesus returns. But until then, we must take good care of all the resources God has given us.

If you had found that snake, what would you have done? Are stray animals cared for in your community? Do you live close to a public park, wildlife preserve, botanical garden, zoo, or natural museum? Why not plan to visit one or more this summer and ask those in charge how they care for animals.

God says, "Use them, don't abuse them"

Q

How can I help protect our natural resources?

A

I should care for our natural resources until Jesus comes again.

God packed plenty in a peanut shell!

Q

How can I enjoy the resources God has given me?

A

I can enjoy and appreciate resources by learning more about them.

PARENT:
Encourage your child's interest in nature. With a magnifying glass, study an insect, leaf, or flower.

George Washington Carver, the great scientist, often talked to God about His creation. Listen as he describes one conversation:

" 'Dear Mr. Creator,' I said, 'please tell me what the universe was made for.'

"The Creator answered, 'You want to know too much for that little mind of yours. Ask something more your size.'

" 'Dear Mr. Creator, tell me what man was made for.'

"Again the Creator replied, 'You still ask too much.'

"So then I asked, 'Please, Mr. Creator, will you tell me what the peanut was made for?'

"God responded, 'That's better, but even then it's infinite. What do you want to know about the peanut?'

" 'Mr. Creator, can I make milk out of the peanut?'

" 'What kind of milk do you want, good Jersey milk or just plain boarding-house milk?'

" 'Good Jersey milk,' I answered. And then God taught me how to take the peanut apart and put it together again."

(Copyright 1944, 1971 by Shirley Graham and George D. Lipscomb. Taken from *Dr. George Washington Carver, Scientist,* published by Simon & Schuster, Inc. Used by permission.)

◆ TAKE A LOOK / Psalm 8

From his childhood, George Washington Carver studied growing things. As a scientist at Tuskegee Institute in Alabama, he carefully explored the humble peanut and discovered over 300 products that could be made from it! Milk, cream, cheese, plastics, paper, flour, insulation, and more can be made from this one amazing resource.

Some people have a wonderful curiosity about the world of plants and animals; others about the wind, water, and weather systems of our planet or the structure of the earth itself. David had an appreciation for the world God made, as you'll find out by reading Psalm 8.

▲ TAKE A STEP

David praised God for giving man a place of responsibility in His creation. He said,

You made him ruler over the works of your hands; you put everything under his feet (Psalm 8:6).

Praising God for His creation is one way you can enjoy it. Closely observing it is another way. Let each member of the family choose an animal or plant to learn more about. Do some research; then share what you have learned.

BIBLE

*H*ave you ever noticed how many words and phrases from the Bible have become part of our everyday speech? For example:
• Help someone in distress and you'll be called a "Good Samaritan"; question something another person claims to have seen and you'll be called a "Doubting Thomas."
• Demonstrate longsuffering and people will say you have the "patience of Job"; make a smart decision and they'll say you have the "wisdom of Solomon."
• Run away from home and you'll be known as a "prodigal"; grow too tall and you'll be called "Goliath."
• Come through hard circumstances and they'll say you've faced a "fiery furnace"; do something that seems impossible and they'll say you can "walk on water."

◆ THINKING ABOUT THE BIBLE

The all-time, number-one bestseller, the Bible, has affected our lives and language. You can find its words on the walls of public buildings and monuments, in hotel and motel rooms, and in the minds and hearts of countless believers.

The word *unique* means "one of a kind," and the Bible is certainly unique! It is different from any other book ever written because of its Author, its amazing durability, and its life-changing contents. The Bible is **God's special message to all people** for all times and in all places.

● KEY VERSE ON THE BIBLE

All Scripture is God-breathed and is useful for teaching, rebuking, correcting and training in righteousness, so that the man of God may be thoroughly equipped for every good work (2 Timothy 3:16-17).

▲ LOOKING AHEAD

This week we'll explore the Bible.

To start your study of the Bible, read Psalm 119:160 and Matthew 24:35 to find out how much longer it will be a "bestseller"!

*"No, Billy. The prophets weren't under court order. They **wanted** to reveal their sources."*

Thirty-nine books make one-half of "the Book"

H ey, Greg," Tony whispered to his friend as they walked out of the classroom, "that was a dumb stunt you pulled—disagreeing with Professor Jones. He's forgotten more about ancient history than you'll ever know!"

"I wasn't trying to be rude, Tony," Greg answered, "but that book he was using is 20 years old. When he claimed that almost nothing in the Old Testament is historically true, I knew he had his facts wrong. Was I supposed to say nothing?"

"Well, he's entitled to his opinion, just like you are."

"Tony, Prof. Jones wasn't expressing an opinion. In the last few years, archaeologists have uncovered civilizations that aren't mentioned anywhere else except in the Bible. What people once thought were fables and myths have turned out to be real. That's not opinion, it's fact. And Prof ought to know it!"

◆ TAKE A LOOK / John 5:39; Luke 24:25-27

Some people have claimed that the people and places in the Old Testament were just myths. But in the last few decades, archaeologists have uncovered many of the ancient civilizations mentioned in the early chapters of Genesis. They have also discovered complex written languages and records of laws existing long before Moses wrote the first five books of the Bible—though many thought writing hadn't been invented yet!

The Bible is God's Word, so it's accurate even in historical details. But more important, the Old Testament also looked ahead to Christ—and the salvation He would bring—long before He was born. Read John 5:39 and Luke 24:25-27 to learn what Jesus said about how reliable the Old Testament is.

▲ TAKE A STEP

The Old Testament is made up of 39 separate sections that we call "books." These books are divided into four categories: law (the first 5 books); history (12 books, Joshua–Esther); poetry (5 books, Job–Song of Solomon); and prophecy (17 books, Isaiah–Malachi). The books of law and history tell the story of Israel from its beginning to the time of Malachi, 400 years before Christ. The poetical books focus on experiences of life and our relationship with God. And the books of prophecy reveal both God's judgment and His rewards in the future.

Close your family time by naming the Old Testament books, section by section, using the table of contents in your Bible.

Q

What parts make up the Old Testament?

A

The Bible's 39 Old Testament books look forward to the Messiah, Jesus Christ.

PARENT: Make it a family project to memorize the names of the Old Testament books.

A scholar who didn't believe in God often lectured against Christianity, mocking God and His Word. But late in his life he confided to a friend: "Something secretly troubles me; in fact, I have no peace of mind day or night."

"What could bother you so greatly?" his friend asked.

"I do not have peace of mind," the scholar replied, "because I cannot know for sure what happens after death. I've always taught that death is the end of existence, that there is simply nothing after it. But what if the Bible is true after all? I don't believe it, and I've even taught and written against it. But what I've read in the Bible about the man who doesn't know God describes me perfectly. So if the Bible is true, then there is a hell . . . and I will be lost forever."

◆ TAKE A LOOK / 1 John 1:1-5; 2:1, 7-8

Many people have tried to prove that the Old Testament is false. Others don't want to hear the message of the New Testament, which teaches that a person must trust in Jesus to be saved from eternal punishment.

The Old Testament points to the coming of Christ. The New Testament records and explains His coming. The first five books of the New Testament are history, describing the life of Christ and the spread of Christianity.

The next 21 books are actually letters to churches or individuals. These letters were written either by the apostle Paul (13 letters) or other apostles such as Peter, James, and John (8 letters). The final book, Revelation, is about what will happen before Jesus returns. Read 1 John 1:1-5; 2:1 and 7-8 to discover why John (and the other New Testament authors) wrote their books.

▲ TAKE A STEP

In writing both the Old and New Testaments, godly men were guided by God's Spirit. The apostle John described his reason for writing this way:

We proclaim to you what we have seen and heard, so that you also may have fellowship with us. And our fellowship is with the Father and with his Son, Jesus Christ (1 John 1:3).

The scholar in the opening story realized that if what he read was true, he had two choices—to suffer eternal punishment, or to acknowledge his sins and confess Christ as Savior. Everyone faces those same choices. Have you made your choice yet?

New Testament history is really "His story"

Q

What parts make up the New Testament?

A

The Bible's 27 New Testament books tell me about Jesus and how He died for my sins.

PARENT:
After your family memorizes the Old Testament books, the New Testament books will be easy.

People, parchments, and pens: tools in God's hand

Q

How could the Bible be around so long and not get lost or changed?

A

The Bible has been preserved by God so that I can read and obey it today.

PARENT:
For information on how the Bible was preserved, see Josh McDowell's Evidence That Demands a Verdict.

*C*enturies ago scribes followed these rules to make sure they didn't make mistakes when they copied the Old Testament.

1. A scroll used in a synagogue must be written on the skins of certain animals that were prepared only by Jews.

2. Each skin must contain a certain number of columns for writing. Each column must not be less than 48 lines, or longer than 60 lines, and must be 30 letters wide.

3. The scribe had to look at every letter on the original before he copied it. He was not to trust even one letter to his memory.

4. The scribe had to leave the space of a hair between every consonant, the space of nine consonants between each section, and the space of three lines between each new book.

5. If a scribe made a mistake in copying, the entire scroll had to be burned or buried.

If you had to do assignments using those rules, how many reports would you turn in?

◆ TAKE A LOOK / Matthew 5:17-20; 24:35

Because scrolls were written on papyrus (made from a plant) or parchment (made from animal skins), none of the originals have survived. But when scholars compare the many copies that do exist from different time periods, they can tell that the later scribes produced almost error-free copies.

Read Jesus' words in Matthew 5:17-20 and 24:35. Learning how the Bible has been preserved shows us that God Himself protected His Word—so we could read and obey it today!

▲ TAKE A STEP

"Until heaven and earth disappear, not the smallest letter, not the least stroke of a pen, will by any means disappear from the Law until everything is accomplished" (Matthew 5:18).

The New Testament was written in the Greek language and was carefully preserved by the early church. Later the Bible was translated into Latin and was used during the Middle Ages. About 1380, John Wycliffe used that Latin version to make the first English translation so that ordinary people could understand God's Word. Since that time many translations have been made which help us understand what God is saying to us. Sometime this week, plan to purchase a recent translation to use in your family's devotional or study times.

W ith her Bible in hand, nine-year-old Ramona strolled into the kitchen. "Mom, can I ask you an important question?"

"Sure, honey," Mrs. Morris answered. "If I know the answer, I'll tell you!" They sat at the kitchen table.

"Mom, when I read the Bible by myself, I get real confused. I know I'm supposed to do what God says, but what if I don't understand? Will God be mad at me?"

"Oh, no, Ramona, God wants you to enjoy reading His Word. Why not do this: Before you read the Bible, ask God to help you understand what you read. Next, read a sentence or two. Then put what you've read into your own words, and picture it in your mind. Ask God to show you how it can make a difference in your life. Hey, why don't we try it right now?"

◆ TAKE A LOOK / Psalm 119:33-40

Everyone has questions about the Bible. Even adults who have studied God's Word for a long time don't understand what every verse means. But whether you're young or old, the Bible is still God's message for you. And He can help you understand it . . . if you'll let Him.

Even though David didn't understand everything God's Word said, he did realize that a big part of understanding is being willing to obey. As you read Psalm 119:33-40, find five ways David asked God for understanding.

▲ TAKE A STEP

Turn my heart toward your statutes and not toward selfish gain (Psalm 119:36).

Asking God for an understanding heart is an important part of Bible study. Every father wants his children to understand his thoughts, commands, and loving encouragements. And that's true of our heavenly Father too.

Each time you begin to read the Bible, tell God you will obey what you read. Ask Him to help you understand what He is saying to you in the verses you're reading. If the passage seems difficult, try reading it sentence by sentence. Keep reading until you understand a sentence or two. If you still have questions, don't be shy about asking your parent or church school teacher for help.

Do you have a daily time of prayer and Bible study? If not, today is the best time to begin. If each family member studies the same Bible book, you can learn from each other!

When you eat, bite off only what you can chew

Q

How can I understand the Bible when I read it myself?

A

The Bible can be understood by anyone willing to obey it.

PARENT:
Keep your own spirit refreshed in God's Word by getting involved in a Bible study group in your church or neighbor-hood.

PARABLES

On the first day of school a teacher told her class this story:
"There once was a student who took one look at the English textbook and was sure he would make an A. He had used the same textbook for another English course, so he thought this class would be a snap. Besides, he was a pretty good student and never had to study much.

"So, after the first day of class, the student didn't bother to listen. He never took notes, didn't participate in group activities, and rarely turned in homework assignments. He was late to class nearly every day.

"When mid-terms rolled around, he squeaked by with a D, but told himself not to worry—he'd do better on the final. And when his final exam was returned, that was exactly what his teacher had written: 'Don't worry. You'll do better when you take this course again next year!' "

◆ THINKING ABOUT PARABLES

That teacher could have simply said: "The way to pass this course is to pay attention, take notes, do your homework, and pass the tests." Instead, the teacher grabbed her students' attention. She put her good advice in the form of a story to help them experience in their imaginations the problems she wanted them to avoid.

Stories with a hidden meaning are called *parables*. They may illustrate a hard-to-understand truth, give instructions, or explain good behavior. We call the parables of Jesus **earthly stories with heavenly meanings.** By speaking in parables, Jesus fulfilled a prophecy written about Him in Psalm 78:2.

● KEY VERSE ON PARABLES

"I will open my mouth in parables, I will utter things hidden since the creation of the world" (Matthew 13:35).

"It's the weekend, Dad.
Read me one without a moral."

▲ LOOKING AHEAD

This week we'll ask questions about four parables.

By the way, what did the teacher's "parable" teach you about studying? How would you have felt if you were in her class?

*O*ne student from Central High was chosen to compete at the state academic tournament. Five students from nearby Northside High participated.

Late at night on the second day of the tournament, two of the Northside students were returning to their hotel rooms. As they passed the room where the girl from Central was staying, they heard muffled sobs. "Shh! Listen . . . " one said, and they put their ears to the door, snickering to each other. "She's probably homesick," one whispered as they walked away quietly. "All the better for us," the other replied. "She might not do so well tomorrow if she doesn't get enough sleep tonight."

A few minutes later, two more Northside students came down the hall. They too heard the sobbing and paused to listen. "Aw, poor baby!" one said sarcastically. "She's probably upset because she missed one question today. I hope she misses them all tomorrow!" They laughed as they walked on.

The last Northside student was hurrying to her room when she heard the sobs. She paused to listen, knocked softly, and went in. Soon she hurried out and went to her room . . . only to return a few minutes later with her overnight bag, pillow, and notebook.

◆ **TAKE A LOOK / Luke 10:30-37**
In many ways, that story is similar to Jesus' parable of the good Samaritan. According to God's Word, one of the two most important commandments is this:
Love your neighbor as yourself (Leviticus 19:18).
A Jewish religious leader tried to trick Jesus by asking Him who his "neighbor" was. In reply, Jesus told a story, which you can read in Luke 10:30-37. What do you think Jesus was teaching His followers to do by telling that parable?

▲ **TAKE A STEP**
Stories like the good Samaritan and the one about the students help us think about how we might react to a situation before we actually experience it. Jesus' parables gave His followers the opportunity to learn attitudes and actions that would please God in those situations.

It may be hard for you to imagine traveling on the road from Jerusalem to Jericho and finding a beaten man. But you can imagine being a student from Northside High. What would you have done? Can you think of a hurting "neighbor" you know who needs some tender loving care right now?

Take a look through your neighbor's eyes

Q

What does the parable of the good Samaritan teach me about love?

A

The parable of the good Samaritan prepares me for real-life situations by teaching me to respond to them with God's love.

I may not be perfect, but I'm still important!

*A*ndre was having trouble. It seemed the harder he worked on his math problems, the more he got wrong. None of the other students wanted to be in Andre's reading group because he was so slow. And thanks to him, his spelling team always lost.

One day Mrs. Baxter, the teacher, decided that since all the other students were doing well, she would concentrate on Andre. She began tutoring him after school and gave him special help while the rest of the class was busy on other assignments.

At the end of the term, Mrs. Baxter beamed as she handed out report cards. "Class, I want you to know I'm very proud of everyone's work this term, but I'm especially proud of Andre. He has caught up with the rest of the class and is doing very well."

Q

What does the parable of the lost sheep teach me about God?

◆ TAKE A LOOK / Luke 15:1-7

What is that story about? You could answer: It's about how lost you feel when you're not part of the group, or it's about a teacher who really cares about her students. But the point is that after much effort by Mrs. Baxter, her class is once again together.

The story of Andre and Mrs. Baxter is a modern parable, similar to one Jesus told. Mrs. Baxter cared about her whole class, but she also cared about Andre as an individual. And you know what? God loves His people in much the same way. You'll see that truth shine through the story found in Luke 15:1-7.

A

The parable of the lost sheep teaches me that everyone is important to God.

▲ TAKE A STEP

In Jesus' time, some of the very religious Jews thought that people who weren't "perfect" were worthless. They felt that if a person was crippled or blind or—worst of all—a tax collector, he could never get into God's kingdom. That's why the self-righteous Pharisees were so shocked at Jesus' behavior that they said:

"This man welcomes sinners and eats with them" (Luke 15:2).

But Jesus invited everyone—men and women, boys and girls—to become God's children and enter His kingdom regardless of how sick or poor or "bad" they were.

Can you identify a group of people you might find it hard to care for—those of another race, or from another country, or convicted criminals, or maybe those who dress differently? How would you feel if someone like that moved in next door? According to the stories you read today, how would Jesus want you to act?

*T*hat's a serious matter," Mr. Barrett said after learning from another teacher that one of the students had been through her test files. "Do you have an idea who it could be? Maybe you should question your students one by one."

"No, I don't think so," Mrs. Sanford replied, shaking her head. "It's not fair to upset all the innocent students just to find the guilty one. Besides, if I accused someone unjustly, I might hurt his reputation. I think the best thing to do is to wait until exam time. I'll give a completely different test, and maybe the culprit will give himself away by not studying. Anyone who just memorizes the answers to the old test will fail."

◆ TAKE A LOOK / Matthew 13:24-30, 36-43

Jesus' disciples once asked Him why He told parables. He answered:

"The knowledge of the secrets of the kingdom of heaven has been given to you, but not to them"(Matthew 13:11).

Through His parables, Jesus was announcing the good news that God's kingdom is open to anyone willing to enter it. The people who understood that and believed in Him became members of His kingdom and could understand His stories.

Today you'll read a parable that teaches something else about God's kingdom on earth. After you read Matthew 13:24-30, skip down to verses 36-43 and read how Jesus Himself explained what the parable meant.

▲ TAKE A STEP

Mrs. Sanford allowed the cheater to remain in the class. But when exam time came, that student would be revealed. The parable you just read tells the same kind of story. The good seed stands for the members of the kingdom—those who have received Jesus as Savior. The all-knowing God is in control, but His people must live together with the wicked people in this world until they are separated at the "harvest," the time of judgment. Peter warned:

So then, dear friends, since you are looking forward to this, make every effort to be found spotless, blameless and at peace with him (2 Peter 3:14).

Close your family time today by answering this question: By the way I live my life daily, do I look more like wheat or a weed?

Wheat or weed—which one do I look like?

Q

What does the parable of the weeds teach me about life?

This parable teaches me that the righteous and the wicked live together until the day of judgment.

There's no excuse for ignoring God

Mr. Goodman leaned back in his chair and thought about the banquet he had planned for his employees. The banquet hall would be beautifully decorated, the food fit for a king, and the entertainment superb. He had spared no expense. He'd even given his workers time off to get ready for the celebration.

Suddenly the phone interrupted his thoughts. "Sir," his secretary said, "Mr. Lake called and sends his regrets about tonight. He's in the middle of a big real estate deal, and he might lose a large commission if he's not there."

That made Mr. Goodman a little sad. But by the time he had hung up the phone a second time, he was pretty angry. "A friend gave me tickets for a ball game," Mr. Merritt said. "Sorry I have to miss tonight." One employee after another called to excuse himself from the big banquet. The last straw came when Miss Hooper stopped him in the hall. "Oh, Mr. Goodman," she gushed, "I meant to let you know, but I won't be coming tonight. My boyfriend and I are going to look at engagement rings."

Mr. Goodman rushed angrily into his office and buzzed his secretary. "Call the downtown mission," he said brusquely. "Invite everyone there—the poor, the homeless, the underprivileged—to come to my banquet. And send a memo to all employees. It should read: 'Invitation cancelled.'"

◆ TAKE A LOOK / Luke 14:15-24

When Jesus was on earth, he spent time feasting with the outcasts of society—sinners and tax collectors. But on one occasion, He was invited to the home of a prominent religious leader, where He was carefully watched (Luke 14:1). While He was there, Jesus told a story similar to the one you just read. As you read the story of the great banquet in Luke 14:15-24, imagine how you would feel if you were the host.

▲ TAKE A STEP

In Old Testament days, the time of the Messiah's coming was often compared to a wonderful feast. Isaiah wrote:

The LORD Almighty will prepare a feast of rich food for all peoples (Isaiah 25:6).

In Jesus' parable, the people you'd expect to come were the ones who were eventually left out. Think about the excuses the people gave in today's story and in the parable. The people weren't doing anything wrong, were they? Then why were their excuses not acceptable?

Q

What does the parable of the great banquet teach me about honoring God?

A

The parable of the banquet teaches me that I honor God by obeying Him, and that He rewards obedience.

ENCOURAGEMENT · ·

A *group of 11-year-olds defined the word* encouragement *by using each letter of the word to make this acrostic:*
> **E**ncouragement
> **N**ever uses force,
> **C**ares what happens to someone else.
> **O**ffers love,
> **U**nderstands,
> **R**eally listens,
> **A**lways helps,
> **G**ently persuades.
> **E**ncouragement is
> **M**aking
> **E**ach person feel
> **N**eeded, and
> **T**aking special care of those who need a little more help.

◆ THINKING ABOUT ENCOURAGEMENT

You may not realize it, but you're always either encouraging or discouraging the people around you by what you say and do. Everyone wants to feel loved and accepted. Don't you?

Sometimes people are afraid they don't quite "measure up." That's when they need encouragement.

Encouragement is **the loving concern that helps a person overcome feelings of rejection or failure**. The Bible encourages us to . . .

● KEY VERSE ON ENCOURAGEMENT
Encourage one another daily (Hebrews 3:13).

▲ LOOKING AHEAD

Read about one of the best-known encouragers in the Bible—Joses. Never heard of him? Perhaps you know him by his nickname—*Barnabas*, which means "Son of Encouragement"! Read Acts 4:36-37; 9:26-27; and 11:20-24. In what specific ways did Barnabas encourage others?

$$\begin{array}{r} 20° \\ +\,17° \\ \hline \cancel{27}° \\ \cancel{33}° \\ 34° \end{array}$$

"Keep going. You're getting warmer."

Gentle people + kind words = encour- agement

Q

Who needs encourage- ment?

A

Everyone needs encourage- ment from time to time.

I feel funny being in class with all those teenagers," Mrs. Allen sighed, *"and the work sure isn't easy. I wonder if going back to college was the right thing to do."*

Seventeen-year-old Janna looked at her mother tearfully. *"I never dreamed Rod and I would break up. I miss him so much."*

Five-year-old Christopher slowly pushed his new bicycle back to where his dad was waiting. With his head down he muttered, *"Daddy, I'm afraid I'll fall off again. Can we go inside now?"*

"I'm just not hungry, honey," Mr. Franklin said as he slowly removed his suitcoat. *"That contract I've been working on for months went to another firm. I don't know—maybe starting my own business was a big mistake."*

Debbie could feel her face blushing and could hear the class snickering. *"Why did I raise my hand?"* she asked herself. *"I must be really dumb not to know the answer to that question."*

◆ TAKE A LOOK / Mark 14:27-42
Everybody has times of discouragement, fear, or frustration. From the toddler to the business executive, there's not a person alive who doesn't benefit from a little honest encouragement now and then.

Even Jesus knew times of loneliness and discouragement—especially when He faced the final hours of His life. From the account in Mark 14:27-42, do you think Peter, James, and John gave *encouragement* or *discouragement* to Jesus?

▲ TAKE A STEP
We all need someone to believe in us, to appreciate our strengths, and to accept us even when we make mistakes. God's Word actually commands us to encourage others.

Let us encourage one another—and all the more as you see the [last] Day approaching (Hebrews 10:25).

The disciples couldn't really have stopped Jesus' arrest and crucifixion from happening, but if they had been more sensitive to Jesus' needs, they might have encouraged Him during some of His darkest hours on earth. You too can become an encourager as you put other people's needs above your own and listen to them with your heart.

Pick one of the five situations above. How do you think the person feels? What would you say or do to encourage that person?

*T*he spectators' excitement grew as the two wrestlers grappled on the mat. Their coaches shouted moves and countermoves to them. "Come on, Bob!" Coach Kyzer yelled enthusiastically. "Go for it. Chicken wing; chicken wing. That's it; that's it. Great move, man! Hold him right there."

Across the mat, Coach Brown bellowed angrily, "What do you think you're doing, dummy? You think we never practiced that escape? What have you got for a brain?"

Minutes later the referee raised the winner's hand. Coach Kyzer gave Bob a bear hug, and his team cheered and walked forward to slap him on the back. On the other side of the mat, Coach Brown turned away from his defeated wrestler with a shrug of disgust.

◆ **TAKE A LOOK / 1 Samuel 30:3, 6, 8-10, 17-25**

Year after year, Coach Kyzer turned out winning wrestling teams. And year after year, Coach Brown complained about the lack of commitment of his wrestlers—who consistently lost. But nobody who saw the two coaches in action really wondered why.

Coach Brown's team worked out just as hard, learned just as many moves, and practiced just as often as Coach Kyzer's team. But Coach Brown's angry shouting and sulky attitude humiliated his wrestlers and made them feel guilty for losing.

Coach Kyzer expected—and encouraged—every member of the team to do his best. But win or lose, each wrestler felt like part of the team. The difference between the two coaches was the difference between success and failure.

Before David became king of Israel, a small group of men became his followers. Though they were vastly outnumbered by King Saul's army, their loyalty to David never wavered. Read 1 Samuel 30:3, 6, 8-10, and 17-25 to see how David's encouragement built trust among his men.

▲ **TAKE A STEP**

If a man's gift is . . . encouraging, let him encourage (Romans 12:6, 8).

One reason David's mighty men remained loyal throughout his life was because David encouraged them . . . both as individuals and as a team. Think about the "teams" you belong to—in sports, at school, on the job, at church, and even your family. How does the leader of each of those teams encourage you? What's one way you can encourage your teammates?

What difference does encouragement make?

Encouragement motivates me to do my best in whatever I do.

Walk in my shoes to know why my feet hurt

"**I** don't understand it. Clem plays so well when Debbie is here, but he doesn't play nearly as well when we come to watch him," Mrs. Crawford said to her husband as they waited for their six-year-old son after his T-ball game.

Debbie, Clem's 16-year-old sister, often watched her little brother's team practice. She knew that Clem worried about not making the right plays. So when Debbie attended Clem's games, she sat in the stands cheering loudly. He could hear her shouting, "Run, Clem! Go on to second," or "Yea, Clem! Great job!" when he crossed home plate for a score. He knew she would be waiting for him at the players' gate, rain or shine, win or lose. And if he made a mistake, he knew exactly what she'd say: "Don't worry about it. You'll do better next time."

◆ TAKE A LOOK / Luke 7:36-50

Clem's parents hadn't learned the "secret" of sincere encouragement, but Debbie knew! Debbie could sense how her brother felt. Because she understood, supported, and gave him hope, he was encouraged to do his best.

Many people miss great opportunities to encourage. Some people just don't think to do it. Some are afraid to reach out, or simply don't know what to say. But if you love people with God's kind of love, you'll encourage them.

People who came to Jesus always found encouragement because He accepted them. He hated their sin but He loved the sinner. Read Luke 7:36-50 for one example of how He did this.

▲ TAKE A STEP

Jesus certainly didn't encourage the Pharisees and Sadducees who tried to trap Him! But everyone who came to Him with a genuine desire for forgiveness, understanding, or compassion went away with encouragement, hope, and rejoicing. Through Jesus,

[God] gave us eternal encouragement and good hope (2 Thessalonians 2:16).

In order to encourage others, you must first see a person's need and then show him God's kind of love—love that is willing to accept that person "as is" . . . and willing to get involved.

What advice would your family give Mr. and Mrs. Crawford about their son? Close your devotional time today by letting each person share an area of life in which he or she needs encouragement right now.

Q

Why is encouragement so difficult?

A

Encouragement involves responding to others' needs with God's kind of love.

PARENT:
People blossom in an atmosphere of encouragement. Let your child tell you how he or she perceives the "atmosphere" of your home—and work on necessary changes.

Which sentence in each pair do you find more encouraging?

Mother to daughter: (a) "Hey, if you keep biting your nails, you'll be the ugliest girl around!" Or, (b) "Honey, I know you're trying hard not to bite your nails. Would it help if we worked out a 'warning signal' to help you realize what you're doing?"

Wife to husband: (a) "This house could fall apart for all you care. The least you could do is change this lightbulb!" Or, (b) "Dear, I can't reach the socket in the bathroom to change the bulb. When you get a chance, would you mind doing it?"

Youth leader to group: (a) "Anyone who wants to go on the summer trip must participate in every fund-raiser." Or, (b) "Okay, gang, we can only take so many kids on the summer trip. We've got to find a fair way to decide who will be eligible. Anybody got any ideas?"

◆ **TAKE A LOOK**
Proverbs 12:18; 15:1; 17:27; 26:21; 29:20
Words either help or hurt. They can open a door for someone who's discouraged . . . or slam it.

Many comedians today joke with sarcastic re-marks that can cut and hurt. Some people find this funny . . . unless the teasing is directed toward them! But an encourager uses carefully chosen words to build others up rather than tear them down.

The tongue that brings healing is a tree of life,
but a deceitful tongue crushes the spirit
(Proverbs 15:4).

The proverbs below will help you understand how an encourager should speak to others. As you read, match each verse with the phrase at the right that best summarizes it.

This verse tells me . . .   **that an encourager is:**
1. Proverbs 12:18   a. not quarrelsome
2. Proverbs 15:1   b. slow to speak
3. Proverbs 17:27   c. careful about what he says
4. Proverbs 26:21   d. gentle
5. Proverbs 29:20   e. not reckless, but soothing

▲ **TAKE A STEP**
An encourager uses words that are soothing, gentle, carefully chosen, and understanding.

Look again at the (a) and (b) statements at the top of the page. This weekend, evaluate (with a lov-ing spirit) what others in the family say to you: "That sounded like an '(a) statement.' Could you rephrase it?" or "Thanks—I needed that '(b) statement'!"

Do my words build up or tear down?

Q

How can I encourage others?

A

Encourage-ment means carefully considering what I say and how I say it.

PARENT:
Answers to the matching quiz are 1-e, 2-d, 3-c, 4-a, 5-b.

FATHERS

*R*ecently you answered some questions about your mother. Now fill in the blanks below to see who knows father best!

Dad's hobbies are _____ .
Dad was born in the state of _____ .
Dad's middle name is _____ .
The sport Dad likes to watch most is _____ .
Dad is _____ years old.
When Dad has time to himself, he likes to _____ .
Dad's favorite meal is _____ .
Dad's favorite kind of book is _____ .

◆ THINKING ABOUT FATHERS

You may know a whole lot about your father, or maybe he hasn't told you very much about himself. He may spend hours every week playing with you, helping with homework, just talking with you, or maybe you see him only on weekends.

Fathers come in all ages, shapes, and sizes, and with an assortment of jobs, hobbies, and habits. No two fathers are alike. But every father has the same privilege of helping his child be the best he or she can be. As **head of his family**, a father has the awesome and challenging responsibility for each family member's well-being.

This key verse tells how fathers can fulfill their God-given goal.

● KEY VERSE ON FATHERS

For you know that we dealt with each of you as a father deals with his own children, encouraging, comforting and urging you to live lives worthy of God (1 Thessalonians 2:11-12).

▲ LOOKING AHEAD

This week we'll use the key words in that verse to look at the role of fathers.

Most children inherit something from their fathers: the shape of his nose, an interest in sports, a funny habit, or even an aptitude for math or science. Can you think of three ways in which you are like your father?

"What are you, Dad? The breadwinner or the vegetablewinner?"

E ven though he was now a young man, Ray
Marshall could still remember his father's hurtful
words. He realized now that his dad didn't mean to
hurt him, but Ray could still feel the pain he had
experienced 15 years ago.

Ray was five then. He and his older sister were
driving with their parents to visit Aunt Judy, Uncle
Vaughan, and their new baby—a little boy who joined a
family of three girls. The entire family—grandparents,
aunts, uncles, even cousins—were thrilled with the new
arrival. As they rode, Ray and his sister tried to imagine
how excited everyone had been when they were born.
Mr. Marshall, concentrating on driving in the pouring
rain, wasn't paying much attention.

Suddenly five-year-old Ray leaned forward and put
his arms around his father's neck. "I'll bet you were
glad to get a boy when I was born, weren't you, Dad?"

"Let go, Ray!" Mr. Marshall shouted. "No, we
didn't really care whether you were a boy or a girl; we
were just glad you and Mom were alive."

◆ **TAKE A LOOK**
Proverbs 1:8-9; 2:1, 5; 3:1-2; 4:1-6
Ray wanted his father to say how happy he was
to have Ray for a son. Instead, it seemed that Dad
didn't care. But Mr. Marshall had been thinking
about his wife's difficult labor before Ray was born.
Immediately Mr. Marshall tried to explain that he
had been more concerned about the baby's safe
arrival than whether it was a boy or a girl. But his
explanation didn't take the sting out of the words.

Words have an awesome impact—they can
either help or hurt. A father's words of encouragement tell his child how much he is loved. They help
the child do his best in whatever he does. King
Solomon, who wrote the book of Proverbs, was a
wise father. Read Proverbs 1:8-9; 2:1, 5; 3:1-2; and
4:1-6. What can you tell about Solomon's father,
David?

▲ **TAKE A STEP**
David taught Solomon to . . .
*Lay hold of my words with all your heart; keep
my commands and you will live (Proverbs 4:4).*
A father's encouraging words and the way he
lives work together to teach his child how to
handle life's situations in a godly way. Whether
you're a child or an adult, think of a time your
father encouraged you. Then make time today to
encourage him!

Children are fragile— handle with care

*Why should
a father
encourage
his child?*

A

*A father's
encourage-
ment helps
his child
live wisely.*

PARENT:
*An outstand-
ing book
written for
fathers is* The
Blessing *by
Gary Smalley
and John
Trent.*

Thy rod and thy paddle, they comfort me . . . ?

"Why do I have to have the smallest room in the house?" 13-year-old Terry complained to his father. "All my friends have big rooms, and I'm stuck in this closet!"

"Keep complaining like that, son, and we'll be glad to put you in a real closet," his father replied. "After all, the way business has been lately, you should be thankful you have a roof over your head, food to eat, and clothes to wear."

That evening, Terry came to his father. "Dad, I'm sorry I complained this afternoon. I guess I was envious of everything Jason has—a VCR, a computer, a swimming pool, and a place to put it all. But I was thinking: Jason's dad has a lot of money, but there's one thing you give me that he doesn't give Jason."

"What's that, son?" Terry's dad asked with interest.

"You give me rules. It sounds corny, but that tells me you care about me. A lot of kids I know can't say that about their dads."

Q

What are some ways a father comforts his child?

A

A father comforts his child by providing for basic needs, loving guidance, and healthy discipline.

◆ **TAKE A LOOK / Luke 11:11-13**

This week's key verse, 1 Thessalonians 2:11-12, states that one thing a good father does is comfort his child. We often think of comfort as the care we get when we're hurt or feeling sad. But it also means making someone comfortable by meeting that person's basic needs. Fathers make their children comfortable by providing shelter, food, clothing, transportation, and medical care. And when they can, most fathers give more than just the bare necessities of life.

Read Luke 11:11-13. How does Jesus say *earthly fathers* are like your *heavenly Father?* What does that tell you about God?

▲ **TAKE A STEP**

A father's rules are "comforts" too. They're not made just to keep you from having fun, but to protect you from dangers you may not realize are there. When those rules are broken, even the discipline that follows is part of the "comfort" a father gives.

We have all had human fathers who disciplined us and we respected them for it (Hebrews 12:9).

Terry was old enough to appreciate his father's "comfort" for him through guidance, rules, and discipline. Think of three rules your parents have made. How does each one protect you? In what other ways does your father comfort you?

*A*s the pastor listened to the choir sing, his gaze scanned the congregation. He noticed Mr. Clayton and his grown sons sitting in the second row. Both sons were now successful businessmen like their father, but rarely came to church. "Why does God mean so little to them?" the pastor wondered.

Next he saw Mr. and Mrs. Bentley sitting behind the Claytons. The pastor had sometimes been irritated by Mr. Bentley's refusal to serve on some church committees because it would take time from his family. But at least Mr. Bentley was consistent: He had also turned down a big promotion because it would have meant weekly travel and moving the children away from their church and school. And probably no other man he knew showed his wife more love.

Yes, for practicing his faith before his children, Mr. Bentley got top marks. No wonder his son was serving as a missionary and his daughter was studying to be a nurse. It seemed the faith Mr. Bentley taught them had certainly been caught by them.

◆TAKE A LOOK / 1 Corinthians 4:14-17

The word *modeling* describes what happens when a person's life influences the way others think, act, and talk. When children talk, walk, and behave like their parents, it's usually because of the parents' influence in their lives.

When the church was just beginning, the apostle Paul was a model or example for many new believers. In 1 Corinthians 4:14-17, Paul speaks to them as a father because he had led them to Christ. As you read those verses, you'll find that Paul urged them to imitate him. What do you think he meant by that?

▲ TAKE A STEP

Like all fathers, Paul set an example for his "children." He was their role model. And when he could not be with them personally, he sent Timothy to . . .

Set an example for the believers in speech, in life, in love, in faith and in purity (1 Timothy 4:12).

Like Mr. Bentley and the apostle Paul, fathers can urge their children to love God and live a life that pleases Him. How? By living that kind of life themselves and setting a godly example. Can you think of a regular activity your father does that encourages you to know and please God better? (And Dad, if your children have trouble thinking of your God-pleasing activities, what does that tell you?)

Will you fill your father's big shoes?

Q

How can a father urge his child to live a godly life?

A

A father urges his child to live for God by setting a godly example.

DAD:
One major example you provide is as a husband. Study Proverbs 5:18-19; Ephesians 5:25-33; 1 Peter 3:7.

Honoring your father is a lifelong job

Q

How can I honor my father as God has commanded?

A

I honor my father when I obey, respect, and care for him throughout his life.

Honey, I think you ought to read this," Mrs. Rhodes said as she handed the smudged sheet of notebook paper to her husband. "Clayton's teacher gave it to me at our conference today." It was an essay his third-grade son had written, entitled "My Dad":

"My dad's not perfect. But he's special. He makes money so Mom and my sister and me can have the things we need.

"I know he loves me because he takes me fishing and plays catch with me in the backyard. He helped me build a treehouse. Sometimes after we turn into our driveway, he lets me sit on his lap and drive. It's fun. Dad helps me with my homework. He said he had trouble learning times tables when he was in third grade. Dad says I'll be okay, just keep practicing.

"I think Dad is worried about getting old like Grandpa did. Maybe I should tell him not to worry. I'll look after him."

After he read the paper, Mr. Rhodes looked at his wife with tears in his eyes. "You know, this makes it all worthwhile. Do you think we could get this framed?"

◆ TAKE A LOOK
Genesis 46:28-30; 47:28-30; 50:12-14

Clayton's essay showed that he recognized and appreciated the ways his father provided for, taught, and encouraged him. It showed how much Clayton admired and enjoyed being with his dad. His essay honored his father.

God's Word clearly tells people:
"Honor your father and your mother, so that you may live long in the land the LORD your God is giving you" (Exodus 20:12).

This command is true for you during your childhood, youth, and adulthood—as long as your parents live.

When Joseph was sold into slavery, his father, Jacob, grieved because he thought his son was dead. Years later after much suffering, Joseph was a powerful man in Egypt when God reunited him with his family. Read about Joseph and his father in Genesis 46:28-30; 47:28-30; and 50:12-14.

▲ TAKE A STEP

Joseph honored his father by caring for him during the last years of his life, and by respecting his wishes about his burial place. Clayton honored his father with an essay of appreciation. You might want to write your own essay about your father. Write it neatly on clean paper, and give it to him on Father's Day!

NEW BIRTH

*T*he story of my new birth has two parts. My family was active in church, and I believed in God. As a child I never doubted that I would go to heaven when I died. But when I was nine, I was challenged in an evangelistic service: 'You must accept Christ as your Savior and believe that He died for your sins.' Right then I realized I wasn't automatically a Christian, so I accepted Christ as my Savior.

"Later my life changed when my parents divorced. I was bitter. In my teens I became rebellious and withdrawn. I didn't turn my back on the Lord totally, but I wasn't listening to Him either. He drew me back to Himself by letting my life hit rock bottom. I was sent to a large church one night for counseling, but I skipped the session and was walking around when I heard music in the gym. Before I knew it, someone pulled me into the group. In that youth meeting my hardness melted and I surrendered my life to Jesus."

◆ THINKING ABOUT NEW BIRTH

The Bible uses phrases like "being born again," "becoming a new creature," "conversion," and "new life" to describe **the complete change from one form of life to another that happens when a person accepts Jesus as Savior.** Just as physical birth takes a baby from the mother's womb into a totally new way of life, so spiritual birth brings people into eternal life. New life is necessary because all people are under a death sentence for their sins, which separates them from God.

● KEY VERSE ON NEW BIRTH
Jesus declared, "I tell you the truth, no one can see the kingdom of God unless he is born again" (John 3:3).

▲ LOOKING AHEAD

This week you'll read the stories of five people who experienced new birth in Christ. With some, it's a sudden, dramatic event. For others it's a quiet experience. But for each person, it's the most important event of his or her life.

Read in Acts 9:1-19 what happened to the apostle Paul.

SUNDAY SCHOOL CLASSROOMS →

"Must've been a candy apple. I can't believe Adam and Eve would do us in for plain fruit."

People without Jesus are the "walking dead"

When I was in tenth grade, my family edged away from the church. When I started college, my parents divorced and we weren't the same family anymore. It was really hard.

"My older brother accepted Jesus as his Savior during college, and after he graduated he went to seminary. I was still pretty mixed up and frustrated by all that was happening at home, so I went to spend a summer with my brother. He was really patient and let me ask a lot of questions. He knew there was a lot I didn't understand. He showed me what the Bible says about important issues. When we read the Bible together, I finally saw that God was talking about me as an individual who needed new life. I accepted Jesus as my Savior that summer and I became a different person."

Why do I need a new birth?

◆ TAKE A LOOK
John 3:16; 10:10; Ephesians 2:4-5

The confusion and frustration that this young woman and her family experienced were the results of humanity's sinful condition. People were created to have fellowship with God. But when the first man—Adam—chose to disobey God, that fellowship was broken for everyone. All human beings are born with a sinful nature. Their sin keeps them from God and causes unhappiness, pain, and evil.

The Bible describes the human problem this way:

As for you, you were dead in your transgressions and sins (Ephesians 2:1).

Jesus came to bring life where there was sin and death. Read John 3:16; 10:10; and Ephesians 2:4-5 for God's own description of the life He wants each of us to experience.

New birth is necessary because sin separates people from God.

▲ TAKE A STEP

Sin keeps people from the life God wants them to have. People who have not invited God into their lives may feel frustrated, sad, or angry. They will do things that they know are wrong. Many people without God try to fill the emptiness of their lives with money, possessions, pleasure, fame, drugs, sex, or success. But no one can find true happiness apart from God. And no one can find God without experiencing the new birth.

Close your family time today by thinking about your life. Have you experienced the new birth? If you haven't, read Ephesians 2:1 again . . . and then agree with God that sin in your life is serving as your "coffin." He can free you from that coffin!

I grew up in a Christian home and always believed what I was told about God, so I can't pinpoint the moment of my new birth. Now I realize I had only a kind of mental belief.

"I worked a few years after high school, then wanted to go into Christian work. I wrote to a Bible college about working my way through. The reply came that I could be secretary to the college president and have time off for classes. So I went. There my eyes were opened: I saw people who had a quality of life I didn't have.

"The Holy Spirit began to use the sermons I was hearing to convict me, and after about a year of struggling, a friend invited me to an evangelistic meeting. I thought I needed to improve myself and do more for God. But I soon realized I really needed to have Jesus as the Savior and Lord of my life. At that time, Jesus took control of my life. I've belonged to Him for 39 years now and He's never let me go!"

◆ **TAKE A LOOK / 1 Timothy 2:5; John 1:12; Ephesians 2:4-5, 8-9**

No two babies are born in exactly the same way. And there are as many different experiences of the new birth as there are Christians. But one thing is the same with everyone. As Jesus said, *"I am the way and the truth and the life. No one comes to the Father except through me"* (John 14:6).

By paying the penalty for our sin, Jesus Christ bridged the gap between sinful people and a holy God. His death and resurrection make new birth possible for all who trust in Him. Read 1 Timothy 2:5; John 1:12; and Ephesians 2:4-5 and 8-9 to find out how He makes this possible.

▲ **TAKE A STEP**

God has provided the only way to Him. But we must respond to His invitation. Here's how:

1. Admit that your sin has separated you from God.
2. Be willing to turn from sin and toward God.
3. Believe that Jesus suffered for *your* sins when He gave His life on the cross.
4. Ask God to forgive you, to take control of your life, and make you a new person.
5. Believe that God has heard your prayer, and thank Him for it.

The path is open, but you must take the step

Q

How can I experience a new birth?

A

New birth happens when I turn from sin and put my trust in Christ, who died for me and rose again.

"Let the little children come to me," Jesus said

I was five years old when my dad became pastor of a small country church. A year later, during summer revival services, I realized that what my dad and the evangelist had been preaching about included me: I was one of those sinners who needed Jesus. I didn't want to be separated from God forever. At that moment I trusted in Jesus' death for me, and I asked Him to be my Savior.

"After the service, I told my mom and dad that I now belonged to Jesus. They questioned me to make sure I understood what I was saying, but I was already a 'new creature in Christ.'

"My clearest memory of that night is of overwhelming joy. Though I can hardly explain it, I remember how it felt. All during the long ride home, I sat between my mom and dad, joyfully singing songs about Jesus, praising Him. It was as if I were singing with an angel choir. The night was clear; the stars were bright; and for me, heaven seemed only a step away."

Q

Do I have to be a certain age to experience new birth?

A

New birth can happen to anyone—even children.

◆ **TAKE A LOOK / Matthew 18:6; 19:13-15**

Everyone needs to know Jesus—including children! But because each child is different, there is no specific age at which a child suddenly understands he or she needs to be born again. Even young children can understand that because they are human, born into Adam's family, they sin (which makes God sad).

Sometimes adults wonder whether a child who accepts Christ really understands what the new birth means. The truth is that no one—adult or child—knows everything about that wonderful experience. But when a Christian of any age studies God's Word, prays, and lets God work in and through his life, then understanding grows.

Even in Jesus' day some adults overlooked children, thinking they couldn't really understand what Jesus taught. But Jesus knew that children could understand and believe in Him. He also knew that a child's faith was often greater than an adult's. What evidence do you find in Matthew 18:6 and 19:13-15 that the children believed in Jesus?

▲ **TAKE A STEP**

Jesus said, "Let the little children come to me, and do not hinder them" (Matthew 19:14).

Perhaps someone in your family experienced the new birth as a child. If so, now would be a good time for that person to share the story of his new birth. Can you think of a Bible character who started serving God as a young child?

I n college I saw that Bill (who is now my husband) and his family had a serious, joyful, living relationship with this mysterious being they called God. The more I got to know them, the more I saw they had something I wanted. But I wasn't ready to give up my way of life; I thought Christianity was just a lot of do's and don'ts.

"After a couple of years I started going to a Bible study. The teacher had a real knack for explaining who God is and what He does for us. It was amazing. One day I couldn't put it off any longer—I had to come to God in faith. All those things I was holding onto in my life no longer mattered. I couldn't have the joy I'd seen any other way. So I stopped fighting. I had to say yes to the Lord. And right then that joy became mine."

◆ TAKE A LOOK / Luke 19:1-10

When someone experiences the new birth, life changes. Sometimes the *effect* of past sin lingers, but the new birth gives us a fresh start with God at the controls.

Everyone responds to Christ a little differently. For instance, if a person has been heavily involved in a sinful lifestyle, he or she may now seek a life of purity. One who has strongly opposed believing in God probably will want to soak up the truth in the Scriptures. One who has lived an aimless, selfish life will have a new purpose for living. Even so, God's goal for all believers is the same—that they become like Jesus.

Those who are led by the Spirit of God are sons of God. . . . If we are children, then we are heirs—heirs of God and co-heirs with Christ (Romans 8:14, 17).

As you read Luke 19:1-10, look for the way Zacchaeus became more like Jesus after he met Him.

▲ TAKE A STEP

When you've experienced the new birth, Jesus makes changes that other people can see. It happened in Zacchaeus's life. He returned the money he'd stolen by collecting too much tax because now he wanted to do what was right. It happened to the young woman in the opening story—her whole attitude toward God changed.

How many ways can you think of that you've changed since your new birth? If you've not yet experienced the new birth, perhaps God is speaking to you today.

If so, won't you say yes to Him right now?

The new birth means a new way of life

Q

How will I be different after my new birth?

A

New birth changes me so I become more like Jesus.

PARENT: *Are you keeping a scrapbook for your child? You might also keep a journal of his or her spiritual growth. It will be a record that will later be treasured.*

SELF-CONTROL

I said you may not have any candy today," Mrs. Tucker reminded Butch firmly as she pushed the grocery cart through the checkout lane. But Butch's grip tightened around the candy bar, and he shook his head stubbornly. "Butch, I said put the candy back and I meant it," his mother said with irritation.

Butch closed his eyes and shook his head more vigorously. His mother snatched the candy bar from him. Butch screamed loudly.

"Hush! Everyone is looking at you," his mother hissed angrily.

Her two-year-old continued to bellow. "Okay, Butch, okay. Stop screaming and I'll buy the candy bar. You can have it later." As she paid for the groceries, Butch grinned to the people in line behind them.

◆ THINKING ABOUT SELF-CONTROL

People of all ages occasionally use bad behavior to get what they want. Sometimes we just call them "immature," but what they really need is the character quality of "self-control."

Self-control is **the ability to say no to what we shouldn't do and yes to what we should**. See why self-control is so important in this command from God's Word:

● KEY VERSE ON SELF-CONTROL

Be self-controlled and alert. Your enemy the devil prowls around like a roaring lion looking for someone to devour (1 Peter 5:8).

▲ LOOKING AHEAD

A little girl once heard her pastor preach about "controlling one's self." Soon after that she disobeyed her mother and explained that her "little elf" had taken control!

Proverbs 25:28 pictures someone who lacks self-control. What might happen if your wall of self-control is broken down?

"Her mother told her to quit biting her fingernails, but she went right ahead!"

"Aw, do I have to go?"

"A w, do I have to go?" Darren complained to his mother. "When Dad smokes in the car, I get a headache. Can't I just stay home?"

"Darren, this is the first vacation Dad's had in—"

"But Mom," Deanna chimed in, "why doesn't Dad just quit smoking? We saw a film in health class about smoking and it's an awful habit. Every time you smoke a cigarette, you take eight minutes off your life. And a whole quart of that yucky tar accumulates in your lungs every year. Dad's killing himself and we all know it. I hate it when he smokes."

"I know, honey," her mom replied. "Dad's heard those facts, but he just doesn't want to believe them. He's addicted to cigarettes and it would take a tremendous, even painful, effort to stop. He's not in control of his life—his habit is."

◆ TAKE A LOOK / 2 Peter 2:1-2, 13, 18-20

When you really want something—even if it's not good for you—is it easy to do without it? If you're like most people, instead of exercising self-control you try to get what you want when you want it. Marriages often break up when a partner leaves to seek "personal happiness." And many people become addicted to tobacco, alcohol, drugs, or even certain foods.

But God has commanded His children to exercise self-control, because He knows we're at war with our own sinful desires. First Peter 5:8, this week's key verse, warns believers to be self-controlled because the Enemy (Satan) is looking for someone he can control. Peter also warns:

Dear friends, I urge you, as aliens and strangers in the world, to abstain from sinful desires, which war against your soul (1 Peter 2:11).

In 2 Peter 2:1-2, 13, and 18-20, Peter foretells that false teachers will actually encourage men and women to give in to sinful desires. How do you think God feels about those false teachers?

▲ TAKE A STEP

The world under Satan's control says, "If it feels good, do it." But God says, "Be self-controlled and obey My commands." Share with one another a time when you didn't get what you wanted. You may have been upset at the time, but looking back, did it really hurt you not to get what you wanted?

Who's calling the shots in your life?

Q

Why should I control myself?

A

I need self-control because my desires are sometimes wrong.

Be mastered by the Master's plan

Q

How can I control my body?

A

Self-control is possible with God's help when I do not let anything master me.

PARENT:
Your personal habits set the pace for self-control in your home. Examine yourself honestly, and make the needed changes in your lifestyle.

I've had a terrible day. I deserve an extra piece of chocolate cake tonight."

"Sure, if I wanted to I could stop smoking, but I really don't want to. So why should you complain?"

"I know I ought to face up to my problems, but just one little drink never hurt anybody."

"I wish I'd worn my headpiece like the orthodontist told me to. I'd be out of braces by now if I'd listened to him."

"I should have gone to the library instead of watching TV. Now I don't have the material I need for my report."

"I knew what we were doing was wrong—but I never thought there'd be a baby. What are we going to do now?"

◆ **TAKE A LOOK / 1 Corinthians 6:12-20**
Lack of self-control affects many areas of life. It can
   • create health problems,
   • cause embarrassing predicaments at school or work,
   • bring heartache because of an unplanned pregnancy.
   As Christians, we are to exercise self-control in all areas of life, even in such things as eating, sleeping, and the physical relationship God intended for marriage. Read 1 Corinthians 6:12-20, which contains God's instructions about controlling your body.

▲ **TAKE A STEP**
God intends for us to enjoy life. But some people try—without success—to find fulfillment in harmful things. And because of sin, some let even good things become their masters. For this reason, the apostle Paul wrote:
   "Everything is permissible for me"—but not everything is beneficial. . . . I will not be mastered by anything (1 Corinthians 6:12).
   Some Christians keep themselves in tip-top physical shape, but do not exercise the self-control needed to grow spiritually by spending time alone with God in prayer and Bible study. God expects us to have self-control in every area of life.
   Pick one of the examples at the top of the page. How can he or she regain self-control? Is there something harmful mastering you? Are you willing to do what it takes to regain control? Work out a "plan of attack" with your family right now. God is ready to help!

Dianna Lynn's eyes were glued to the pages of the romance novel. How wonderful it would be to live an adventurous life, she thought. She saw herself as the gorgeous heroine about to be saved by the nobleman. They'd fall in love, and—

The sudden knock on her door startled her, and before she could turn off the flashlight and hide the book, her father had turned on the light. She shoved the book under her covers.

"You should have been asleep hours ago," he said softly. "What were you reading that's so exciting?" Slowly and guiltily Dianna Lynn pulled the book out and showed him. She blushed when her father read the title and looked at the cover.

Gently her dad sat down on the bed. "Sweetheart, why do you fill your mind with this stuff when there's so much good literature to read? If you put this trash in, eventually trashy thoughts will come out. What you put in your mind usually can't be erased—even when you want to forget it."

◆ TAKE A LOOK / Philippians 4:8-9

"Our minds are mental greenhouses where unlawful thoughts, once planted, are nurtured and watered before being transplanted into the real world of unlawful actions."* King Solomon gave a similar warning:

Above all else, guard you heart [mind], for it is the wellspring of life (Proverbs 4:23).

Yesterday we learned about self-control over the body. But if King Solomon is right (and he is!), then self-control over the mind is even more important, because seeds of trouble planted in your thoughts produce harvests of problems in your actions.

When you think about things that please God, you're exercising self-control over your mind. In Philippians 4:8-9 the apostle Paul tells us the kinds of thoughts that please God.

▲ TAKE A STEP

Dianna Lynn's father knew that our eyes and ears are the "gates" from the outside world into our private thoughts. We can guard our minds by being careful of what we put into them.

Check out the "arrows" you've allowed to pierce your mind this week. As a family, list the TV programs you've watched, the radio stations or tapes you've listened to, and the books and magazines you've read. Does each item fit Philippians 4:8?

*Jerry Bridges, *The Practice of Godliness*, Navpress, 1983, p. 169.

It's mind over matter because your mind matters

Q

How can I control my mind?

A

Self-control over my mind comes when I think about things that please God.

PARENT:
Have your child write out Philippians 4:8 and illustrate it with lovely things. Hang it up to encourage the family to evaluate their thoughts.

If I can't control me, nobody can but God!

I'm not sure I'll ever come to another game,"
Mrs. Young whispered to her husband. "I'm so
embarrassed!"

The Youngs were ashamed to hear spectators
complain about the unsportsmanlike conduct of their
son Elliot. They cringed when they heard one man roar,
"I don't care how good that guy is. If I was the coach,
he wouldn't play on my team!"

Elliot had a talent for basketball, but also a lack of
self-control. Tonight he had gotten into a fight with an
opposing player, then argued loudly with a referee,
resulting in just one of many technical fouls. (In fact,
many people called him "Mr. T"—for "Technical"!)

When Elliot's team fell behind and he lashed out at
his teammates, the coach took him out of the game.
"That does it," Coach said. "Until you can control your
anger, you're off the team!"

How can I control my emotions?

◆ **TAKE A LOOK / Galatians 5:16-23**

God made us with many different emotions, or
feelings. Emotions in themselves are not bad, but
the ways we express them can be. Emotions like
anger can harm others. Emotions such as bitterness, self-pity, and resentment can harm us. That's
why we need to control them.

In Galatians 5:16-23, Paul explains that self-
control is possible only with the Holy Spirit's help.
In verses 19-21 he lists sins that master the body,
mind, and emotions of a person not controlled by
the Spirit; in verses 22-23 he lists the qualities of a
life under the Spirit's control.

I can control my emotions by letting the Holy Spirit lead in my life.

▲ **TAKE A STEP**

The self-control you need to break bad habits
and form good ones can begin only when you let
God's Spirit take control and give you the power to
be what you should be. The apostle Paul wrote:

I urge you, brothers, in view of God's mercy, to
offer your bodies as living sacrifices, holy and
pleasing to God. . . . Do not conform any
longer to the pattern of this world, but be
transformed by the renewing of your mind
(Romans 12:1-2).

Can you honestly say that the "fruit of the
Spirit" (Galatians 5:22-23) can be seen in your life?
If not, close today's family time in prayer, and do
what Romans 12:1 suggests is only reasonable!

WORK

A hundred years ago, most Americans lived in rural areas and worked on their family farm. They provided their own food, drying and preserving vegetables and fruit for winter. They cared for livestock (which gave them meat and milk), plowed the fields, and reaped crops which they used or sold. They did household chores and repaired equipment. Everyone in the family, from the youngest to the oldest, knew firsthand that farming is hard work!

Today, most people live in cities, doing jobs their great-grandparents never imagined. Their children's favorite foods are not beans from the garden . . . but hamburgers from the nearest fast-food restaurant! Many mothers have to tell their kids that milk comes from cows, not from the supermarket shelf! And by the year 2000, maybe no one will be surprised to hear a child ask, "What's a cow?"

◆ THINKING ABOUT WORK

The kinds of jobs people hold change with time. In the early 1900s, most of the work in America was in farming or manufacturing—occupations which produced goods, things people use.

In the 1990s most jobs will involve providing services for other people. Medical workers, office workers, engineers, scientists, teachers, and computer operators will hold most of the jobs in our country.

Work is **the physical or mental labor used to make a product or accomplish a task.** The apostle Paul showed the purpose of work when he wrote this about people who were lazy:

● KEY VERSE ON WORK
If a man will not work,
he shall not eat
(2 Thessalonians 3:10).

▲ LOOKING AHEAD
Everyone would rather spend time in leisure activities. But if we are to fulfill our responsibilities in life, we must work. Our job this week is to look at work from God's viewpoint.

God wants us to work, but He also desires that we have adequate rest. What does Exodus 20:8-11 tell you about work and rest?

*"My mother **has** a household cleaner."*

Hard work today brings benefits tomorrow

Is work punishment?

Work is one of the ways God provides the basic things we need to live.

"We might as well be on a chain gang!" Gus fumed, counting the rows he still had to hoe in the garden. "This is slave labor."

"Look, if you'd quit complaining and start working, we might finish this before summer's over," Hal replied curtly. "You know Dad said we couldn't spend the night with Jeremy unless we finish this hoeing. So you might as well get to work."

For a while the boys worked steadily, chopping weeds and gently loosening the soil around the corn, beans, squash, peas, and tomatoes in the large family garden. But as the sun rose higher, the boys got more thirsty, sweaty, and tired. When their father checked on them again, Gus could contain himself no longer.

"Why do we have to work so hard?" he blurted. "What are you punishing us for?"

"You're not being punished," his father answered. "But ask me that first question again next winter when we're snowed in, can't get to town, and Mom can still fix all those good vegetables for dinner. If you don't know the answer then, I'll tell you."

◆ **TAKE A LOOK / Genesis 2:4-9, 15-17; 3:17-19**

Whether we have housework, homework, or a nine-to-five job, we sometimes wish we didn't have to work at all. And if our job is hard or boring, or if we get paid too little, we may also think our work is some kind of punishment.

Many people believe if we lived in a perfect world or another Garden of Eden, no one would have to work. But from the beginning God intended people to work. Read Genesis 2:4-9 and 15-17. What kinds of work do you think Adam might have done? Now read Genesis 3:17-19. Why did God make it harder for Adam to work?

▲ **TAKE A STEP**

Work was meant to be a pleasure. By working, Adam could glorify God. But after Adam sinned, work became much harder. But its purpose didn't change:

That everyone may eat and drink, and find satisfaction in all his toil—this is the gift of God (Ecclesiastes 3:13).

Gus and Hal weren't really happy with the hard work they were doing. But as their father pointed out, they'd enjoy the fruits (or vegetables!) of their labor later.

Make a list of the most disliked jobs at your house. What would happen if no one did those chores?

J osh leaned against a stack of plywood and wiped his forehead with a handkerchief. "Whew! Will I ever be glad when this day is over," he moaned. "I can't wait till five o'clock."

Just then his boss barked, "Get back to work, Josh. You'll never get those two-by-fours moved at that rate!"

Reluctantly Josh began moving the pieces of lumber again. He remembered how excited he had been when he'd gotten this job working on a construction crew. But now that early excitement had worn off. This job was nothing but hard work, and Josh hated every minute of it.

Soon he spotted his boss driving off in his pickup truck.

"Good," Josh thought, "now I can let up until he gets back." He motioned to his pal. "Come on, Pete. The boss is gone. Let's get a soda and relax a minute. That's about the only thing I like about this job— except payday, that is."

◆ TAKE A LOOK
Proverbs 12:24; 13:4; 15:19; 18:9; 20:4

Josh was doing just enough to get by, looking forward to the time when he would have a "real" job doing something he enjoyed.

What he didn't realize was that the work he was doing then was as important as any he might do in the future. Though his job was difficult and he didn't like his boss, Josh needed to understand that his real boss is God. And God's instructions are to work with wholehearted diligence:

Whatever you do, work at it with all your heart, as working for the Lord, not for men. . . . It is the Lord Christ you are serving (Colossians 3:23-24).

Josh worked fast and furiously while the boss was watching. But the minute his boss's back was turned, Josh slacked off. Simply put, he was lazy. According to Proverbs 12:24; 13:4;15:19; 18:9; and 20:4, where does laziness lead?

▲ TAKE A STEP
Laziness (or "sloth" as it is sometimes called) is foolish behavior. The Bible tells us it can lead to difficulties ("thorns"), poverty, hunger, forced labor, and even self-destruction.

If you worked with Josh, what advice would you give him? Now think about your own attitudes toward your schoolwork and chores around the house. Are you following your own advice?

The boss who is always on the job

What should my attitude be toward work?

A

Work should be done as if I were doing it for the Lord.

PARENT:
Help your younger child learn to complete tasks. Provide incentive by using a poster with a star for each completed chore.

Anything you can do, I can do better!

Roy slumped into his easy chair in the family room. "I didn't get the promotion to sales manager," he said quietly to his wife. "Elliot Mason did."

"Elliot Mason!" his wife exclaimed. "Didn't you give him some of your sales leads when he came into the department?"

"Sure. I gave him more than a few good leads. And I did all the legwork on this last big job, but he closed the sale—and I didn't get any credit. In fact, he was making mistakes right and left. If I hadn't corrected his paperwork, it would have cost the company a lot of money and he would've probably gotten fired. Instead, he's been promoted. I know I'm a better salesman, but Elliot likes to take the credit and get ahead, even if it means treating other people like dirt."

"Don't worry, honey," his wife reassured him. "The boss can't be fooled forever. And if it takes cheating to get ahead, we can do without the extra money. Besides, if Elliot's that bad a salesman, you'll probably end up with that promotion after all."

◆ TAKE A LOOK / Matthew 20:20-28

Have you ever heard the phrase "rat race"? It's what many people call the competition of the working world. But in some ways the rat race is more like a stampede in which people are trampled by those who will do anything for success.

In the business world people compete for prestige, power, money, and success. We can selfishly join the "herd" and trample others so that we will succeed. Or we can obey God and live by His principles. That may not be easy, but even in the working world we can obey this command:

Do nothing out of selfish ambition or vain conceit, but in humility consider others better than yourselves (Philippians 2:3).

Read Matthew 20:20-28 to see how easy it is to fall into the trap of selfishness and competition.

▲ TAKE A STEP

In all our relationships—at work, school, on athletic teams, even in church or at home—we need to be humble, not selfish or conceited. But, like the disciples, we may sometimes be tempted to seek personal benefit or power in a way that might hurt someone else. That's what Elliot did. But was Roy's attitude really much better?

From what you read today, what attitude should Christians have—even toward someone who treats them unfairly?

Q

Should I be competitive with others in my work?

A

Work gives me the opportunity to be a humble helper, not a selfish competitor.

*T*he alarm buzzed. Goldie reached over and turned it off, then automatically grabbed her Bible and flipped on the light.

Refreshed after reading a chapter and praying, Goldie started to dress. She thought about what she needed to do that day.

"I'll pick up those papers for Mr. Ramsey on the way to work," she thought. "He needs that report today." Goldie's boss carried a heavy load, so she wanted to help him all she could.

Meanwhile, in the apartment next door, Alice reached over, pushed the snooze button on her alarm clock, and groaned. "I've got to have more sleep. I shouldn't have stayed up so late last night."

When the alarm rang again, Alice reluctantly grabbed her robe. "Oh—I can't wait till this day is over," she grumbled. "Maybe I'll call the office and tell them I'm sick. I don't think I can face another day with that grouch I have for a boss."

◆ TAKE A LOOK
Philippians 2:3-4; Ecclesiastes 9:10

In one way or another, you will almost certainly spend most of your life working. And as we've learned this week, Christians work not just for a boss but for the Lord, who is concerned about the way we do our job—and our attitudes toward it.

In the Bible, God gives us some guidelines to follow as we work for Him. As you read each of the verses below, jot down the character quality called for in a worker who pleases God.

God's Word says . . .	a worker should be:
Philippians 2:3-4	_____
Ecclesiastes 9:10	_____
Matthew 20:25-28	_____
Proverbs 10:4	_____

▲ TAKE A STEP

In God's perspective, a job is much more than just a way to make money. It's an opportunity to glorify Him by being a humble, hardworking, and diligent servant to others. The apostle Paul, who was a hard worker himself, wrote:

Whatever you do, do it all for the glory of God (1 Corinthians 10:31).

The thoughts and attitudes Goldie and Alice had as they dressed for work showed how they felt about their work. Which one do you think had a better day at work? How did she show those four scriptural qualities of a good worker?

Honor your "Boss" by the way you work

Q

How can I become a better worker?

A

Work gives me the opportunity to honor God by being a hardworking servant.

PARENT:
Your attitude toward your own work sets an example for your child. Take time to assess your own feelings about your job.

BEAUTY

*B*eautiful!" *the traveler exclaimed as he watched the sun set brilliantly over the calm, green sea.*

"Beautiful!" the astronomer whispered as he gazed at a distant galaxy through his telescope.

"Beautiful!" the scientist said as he looked at the complex design of the cell with his electron microscope.

"Beautiful, beautiful!" the applauding audience shouted as the symphony ended and the orchestra members bowed.

"Beautiful!" the coach yelled as the gymnast executed a leap.

"You're beautiful," the groom whispered to his new bride.

"It's beautiful, Dad!" the teenager said, stroking his new car.

"Oh, sweetheart, she's beautiful!" the new father beamed as he looked at his newborn daughter.

"That's so beautiful," the woman whispered when she heard that her sins were forgiven through Jesus' death on the cross.

◆ THINKING ABOUT BEAUTY

What comes to your mind when you think of beauty? As you can see from the statements we read at first, beauty can mean different things to different people. People, places, and things . . . ideas, art, and music . . . can all be called "beautiful."

Beauty is **the quality in something which brings delight when we experience it**. The Bible doesn't define beauty, but it does tell us that God created beauty, and so it is important to Him.

"I'm clean inside where it counts. Why can't we let it go at that?"

● KEY VERSE ON BEAUTY

[God] has made everything beautiful in its time (Ecclesiastes 3:11).

▲ LOOKING AHEAD

This week we'll see why beauty is an important part of a life that pleases God.

Begin your study of beauty by reading Ecclesiastes 3:11-14. According to verse 14, what might be the purpose of beauty? Name two things in God's whole creation that you find most beautiful. Why did you choose those two?

Dad, why did Uncle Roger marry Denise?" David asked his father as they drove away from the wedding reception.

"I'm sure it's because he loves her, son," Mr. Baxter replied, a bit startled by the question. "Why do you ask?"

"Well," David replied hesitantly, "It's just that Uncle Roger's so good-looking and smart, he could have married almost anybody. And Denise is . . . well, you know . . . Denise is sweet, but she's not very pretty. I like her and all that, but Uncle Roger didn't have to marry somebody so plain."

Mr. Baxter thought a moment. "You're right. Denise would never win a beauty contest. But Roger sees her inner beauty—her character and spirit. Haven't you ever noticed how his eyes light up when she walks into the room?"

◆ TAKE A LOOK / Revelation 21:10-11, 18-27

Throughout history, artists and philosophers have tried to explain what makes something beautiful. But society's definition of beauty constantly changes—just glance at fashion pictures of a hundred years ago. And for some, even last year's styles are out of date!

When you look at the art and architecture of countries all around the world, you'll see that different people have far different ideas about what is beautiful! The pyramids of Egypt, the pagodas of China, and the Parthenon of Greece are all examples of beautiful architecture. They're all different, but their designs pleased the people who made them.

The Bible itself often mentions beautiful cities, people, buildings, and natural wonders. But nothing is more beautiful than the city the Bible calls the New Jerusalem. As you read Revelation 21:10-11 and 18-27, imagine how you will feel walking on streets of gold every day!

▲ TAKE A STEP

The great street of the city was of pure gold, like transparent glass (Revelation 21:21).

What makes something beautiful? Heaven is beautiful because Jesus is there! Nothing impure, shameful, sinful, or deceitful is found there. And you can use those same standards to measure beauty on earth too!

Denise was beautiful because her life reflected Jesus from the inside out. Think of a person you feel is beautiful—not because of looks, but because God's love is seen through him or her. Would others think you are beautiful for the same reason?

Heaven's a beautiful place, full of glory and grace

Q

What makes something beautiful?

A

Beauty can be seen wherever God's character is reflected.

Maybe I can't see it, but it's still beautiful!

There's not a tint that paints the rose
  Or decks the lily fair,
Or marks the humblest flower that grows
  But God has placed it there.
There's not a star whose twinkling light
  Illumes the spreading earth;
There's not a cloud, so dark or bright,
  But wisdom gave it birth.
There's not a place on earth's vast round,
  In ocean's deep or air,
Where love and beauty are not found—
  God is everywhere.*

Q

What is beautiful to God?

A

Beauty can be seen in actions and attitudes that please God.

*"God Is Everywhere" by Esther Gillespie, from A Child's Treasury of Verse, compiled by Eleanor Doan. Copyright 1977 by Zondervan Publishing House. Used by permission.

◆ **TAKE A LOOK / Genesis 1:31; Proverbs 1:8-9**

Many different things in life can be called "beautiful." But they're beautiful in different ways. For instance, mighty ocean waves crashing on a rocky shore would be a beautiful sight . . . but if a woman had a big rock for a head and soggy seaweed for hair, we might not think she was so beautiful! Many consider good music and attractive buildings to be beautiful, though they are very different things.

People say that many things are beautiful. But God considers many other things beautiful too, some that we may not even think about. The verses below will tell you what some of those beautiful things are. Jot them down on the lines at the right.

These verses tell . . .   what God thinks is beautiful:
Genesis 1:31   _____
Proverbs 1:8-9   _____
Zechariah 9:16-17   _____
Mark 14:3,6   _____
Romans 10:15   _____
1 Peter 3:3-4   _____

▲ **TAKE A STEP**

"*The LORD does not look at the things man looks at. Man looks at the outward appearance, but the LORD looks at the heart*" (1 Samuel 16:7).

A gentle spirit . . . witnessing . . . worship . . . obedience—just some of the things God finds beautiful. Without considering their outward appearance, turn to the family members on either side of you and tell one thing about them you find beautiful.

Mirror, mirror on the wall, who's the fairest one of all?" Mrs. Gilmer read dramatically from the story of "Snow White" to six-year-old Gretchen and three-year-old Bethany. The girls knew their favorite bedtime stories almost by heart, sometimes even beating their mother to the next word. But tonight, Gretchen was strangely quiet. When her mother paused to turn the page, Gretchen asked, "Mommy, am I beautiful?"

Mrs. Gilmer looked down and kissed her daughter's upturned nose. "You sure are. And so's Bethany. But why do you ask?"

"Because kids at school think I'm ugly. They call me 'Gretch the Wretch,' and everybody laughs."

Mrs. Gilmer smiled. "They're just not smart enough to think of a nice rhyme for your name. But your Daddy's nickname for you always reminds me that you're beautiful in the nicest way."

A twinkle crept into Gretchen's eyes. "Yeah," she whispered, " 'Gretchen the Blessin'.' That is pretty neat!"

◆ **TAKE A LOOK / 1 Peter 3:3-9**
The wicked queen in "Snow White" isn't the only one who values physical beauty. Today more than ever, beauty contest winners are celebrated and star athletes are spotlighted. And as a result, ordinary people—especially children and teenagers —sometimes feel as if they don't measure up to the world's false standard.

Though society often judges people by outer beauty, God's Word tells us what really matters is inner beauty. One of the verses we looked up yesterday is worth thinking about again:

Your beauty should not come from outward adornment. . . . Instead, it should be that of your inner self, the unfading beauty of a gentle and quiet spirit, which is of great worth in God's sight (1 Peter 3:3-4).

True beauty is a gentle and quiet spirit—and that comes from inside, with the Holy Spirit's help. As you read 1 Peter 3:5-9, look for characteristics of a beautiful wife (in verses 5-6), a beautiful husband (verse 7), and a beautiful person (verses 8-9).

▲ **TAKE A STEP**
Gretchen was an ordinary-looking little girl— not exactly gorgeous, but certainly not ugly. How were her parents trying to help her understand what true beauty is? What should you do to be a truly beautiful person in God's sight?

Mirror, mirror on the wall, am I not indeed a doll?

Q

How can I be truly beautiful?

A

Beauty that pleases God comes from my inner self and is seen in the way I treat others.

Little drops of water, tiny grains of sand

*T*he blazing sun seemed to hang in the July sky. "Hey! Come look at this shell I found!" Tad waved wildly to his brother.

Jess ran along the shore to the spot where Tad was kneeling in the surf, examining his treasure. Jess leaned over with his hands on his knees and stared at the delicate object in Tad's hand.

"That's neat," he whispered. "Let me hold it." Jess held the shiny spiral shell in his hand. "I remember seeing this in the shell book at home. It's a conch shell." The brothers sat in the green water and let it splash over their legs. The sun was warm on their shoulders, but the mist from the surf's spray cooled them. Jess lay back and let the water lap over his body.

"Boy, what a great day to be at the beach," Tad sighed with satisfaction. The only sounds were the rush of the water lapping against the shore and the cry of a seagull circling above in the transparent sky. The beauty all around seemed to hug them.

◆ TAKE A LOOK / Job 37:5-13

God's beautiful creation is His gift to all of us. He wants us to appreciate and enjoy it.

Consider a raindrop. From one square mile of ocean surface, the sun draws about 5,435 tons of water into the upper atmosphere. As this water vapor moves across the continents, it cools and condenses into tiny droplets so small that it takes about 8 million of them to form a single drop of rain.

During this condensation process, clouds form and the tiny droplets join together into larger drops. When they get so large the air can't hold them up, they fall to the earth as rain. And rain enables beautiful flowers, lush greenery, and healthy crops to flourish.

During the time of Job, everyone was involved in growing things to eat. Snow or rain caused people to stop working in the fields, so they had time to think about God. According to Job 37:5-13, what qualities about God can be seen in the beauty of His creation?

▲ TAKE A STEP

So that all men he has made may know his work, he stops every man from his labor (Job 37:7).

Think back to the opening story. What were Tad and Jess doing to appreciate and enjoy God's world? What's one thing you can do today—as an individual or as a family—to enjoy the beauty of God's world?

Q

How can I enjoy the beauty of God's world?

A

Beauty can be enjoyed when I take time to appreciate God's creation.

SATAN

Janet burst through the kitchen door, yelling frantically, "Momma! Momma! Oh, Momma—"

"Janet! What's wrong? You're white as a sheet! Are you hurt?"

The five-year-old wrapped her arms around her mother's legs and began to cry. "Momma, is the Devil going to get me? Is he?"

Mrs. Warner picked up her sobbing daughter and held her. "What makes you think the Devil's going to get you, honey?"

Janet was sniffing between her sobs. "Momma, I took a candy bar from the snack bar at the swimming pool, and I didn't pay for it. Barbara called me a thief because I stole the candy. She said the Devil's gonna get me for it. Is that true, Momma? I'm scared!"

◆ THINKING ABOUT SATAN

Janet didn't know much about the Devil, but she pictured him as a monstrously evil figure, wrapped in black and lurking in the dark. And like any normal person, she was frightened by that idea.

You probably have a picture of the Devil, or Satan, in your mind too. You may see him as a red demon with a tail, horns, and a pitchfork . . . or as a huge black snake. But your mental picture of Satan is wrong—unless it comes from what the Bible tells us about him.

Satan is an actual being. He is **the enemy of God and of God's people**. Here's one way the Bible describes him:

● KEY VERSE ON SATAN

Be self-controlled and alert. Your enemy the devil prowls around like a roaring lion looking for someone to devour (1 Peter 5:8).

▲ LOOKING AHEAD

Even Satan's name means "adversary" or "enemy." Knowing your enemy's strengths and weaknesses is a good way to prepare yourself for his attacks. This week we'll do just that.

One time Satan tried to defeat Jesus on earth (read Luke 4:1-13). How did Jesus keep from giving in to Satan's temptation?

"First the serpent in the garden. Now the one in Mom's bathtub."

"My way" is not always the right way

If I needed your help, I would have asked you for it!" Charles shouted at his classmate Al. The class was working on group projects, but Al had noticed Charles at a table by himself.

Al was stunned by the outburst. "I—I was just . . . trying to help," he stammered.

"I don't need any help," Charles replied curtly. "I can handle this on my own, thank you."

Later Al confided to another class member. "I don't know what I said to make him angry."

"Hey, don't worry about it, Al," his friend replied. "You don't know Charles very well; the best thing to do is just to stay away from him. He thinks he can do everything better than anyone else. One time I invited him to my youth group, and you know what he said? 'God never did anything for me, so I'm not going to do anything for Him!' That's right! He's just too proud for his own good."

Q

Why is Satan the enemy of God?

A

Satan became God's enemy because of his sinful pride.

◆ **TAKE A LOOK / Isaiah 14:12-14; Ezekiel 28:14-17**

At first glance, Charles's attitude seems to have little to do with the question we're asking today: "Why is Satan the enemy of God?" But Charles has the same kind of pride that made Satan become God's enemy.

The Bible describes Satan as being one of the wisest and most attractive of all the angels God created. But Satan's deliberate sin against God caused him to lose his position.

Though Satan's name is not mentioned in today's passages, many Bible scholars think he is the one described by two Old Testament prophets. As you read Isaiah 14:12-14 and Ezekiel 28:14-17, find statements about Satan's pride.

▲ **TAKE A STEP**

Satan's sinful attitude is summed up in this verse:

"I will make myself like the Most High" (Isaiah 14:14).

Pride in himself and his accomplishments led Satan to think that he could become like God. Rebelling against God's authority, he tried to take control of creation. The angels who followed him in his rebellion are called demons.

Pride prevents many from realizing how much God has done for them . . . and how much they need God. What do you think Al's friend meant when he said Charles was "too proud for his own good"? Was Satan?

*T*he story is told of the time Satan assembled his demons and asked for a volunteer to go to earth in order to keep people from believing in God. One demon quickly stepped forward. Satan asked, "What strategy will you use to ruin people?"

"I will tell them there's no heaven," the demon replied smugly.

Satan dismissed him. "That won't work; there's a bit of heaven in every heart, so they will not believe you." He turned to a second volunteer and asked, "What would you tell them?"

"I will tell them there is no hell," this demon announced.

"They won't believe you either," his master replied. "For every human heart has a conscience that says good will win and evil will be defeated in the end."

Finally a third demon came forward. "And you, what will you tell them?" Satan asked him.

"I will tell them that you do not exist, so there is no hurry to do good," the demon replied.

"You're the one I'll send," Satan said. "They will believe you—because they want to."

◆ **TAKE A LOOK / John 8:44; Matthew 12:24**
That may not be a true story, but it shows that Satan wants to destroy God's work in any way he can. As a master of disguise, he makes his lies seem attractive, causing many to fall into evil. The apostle Paul warns that . . .

Satan himself masquerades as an angel of light. It is not surprising, then, if his servants masquerade as servants of righteousness (2 Corinthians 11:14-15).

The names used to describe Satan reveal some of his disguises. As you look up each verse, write a word or phrase on the line at the right which describes Satan or his work.

These verses . . .	describe Satan as . . .
John 8:44	_____ & _____
Matthew 12:24	_____ , prince of demons
1 Thessalonians 3:5	_____
1 John 5:19	_____
2 Corinthians 4:4	_____

▲ **TAKE A STEP**
"Everybody's doing it, so it must be okay!" That's an excuse lots of people use when they do something they're not sure is right. Could that be one of the ways Satan makes evil look good? Can you think of another excuse Satan likes to hear?

The prince of darkness behind the angel of light

Q

What is Satan doing today?

A

Satan's purpose—today and always—is to destroy God's work.

Your greatest foe is already on death row

E verything's gone wrong today, Dad," Mickey moaned. "To begin with, I woke up with a yucky feeling in my stomach. I didn't even want to go to school. When I came downstairs for breakfast, I flipped my breakfast plate over and had to clean up that mess. Then when I got to school, I found out I'd studied the wrong chapter for my math test, so I'm sure I failed it."

"Well, son," his dad assured him, "everybody has days like that from time to time."

"But Dad, you say God is in control of everything. That's hard to believe when I have days like today!"

"God never promised life would be easy, Mickey," his dad said. "Maybe He's trying to teach you something."

"But what about people who have really bad things happen to them? How do they keep believing that God's in control? Like the Winstons: Ever since Mr. Winston died and things got so hard for them, Mrs. Winston still tells everyone how God is in control. And she doesn't just say it at church either. She means it!"

Q

What will finally happen to Satan?

A

Satan will be punished forever when he is thrown into the lake of fire.

◆ **TAKE A LOOK / Revelation 20:10**

When you see people like Mrs. Winston suffering, it's easy to think that Satan is winning.

The Bible does describe Satan as the "god of this world," but rest assured—he isn't winning his war with God. He is a created being, and his power is limited. But his pride is so great he thinks he can defeat the all-powerful God of the universe!

In fact, because of Jesus' death on the cross, Satan has already been defeated. Jesus is the Victor! Colossians 2:15 shows how complete Satan's defeat is:

Having disarmed the powers and authorities [Satan's followers], he [Jesus] made a public spectacle of them, triumphing over them by the cross (Colossians 2:15).

But Satan's death sentence has not yet been carried out, so he is still a force for evil in our world. Even so, there's no question about what will happen to him in the end—as you'll learn by reading Revelation 20:10.

▲ **TAKE A STEP**

Jesus Christ has given us "weapons" to fight Satan in the day-to-day battles we will face before he is finally thrown into the lake of fire. In Revelation 12:11, look for three ways God's children will overcome Satan as the time for Christ's return draws near. Which "weapon" did Mrs. Winston use?

What would you do if you suddenly found yourself involved n these conversations:

• "Hey Joe, the librarian's letting us play 'Wizards and Warriors' during our free period. Come on!"

• "Oh, our dinner party will be so unusual. After we eat, Madame Nevsky will read our palms. Are you coming?"

• "How can Christianity be the only true religion? Do you really believe God will close the doors of heaven on the Hindus, Buddhists, and Muslims? You kids need to grow up."

• "May I see the newspaper when you've finished? I'm having such a lousy day, I think I'd better check my horoscope."

• "Aw, don't be silly! It's just a movie; everybody's going. Do you think those demons are going to jump off the screen and get you or something?"

◆ **TAKE A LOOK / Ephesians 6:10-18**
The acts of the sinful nature are obvious: sexual immorality, impurity and debauchery [sinful lifestyle]; idolatry and witchcraft; hatred, discord, jealousy, fits of rage, selfish ambition, dissensions, factions and envy; drunkenness, orgies, and the like (Galatians 5:19-21).

Christians are engaged in spiritual warfare against Satan. This passage shows how Satan tries to attack us head-on through our flesh. But he also often makes "sneak attacks" on our minds; that's what is happening in the opening situations.

God offers protection from all of Satan's attacks. As you read about God's armor in Ephesians 6:10-18, draw lines to match each piece with its description at the right:

I wear this piece of armor . . .   when I . . .
1. belt of truth   a. believe what God says
2. breastplate of
   righteousness   b. tell others of my faith
3. boots of peace   c. know that Jesus saves
4. shield of faith   d. apply Scripture to my
                                        life
5. helmet of salvation   e. understand the Bible
6. sword of the Spirit   f. refuse to dabble in sin

▲ **TAKE A STEP**
God has given His children "spiritual weapons" to fight the Enemy. Practice using those weapons right now by letting each person in the family tell how he or she would reply to one of the situations above.

The armor only your enemy can see

Q

How can I resist Satan now?

A

I resist Satan when I wear God's spiritual armor and know His Word.

PARENT:
The world today is full of occult influences, ranging from horoscopes to outright Satan worship. Help your child identify and understand some of those influences.

(Answers: 1-d; 2-c; 3-e; 4-f; 5-a; 6-b)

··· DEVOTION ···

H *ave you ever heard someone say something like this?*
- *"He sure is a devoted husband. He does everything for his wife."*
- *"That dog is so devoted to his master. He follows him everywhere and hardly ever leaves his side."*
- *"She's really a devoted mother. She's always taking her kids places, doing things with them. I wish I had her energy!"*
- *"I'm sure he'll be a wonderful concert pianist someday. He has devoted himself to his music."*
- *"If you've never eaten one of her souffles, you're in for a treat. She's a devoted cook."*
- *"I don't think I could be a missionary. You have to give up so much. It really takes a lot of devotion."*

◆ THINKING ABOUT DEVOTION

People tend to look up to men and women who get things done by making quick decisions and taking quick action. But devotion to God doesn't seem to fit our fast-paced, action-packed world. Being devoted to God brings to mind such things as quietly reading the Bible or praying. But is that all it means?

When the Bible speaks of devotion, it means having **an attitude toward God that makes us want to please Him in everything we do**. That's why this commandment is so important:

● KEY VERSE ON DEVOTION

"Love the Lord your God with all your heart and with all your soul and with all your mind and with all your strength" (Mark 12:30).

"I'd better not eat any more spinach. I'm saving room for spiritual food."

▲ LOOKING AHEAD

This week we want to talk about the kind of devotion to God that involves every part of life.

According to Psalm 63:1 and Psalm 143:6, what kind of attitude do you need in order to be devoted to God?

Do you ever get that "thirst" just to spend time talking with God and reading His Word?

*T*ake my life, and let it be
    Consecrated, Lord, to Thee;
Take my moments and my days;
    Let them flow in ceaseless praise.
Take my hands, and let them move
    At the impulse of thy love,
Take my feet, and let them be
    Swift and beautiful for Thee.
Take my will, and make it Thine;
    It shall be no longer mine;
Take my heart, it is Thine own;
    It shall be Thy royal throne.
Take my love; my Lord, I pour
    At Thy feet its treasure store:
Take myself, and I will be
    Ever, only, all for Thee.
                        —Frances Ridley Havergal

◆ **TAKE A LOOK / Luke 1:26-38, 46-48**
As the hymn above reminds us, true devotion
is having a life completely focused on doing what
pleases God. Certainly that involves praying,
studying the Bible, and worshiping. But it doesn't
end with those activities.

Many men and women in the Bible—such as
David, Daniel, and Stephen—are good examples of
what it means to be devoted to God. But today's
reading is about another devoted person—Mary,
the mother of Jesus. As you read Luke 1:26-38 and
46-48, what clues can you find that show Mary's
devotion to God?

▲ **TAKE A STEP**
Even though Mary was in a situation she didn't
completely understand, her devotion to God was
clear:
*"I am the Lord's servant. . . . May it be to me
as you have said" (Luke 1:38).*
Sometimes God allows His children to
experience hard times. But no matter what
situations you face, if you are truly devoted to God,
then you know He is in control of your life. When
that happens, you—like Mary—can say, "Lord, I
am Your servant."

Reread any four lines of the hymn above, and
look again at Monday's key verse. Then have each
family member write his own definition of
devotion. After you share yours, think of two
things your family can do to show devotion to God.

"Ever, only, all for Thee"— Lord, is that really me?

Q

What is true devotion to God?

A

Devotion to God means my whole life is focused on pleasing Him.

Devotion sets my life in holy motion

Why is devotion so important?

Devotion causes me to love and obey God—no matter what happens.

PARENT:
Think of some of the other godly character qualities that devotion involves— such as loyalty, obedience, faith, and determination.

L ook, Haley," Rachelle pleaded, "you can come with us to the lake just this once. We're not going to stay overnight, so it's no big deal. You can tell your parents when you get back."

"I told you I'm not going," Haley responded firmly. "My parents have let me make a lot of decisions lately, but one thing they've asked me to do is always to let them know where I'll be."

"But you're going away to college in two months! Are your parents going to run your life by long-distance phone calls?"

"You really don't understand," Haley said quietly. "My folks trust me. They'd let me go if I told them I wanted to go. It's just that I know they'd be disappointed if I went without letting them know. So, since I can't get in touch with them right now, I'm not going to the lake today. It's as simple as that."

◆ TAKE A LOOK / Ezekiel 24:15-18

Haley's love and respect for her parents made her want to please them in every way she could. Though Haley never thought about it that way, she was truly devoted to her parents.

Ezekiel was a prophet who was devoted to God. God told Ezekiel to act out some warnings as signs to the Israelites who were taken captive to Babylon. Then God made Ezekiel unable to speak so he wouldn't say more than God wanted him to.

During the months he couldn't speak, Ezekiel had to cook his food in an unclean way, lie on his side for long periods of time, and even cut off his hair. And his only real friend and companion during those long, difficult months was his wife, whom he loved very much.

Sometime you can read about Ezekiel's strange actions in chapters 1–4 of the book he later wrote. But right now, see how deep his devotion to God was by reading Ezekiel 24:15-18.

▲ TAKE A STEP

In the evening my wife died. The next morning I did as I had been commanded (Ezekiel 24:18).

Devotion can make you—like Ezekiel—want to obey. It can make you want to please God, to be with Him, to admire His work, and to obey His commands—even when you don't understand them or when you find them hard to do. Now answer these questions: "Am I as devoted to God as Haley was to her parents? Would I, like Ezekiel, obey God no matter what He asks me to do?"

Brother Lawrence was a monk who lived in France in the 17th century. He worked at humble tasks, scrubbing pots in the kitchen and working in the shoe repair shop of the monastery.

Even so, Brother Lawrence has become well known because he learned a secret that made every ordinary day extraordinary. Here in his own words is what he discovered:

"I began to live as if there were no one in the world but God and me . . . I adored Him as often as I could, keeping my mind in His presence and recalling it as often as it wandered. . . . At every hour, at every moment, even in the busiest times of my work I put away from my mind everything which diverted me from the thought of God."

◆ TAKE A LOOK
Genesis 5:22-24; Hebrews 11:5

Brother Lawrence's letters to a friend have been put into a book called *The Practice of the Presence of God*. And that's exactly what anyone devoted to God must do. We must live as if God were always with us . . . because He is!

We don't know much about Brother Lawrence's life, but we do remember him for his relationship with God. We don't know much about Enoch in the Old Testament either. In fact, only a few short verses in the Bible tell the story of this man whose life was devoted to God. As you read Genesis 5:22-24 and Hebrews 11:5, you'll see that Enoch "practiced the presence of God" long before Brother Lawrence did!

▲ TAKE A STEP

The Bible often uses the word *walk* to describe a person's entire way of life. To say "Enoch walked with God," means his life was holy in every way.

Like Brother Lawrence, Enoch had to choose to stay in God's presence. Psalm 21:6 describes God's blessing on people like Enoch and Brother Lawrence who are devoted to Him:

Surely you have granted him eternal blessings and made him glad with the joy of your presence (Psalm 21:6).

The first step to staying close to God is to learn how to put Him first in your thoughts. On a 3 x 5 card write the words "Practice the presence of God!" Carry it with you today as encouragement to talk to God continually about everything you do and see. You just might start a holy habit!

God is nearer than you may sometimes think

Q

How can I be devoted to God in my everyday life?

A

Devotion is shown by staying close to God in everything I do.

PARENT: Brother Lawrence's book, The Practice of the Presence of God, *may help you in your devotional life.*

Daily devotions can aid godly devotion

S *plash! Lori's body sliced through the water. As she surfaced, her coach signaled "thumbs up."*

Lori's friend Cheryl was watching. "That was a beauty, Lori!" she gushed. "I'd give anything to dive like that!"

Lori paused a moment before she replied. "Would you really, Cheryl? Would you give anything?"

"Sure I would! " Cheryl replied quickly.

"Well this is really hard work. I have to get up at five o'clock every morning to practice my dives and still go to school. And during the summer I spend my whole vacation in training."

"Why do you do it if it's so hard?" Cheryl asked.

"Simple. It's the price I have to pay to stay on the diving team. And one day I plan to compete in the Olympics. Right, Coach?"

"You bet!" her coach grinned. "Now back up the ladder."

How can I increase my devotion to God?

◆ **TAKE A LOOK / LUKE 10:38-42**

Lori "gave" herself to the art of diving. She exercised self-discipline to practice long hours and keep herself in shape.

Devotion to God requires that same kind of commitment and self-discipline. In fact, a devoted person is one who gives his life to God totally. As you read the story of Mary and Martha in Luke 10:38-42, you'll discover both women cared for Jesus, but Mary was devoted to Him. How did Mary show her devotion?

Devotion grows when I regularly and prayerfully read God's Word.

▲ **TAKE A STEP**

As we've learned, being devoted to God is much more than just having devotions—daily times of prayer and Bible study. From the story of Mary and Martha, it's clear that devotion to the Lord involves having a personal relationship with Him. And that means taking time each day to listen to Him, letting His Word sink deeply into your mind and heart. The psalmist writes:

My soul thirsts for God, for the living God. When can I go and meet with God? (Psalm 42:2).

If you don't have the habit of reading the Bible each day, why not start today? Have each person go to a quiet place for seven minutes to read and think about 1 Peter 1. Plan to read another chapter of 1 Peter each day for the next four days.

Take time to listen to what God is saying to you. You'll be glad you did!

STEWARDSHIP

"*I*t's seventy-five cents," *six-year-old Burt announced after carefully counting the coins on the kitchen table.*

"You're doing great, Burt," his father congratulated him. "And since you're learning to count money, I think it's about time you started learning to spend it wisely too." Mr. Barlow reached into his pocket and pulled out three quarters, two dimes, and a nickel. "I'll give you one dollar each week. But you must put at least ten cents in the church offering and fifteen cents in your bank. Is that a deal?"

"Wow! A whole dollar?" Burt beamed. "Thanks, Dad!"

Three-year-old Jeremy had been listening nearby. He stuck out his hand and said, "Jeremy wants dime too!"

"All right, Jeremy," Mr. Barlow smiled as he handed him one. Jeremy looked at it a moment, then handed it back and pointed to the quarter. "No, Daddy—Jeremy wants a big dime!"

◆ THINKING ABOUT STEWARDSHIP

Advertisers know that even young children have spending power, and a say in what the family buys.

Though we live in an "I Want" culture, it's important for us as Christians to remember that everything belongs to God.

● KEY VERSE ON STEWARDSHIP

The earth is the LORD'S and everything in it, the world, and all who live in it
(Psalm 24:1).

▲ LOOKING AHEAD

Managing God's property wisely is what the Bible calls "stewardship".

Read Psalm 50:10-12 and Haggai 2:8. Then think of one item you "own." On a piece of paper write: "This (name the item)— which belongs to God— has been entrusted to (your name), who promises to be a good steward of it."

"You told him about my room, didn't you?"

All my stuff belongs to my Master— including me!

What does a steward do for the master?

Stewardship means I serve my Master in all I do.

PARENT:
Like so many aspects of the Christian life, stewardship is better "caught" than "taught." This week, ask God to show you how to be an example of a faithful steward.

"Hey, Lane—can you come to my place after school Friday?" Justin asked his new friend. "We can ride the horses and—"

"You have horses?" Lane's voice rose in surprise. "Where do you live that you can have horses?"

"I live on the Rosemont Estate out on Holland Road," Justin replied in a matter-of-fact way. "Have you ever seen it?"

"Sure, but . . . " Lane seemed puzzled. "I thought that belonged to Mr. Winfield, that man who owns all those hotels."

"It does," Justin laughed. "My mom and dad are caretakers of the whole place. Have you seen that TV show where Higgins runs that big estate in Hawaii? That's kind of the set-up my dad has. So we get to use the house and grounds—even the stables. One of my jobs is to look after the horses and run them through their paces. We'll have great fun if you come."

"Count on it!" Lane exclaimed. "Just let me go ask my dad."

◆ TAKE A LOOK / Genesis 24:34-51

Though Justin and his family lived on the estate and enjoyed all it had to offer, they didn't own it. As stewards, they took care of it according to the owner's wishes—not their own.

You'll see the difference between stewardship and ownership in Genesis 24:34-51. Abraham had sent his steward to find a wife for Abraham's son Isaac. When the steward arrived in Abraham's homeland, he prayed that the woman who drew water for the camels would be the right one for Isaac. That's how he met Rebekah, the future Mrs. Isaac! Later he tells Laban—Rebekah's brother and guardian—his own account of his mission.

▲ TAKE A STEP

An owner has the right to say how his money will be spent and how his possessions will be managed. A steward, on the other hand, simply works for an owner.

Did you notice how the steward referred to Abraham? The most noticeable words on a steward's lips are:

"My master" (Genesis 24, eighteen times).

Act out the story. Did the steward's attitude of obedience and service shine through? If it didn't, try it again. A good steward knows who his master is and how best to serve him!

When you were preaching about good stewards this morning, I kept thinking about Hamilton Kenyon," Mrs. Barrett said to her husband over Sunday dinner. "He must be the most generous man in our congregation. Just think about all the projects he's funded . . . how much he gives to missions. I wish a few more people took stewardship that seriously!"

"That would be nice," Pastor Barrett agreed. "But, you know, when I think of stewardship, Cliff Morgan comes to my mind."

"Cliff Morgan?" Mrs. Barrett looked surprised. "But he's—"

"Oh, I know, Cliff doesn't have much money. But the way he gives his time and talents is what impresses me. What he's saved the church in repairs and construction costs can't be counted. And he's so faithful to visit the shut-ins in our congregation. The way I see it, a good steward would be a combination of Hamilton and Cliff—one who knows that his time and talents, as well as his material wealth, belong to the Lord. Every church could use more of that kind of steward!"

◆ **TAKE A LOOK / Psalm 39:5; Philippians 4:13**
Whether or not people believe in God, everything they own really belongs to Him. The psalmist puts it this way:
The heavens are yours and yours also the earth; you founded the world and all that is in it (Psalm 89:11).
God has trusted His children with money, possessions, time, abilities, and energy. Take turns reading the verses below. Then draw a line from the verse to the word it talks about on the right:
This verse tells me . . .   that this belongs to God:
    1. Psalm 39:5   a. my money
    2. Philippians 4:13   b. my possessions
    3. 1 Chronicles 29:14 c. my time
    4. Haggai 2:8   d. my strength

▲ **TAKE A STEP**
Paul sums up stewardship this way:
So, whether we live or die, we belong to the Lord (Romans 14:8).
Look for a moment at the things around you—your home, clothes, toys, jewelry, stereo, books, car. It's not much fun to think about, but many families lose everything they have to fires, floods, or tornadoes. How would you react if you lost everything you "owned"?

The cattle on the hills, the cars on the roads

Q

What does God entrust to His stewards?

A

Stewardship means recognizing that everything I own belongs to the Lord.

PARENT:
A good book for youth is God's Guide Through the Money Jungle *by Larry Burkett, Christian Financial Concepts, 601 Broad Street, S.E. Gainesville, GA 30501*

Dollars and cents—handle with sense!

Q

How can I become a good steward?

A

Steward-ship means making the most of the opportunities God gives me.

Do you think I'll have enough to pay for a year of college?" 18-year-old Margie asked excitedly as she climbed the courthouse steps with her parents.

"Maybe," her dad replied. "We'll soon find out."

Sixteen years before, Margie had been injured in an accident. When the insurance claim was settled in court, $1,500 had been put into an account for Margie's education. All those years the court retained control of Margie's money. But today, at last, she would learn how much interest that money had earned.

An hour later, Margie and her parents left the judge's chambers, his apologies still ringing in their ears. "How could they let that happen?" Margie sighed. "Why did they leave my money in a regular savings account when they could have invested it in one that pays a lot more in interest? Didn't they care? I'm thankful for what I got, but if somebody had been paying better attention, it could have been so much more."

◆ TAKE A LOOK / Luke 19:12-26

Though you may not think about it much, you depend on stewards all the time. If you have a savings account, you give the bank officers stewardship of your money and trust them to invest it wisely. Taxpayers want the government to spend their money wisely. When we give others control of our money, we expect them to invest it for our profit, not theirs.

Jesus once told a parable about three servants who were given various sums of money to keep while their master was away on a long journey. As you read Luke 19:12-26, think about this question: Was Jesus talking to his disciples about being good stewards only of money?

▲ TAKE A STEP

In the parable, the master asked his servant the same question Margie asked the judge:

"Why then didn't you put my money on deposit, so that when I came back, I could have collected it with interest?" (Luke 19:23).

Both Margie and the master could have also asked, "Why didn't you make the most of your opportunity to serve me?"

God gives each of His children—including you—opportunities to serve Him. If Jesus were to return right now, which of those three servants would you remind Him of? Are you missing out on an opportunity at your church or in your youth group to serve Him?

*T*his house is a disaster," 16-year-old Kathy muttered. She and her twin sister Karen looked around the cluttered kitchen. "I thought being on our own for four days would be neat, but we haven't done anything the way Mom and Dad told us to."

"Yeah," Karen replied, "I don't even know where we've put Mom's list of instructions. But next time I'll read it before I spend so much money on a steak dinner. I didn't know she intended us to use some of that money at the grocery store. I hope I never see another peanut butter sandwich!"

"You know, I didn't realize how much we still depend on Mom and Dad," Kathy commented. "I'm so used to Mom washing all our clothes, I didn't have a thing to wear this morning."

"Well, we'd better get this place ship-shape before they get back tonight or we'll wish—" Karen cocked her head and ran to the window. "Oh, no! They're here—and they've got Grandma and Grandpa with them! Oh, I'm so embarrassed!"

◆ TAKE A LOOK / Luke 12:42-48

This week we've learned that all we are and have as followers of Christ belongs to Him. As long as we're on earth, we're simply His stewards, here to manage all He actually owns in ways that will bring Him glory.

Jesus knew the role of a steward is often difficult—especially when the Master is away so long. Read the parables He told about how stewards and servants must work during their master's absence (Luke 12:42-48).

▲ TAKE A STEP

Probably the hardest thing about being a steward is remembering you are one! Even though it's been hundreds of years since Jesus ascended to heaven, believers who are waiting for His return are still His stewards. Time has not changed that fact. The apostle Paul explained the responsibility of stewardship this way:

"Men ought to regard us as servants of Christ and as those entrusted with the secret things of God. Now it is required that those who have been given a trust must prove faithful" (1 Corinthians 4:1-2).

If Jesus were to step into your home right now, with whom would you identify the most: Karen and Kathy, the faithful steward, or the unfaithful steward? Well, don't look now, but . . . He is here!

Good stewards serve their master while he's away

Q

What does God expect from His stewards?

A

Stewardship means I faithfully obey God until Jesus returns.

PARENT:
One theme of the novel The Fellowship of the Ring, by J.R.R. Tolkien, is stewardship and service during a king's long absence. If your teenager has read this book, ask him or her about that.

SECURITY

Read the following statements and see if they help you identify a basic need everyone has:

• *"Did the bank say our Social Security check had been deposited?"* the 80-year-old grandmother asked her husband.

• *"Honey, our insurance agent is coming over to talk to us tonight. He thinks we need more coverage so you and the children will have financial security if something happens to me."*

• *"This house has an elaborate security system,"* the real estate agent told the couple. *"You will have nothing to worry about."*

• *"I don't know if I'm going to be able to keep my place on the team,"* the teenager told his father. *"Coach said he'll drop me if I don't improve."*

• *"Timmy want 'blankie,' "* the two-year-old wailed as his mother put him in the crib for his nap. *"Timmy want 'blankie.' "*

◆ THINKING ABOUT SECURITY

Have you guessed what that basic need of life is? Of course—it's security! From the youngest to the oldest, as individuals, and nations, people want to be secure—**free of fear, doubt, or danger**. But security can be hard to find in our complex, uncertain world.

Families experience divorce and financial ruin; elderly people are attacked and robbed on city sidewalks; the threat of war hangs over everyone. Sometimes the very people we put our trust in turn right around and threaten our security. But the Bible teaches us there's one source of security that will never be shaken:

"I am running away and never coming back! P.S. . . . please record cartoon carnival at two o'clock."

● KEY VERSE ON SECURITY
A righteous man . . . will have no fear of bad news; his heart is steadfast, trusting in the LORD. His heart is secure, he will have no fear . . .
(Psalm 112:6-8).

▲ LOOKING AHEAD
God alone is the source of true security. This week we'll see why that's so important.

A good place to start looking for answers to those questions is in Psalm 28:7-9. What words there bring to mind safety, security, and comfort? (If you have time, why not illustrate those verses!)

*T*he loudspeaker blared through the crowded department store: "Attention please: We have a lost child in the office on the third floor." As she ran to the elevator, Mrs. Adams whispered a prayer: "Oh, let it be Mason, please let it be Mason."

Her three-year-old son had been missing for the past 20 minutes. She had frantically retraced her path through the toddler department without success. Finally she had alerted a sales clerk, who called a security guard. As the minutes passed and Mason still had not been found, Mrs. Adams became more and more fearful. Now, as she rushed into the office and spotted her son, relief flooded her heart. Tearfully she hugged him.

"Where did you go, Mommy?" Mason sobbed. "I looked and looked, but I couldn't find you. I was scared, Mommy!"

"I know, honey," his mother replied. "I was scared too. We'll both be more careful next time, won't we?"

◆ TAKE A LOOK / Genesis 3:6-10

Do you remember how you felt when you looked up and your parents weren't where you thought they were? Maybe, like Mason, you got separated from them in a crowd. Or perhaps Dad was late picking you up after school. Possibly you came home to an empty house when you were sure Mom was supposed to be there. Whatever the situation, you probably felt insecure and afraid.

In Genesis 3:6-10, you'll read about the first time anyone ever felt afraid. As you read those verses, put yourself in Adam's place and imagine what his fear must have felt like.

▲ TAKE A STEP

"I was afraid . . . so I hid" (Genesis 3:10).

People experience many kinds of fear. Some fear the future, or death, or heights; others fear water, or darkness, or thunder. Some fear they may fail a test; others fear they're not loved. Sometimes our fear—like Adam's—is the direct result of sin. Whatever kind of fear you experience, one thing is certain: Nobody enjoys feeling afraid!

In order to overcome his fear, Adam had to face God and admit his sin and his fear. You too will overcome your fears only when you face them.

Close your family time today with each of you sharing the one thing you fear most. After you look up 2 Timothy 1:7, pray for each other, asking God to replace that fear with a "spirit of power, of love and of self-discipline."

I'm all alone and so afraid!

How do I feel when I'm not secure?

Security is replaced by fear when I fail to trust God.

PARENT:
Be sensitive to your child's fears as expressed through his words or actions. Encourage him to share his fears with you . . . and with God.

Security is more than a warm, fuzzy feeling

But why wasn't I invited?" Carolyn sobbed. "I just know they're all having a great time and I feel so left out."

Her mother handed her a tissue and gave her a big hug. "Honey, I can't imagine why Cassie invited all the girls in the Scout troop except you to spend the night. I know it hurts—"

"You can't know how bad it hurts!" Carolyn yelled.

"Carolyn, believe it or not, I do know how you feel. I remember that when I was your age some of my best friends were invited to go on a hayride, but I wasn't. I thought I'd die."

Carolyn's tears stopped for a moment. "What did you do about it, Mom?"

"First, I made sure I hadn't offended or hurt any of them. When I found out the problem wasn't my fault, I made some new friends and just kept on living. The world didn't fall apart."

Carolyn looked down for a moment. "But Mom, I want to go so much. I just want to belong."

Q

Where is security not to be found?

◆ TAKE A LOOK
Psalm 146:3; Proverbs 18:11; 28:26

There's nothing wrong with wanting the security of being loved and accepted. We human beings need love. But it's important to realize that other people can never really love us the way we need to be loved. Only God can do that.

According to the Bible, people try to find security by trusting in all kinds of things. As you read the verses below, jot down on the line at the right the false source of security each verse mentions.

A

Security cannot be found in riches, possessions, or people.

This verse warns ... that security is NOT found in:

Psalm 146:3	_____
Proverbs 18:11	_____
Isaiah 31:1	_____
Proverbs 28:26	_____
Jeremiah 17:5	_____

▲ TAKE A STEP

Lasting security cannot be found in leaders, money, possessions, or people. It can be found only in God:

The name of the LORD is a strong tower; the righteous run to it and are safe (Proverbs 18:10).

Carolyn learned that looking to other people for security only leads to disappointment. Tell about a time in your life when someone let you down. How did you feel? Have you learned where you can find true security?

*H*is life seemed to be the American dream fulfilled. He was an honor student in school, an outstanding Marine, the husband of a wonderful woman, and a powerful advisor to the president of the United States. His future seemed secure.

But suddenly the president he served was disgraced, and he himself faced a prison sentence. In desperation, Chuck Colson began searching for God . . . and found Him. Before he went to prison, Chuck sat by the sea one morning and prayed, "Lord Jesus, I believe You. I accept You. Please come into my life."

Chuck explains what happened: "I had succeeded and I had given God none of the credit, never even thanking Him for any of His gifts to me. With these few words that morning came a sureness of mind that matched the feeling in my heart. There came something more: strength and serenity, a wonderful new assurance about life, a fresh perception of myself and the world around me." Though he spent the next few years in prison, Chuck had already found "maximum security."

◆ TAKE A LOOK
Psalm 62:1-2; Philippians 3:4-11

Chuck Colson discovered that true security cannot be found in power, prestige, or prosperity. It comes only from knowing Jesus as Savior and Lord.

In Old Testament times, King David could have looked for security in his powerful position. In New Testament times, the apostle Paul could have put his trust in his past accomplishments. But both men learned that true security couldn't be found in who they were or what they had done. First read David's words in Psalm 62:1-2; then read Paul's in Philippians 3:4-11. Which verse in Philippians do you think is similar to David's thoughts?

▲ TAKE A STEP

My soul finds rest in God alone; my salvation comes from him (Psalm 62:1).
I consider everything a loss compared to the surpassing greatness of knowing Christ Jesus my Lord (Philippians 3:8).

You might not have the prestigious position of King David, the praiseworthy abilities of the apostle Paul, or even the powerful influence of Chuck Colson, but you can experience the security they found when you trust Jesus Christ as Savior. If you're ready to admit your sin to God and to accept the salvation He offers through His Son's death, you can use the very words Chuck Colson prayed in today's story.

Real maximum security isn't found in prison

Q

Where can I find lasting security?

A

Security is found only in knowing Christ as Savior and Lord.

PARENT:
You can read the story of Chuck Colson's conversion in Born Again.

With God as my shield, it doesn't matter how I feel

"*I was on one of the rugged islands off the coast one magnificent day last autumn," the young man began. "I had gone perhaps a mile into the interior of the island when I heard something to my right. I glanced in the direction of the noise and saw a wild boar emerge from the bush, charging in my direction. I was horrified! I had heard what a boar could do to a man, and here I was miles from help with no weapon. I began tearing through the woods, looking for a tree to climb.*

"*I was losing ground when suddenly I spotted a cabin. With one last burst of speed, I dashed inside, bolted the massive door, and stood quivering against the wall. Outside, the boar rammed himself against the door again and again. One minute I would tell myself that even an enraged boar couldn't break that heavy door; the next minute I'd think 'This is it! He's coming in!' I stood there for almost an hour, trembling with fear.*"

Q

How can I know I'm secure in Christ?

A

Security in Christ is a fact based on God's Word, not on my feelings.

◆ **TAKE A LOOK / John 8:31-32**

Once the young man had run into the cabin and slammed the door, he was safe. He knew that was true. But the threatening noise of the boar battering the door caused him to doubt that truth. And so he felt afraid.

You may never have been chased by a wild boar, but you probably have experienced times when your feelings got the upper hand over what you knew to be true. In a similar way, many people rely on their feelings rather than the facts when it comes to their salvation.

Sometimes a person who has believed in Jesus as Savior will feel that God has left him. That may make him doubt that he ever believed God at all. But God never turns His back on us; by our own sin we turn our backs to Him. (If that's true in your life, put 1 John 1:9 to work right now.)

God wants His children to be free from fear. Read John 8:31-32. Can you identify the one thing you must do to be free from fear?

▲ **TAKE A STEP**

"If you hold to my teaching . . . then you will know the truth, and the truth will set you free" (John 8:31-32).

God wants His children to live according to the truth of His Word, not according to their own shaky, changeable feelings. As different family members read John 10:27-30; 2 Timothy 1:12; Romans 8:38-39; and 1 John 4:16-19, tell what "fear-fighting" truth you find in each passage.

RECONCILIATION

A fter you read these headlines, try to think of a big word that describes the situations. (Hint: It's at the top of the page!)
Treaty Signed in Geneva—Nations Agree to Shipping Rights
Lawsuit Settled: Parties Agree to Injury Compensation Plan
$10,000 Restored to Investor; Funds Found in Wrong Account
Feuding Brothers Vow to Settle Their Boundary Dispute
Divorce Proceedings Stopped: Couple Plans Second Honeymoon
Parents Search for Runaway Daughter; Promise Forgiveness

◆ THINKING ABOUT RECONCILIATION

Without the clue at the top of the page, it might have been difficult to think of a word which describes what happens when something is set right legally, or when a damaged relationship is restored. But that's exactly what each of those situations shows . . . and what the word *reconciliation* means.

That word also describes what happens when one's relationship with God is made right. The Bible puts it this way:

● KEY VERSE ON RECONCILIATION

God . . . reconciled us to himself through Christ and gave us the ministry of reconciliation (2 Corinthians 5:18).

▲ LOOKING AHEAD

Sometimes people think of reconciliation as making something "balance" or work out right—like bank statements or mathematical equations. But our relationships with others should also work out right. That calls for reconciliation—**the process of setting damaged relationships right**. We'll learn about that process.

Reconciliation involves starting over with someone who has wronged you. Genesis 45:1-15 describes Joseph's reconciliation with his brothers, who had sold him into slavery in Egypt. Why do you think Joseph was able to set that damaged relationship right?

Bridging the gulf between God and man

Before Mrs. Newton died, she had dedicated her six-year-old son, John, to the Lord and had faithfully taught him God's Word.

But at the age of 11 John began working on his father's ship. By the time he was 17, that rough environment had encouraged him to do every evil act he could imagine. Later, as the captain of a slave ship, Newton's wickedness became so great that even his few friends thought he was insane. His sin separated him not only from God, but from other people too.

Today we know John Newton as the man who wrote the hymn "Amazing Grace"! These words are etched on his tombstone: "John Newton, Clerk [preacher]; once an infidel and libertine, a servant of slaves in Africa, was by the rich mercy of our Lord and Savior Jesus Christ, preserved, restored, pardoned, and appointed to preach the faith he had so long labored to destroy."

Q

Why do people need to be reconciled with God?

A

Reconciliation—made possible by Christ's death—brings me into a right relationship with God.

◆ **TAKE A LOOK / Romans 5:8-11**

What changed John Newton's life so dramatically? The relationship between him and God that had been damaged by sin was set right. He was reconciled to God.

Reconciliation with God is necessary for every man, woman, boy, and girl because sin has damaged all mankind's relationship with God, separating us from Him. In fact, as Paul explains, those who have not been reconciled to God are His enemies:

Once you were alienated [totally separated] from God and were enemies in your minds because of your evil behavior (Colossians 1:21).

But God changed that sad situation between Himself and sinful humanity. Read Romans 5:8-11 to find out what He did to enable us to be reconciled to Him.

▲ **TAKE A STEP**

Your sins may not be as awful as John Newton's, but any sin puts a barrier between you and God. Yet Jesus' death on the cross made it possible for John Newton to repent of his sins and come to God. And it has done the same for you! God will make this reconciliation real in your life if you ACT:

(1) Acknowledge that you are God's enemy, separated from Him by your sin;
(2) Confess your sin to God;
(3) Take Jesus as your Savior. If you haven't been reconciled with God, don't wait another minute!

*T*en years later, Wanda still remembered what caused her to rebel against her father. She had given him one of her school pictures. He already carried pictures of her brothers. Wanda just wanted him to be able to show off her picture too.

But Wanda also remembered seeing that picture a few weeks later in the corner of her dad's sock drawer. That was the moment Wanda believed her father really didn't love her. Soon she became a rebellious teenager and eventually left home.

Now her father was dying. He had called for her to come. "Oh, Wanda, why did you leave home?" he asked weakly. Wanda explained what had happened and how she still felt about it.

Tears came to her father's eyes. "Honey," he whispered, "why didn't you say something? I would have explained. I had a twin sister who was killed at age 14. In that picture you looked just like her, and I couldn't bear to look at it. I didn't want to hurt your feelings so I put that picture away. I figured I'd get another picture of you eventually . . . but I never did. Oh, honey, I'm so sorry." As he gently squeezed her hand, Wanda began to cry.

◆ TAKE A LOOK / Hosea 3

Sin has separated us from God, but it also separates us from each other. Every day people hurt other people emotionally as well as physically. Sometimes the hurt is evil and deliberate. Other times it happens by accident or out of ignorance. But almost always pain and bitterness result, making enemies of people who really belong together. That's when reconciliation is needed.

Read the story of the prophet Hosea and his unfaithful wife in Hosea 3. God wanted Hosea to marry this sinful woman as a picture of the sin-damaged relationship between Israel and God. Thank God, no sin is too great for reconciliation!

▲ TAKE A STEP

It's hard not to become bitter when someone hurts you. But God can help you guard your heart against bitterness.

See to it that . . . no bitter root grows up to cause trouble and defile many (Hebrews 12:15).

What could Wanda have done to keep from becoming bitter toward her father? Ask yourself honestly: Is there something a friend or family member has done to you that's been making you bitter? What can you do about that right now?

Hard feelings can make high fences

Why do people need to be reconciled to each other?

A

Reconciliation is needed because people are sinful and often hurt one another.

PARENT: Many Christian books offer help in working out hurts from the past. Ask at your local Christian bookseller.

The first step is always the hardest

Q

What steps lead to reconciliation?

A

Reconciliation is possible only when I am willing to communicate and to forgive.

PARENT:
A third party may be needed in the reconciliation process. Your pastor or a Christian counselor can offer an objective viewpoint.

If I've told you once, I've told you a hundred times—write the amount of the check in the checkbook before you tear it out!"

Chuck and Shannon had slipped into the kitchen for a bedtime snack and heard their father's angry shouts in the dining room.

"I hate it when they argue," Shannon whispered.

Then they heard their mom's agitated voice. "Well, I'm always asking you to do some little things around the house, but you just ignore me." Chuck and Shannon cringed and tiptoed out.

Next morning at breakfast the children were surprised to see their parents smiling and cheerful. Finally Shannon asked, "Why are you two so happy? Didn't you have a big fight last night?"

"Yep," Mr. Waldrop replied. "But we have a policy never to go to bed angry. So we work out our differences. Right, honey?"

◆ TAKE A LOOK
Matthew 5:23-25; 18:15-16; Colossians 3:13

Reconciliation gives people an opportunity to start over. But it doesn't happen by accident. Those involved in a conflict must take action.

Read Matthew 18:15-16 and Colossians 3:13 to find out how to start the reconciliation process after someone else has treated you badly. Then read Matthew 5:23-25, which tells what to do if you're the one who has hurt someone.

▲ TAKE A STEP

Remember yesterday's story about Wanda? Because she didn't communicate with her father, Wanda made it impossible to heal their damaged relationship. But in today's story, Mr. and Mrs. Waldrop kept communication open. They were committed to solving their problems.

But even with good communication, reconciliation won't happen unless each person is willing to forgive and be forgiven. That's why Colossians 3:13 is a verse worth memorizing:

Bear with each other and forgive whatever grievances you may have against one another. Forgive as the Lord forgave you (Colossians 3:13).

Let's see how this works. Together, think of a situation that might cause an argument in your family. Then divide into two teams—one team to act out what might happen when you're not willing to communicate and forgive, and the other team to show what can happen when you are.

I get the bathroom first," Chuck announced to his sister as they ran upstairs after breakfast.

Shannon grabbed his arm. "Whoa! You got the shower first. It's my turn. Besides, I've already got my curling iron plugged in."

"Listen, Sis. I was late for class yesterday because of you and I'm not going to be late again. So I'm going first."

"Oh, no, you're not!" Shannon said with determination. Then she paused. "Wait a minute. We sound like Mom and Dad did last night. If they can kiss and make up, why can't we settle this argument? Okay, since you have to be at school before I do, I guess you can go first," she said, stepping back from the door.

"You're great, Sis!" Chuck laughed as he reached for his toothpaste. "Always the peacemaker . . . "

◆ TAKE A LOOK / Ephesians 2:11-18

Maybe you haven't noticed, but human beings aren't perfect! At home it's easy to let selfishness rule our behavior or let the strain of daily life affect how we treat others. That's why it's good to practice "the art of making up."

In Bible times, relationships between the Jewish people and and all other people (called Gentiles) were hostile. The Jews believed that God could never accept a Gentile! As you read Ephesians 2:11-18, you will see that Jesus' death and resurrection made a way for both Jews and Gentiles to be reconciled to God. In verses 15-16, you'll see that God also intended them to be reconciled to each other.

▲ TAKE A STEP

Being reconciled to God brings peace with God. And being reconciled to other people also brings peace with them. The verse which applies to Jews and Gentiles can also apply to anyone else:

His purpose was to create in himself one new man out of the two, thus making peace, and . . . to reconcile both of them to God through the cross (Ephesians 2:15-16).

If you're part of a family, you know peace doesn't always reign supreme. It's easy to fall into the habit of arguing. Sometimes it takes sheer determination—with God's power—to break out of that hostile habit. The example Shannon's parents set encouraged her to do just that. Do you need to practice "the art of making up"? You'll be glad you did . . . and so will the rest of the family!

Breaking up (and making up) are hard to do!

Q

What are the results of recon- ciliation?

A

Recon- ciliation brings peace in my relationship with God— and with others.

DISCERNMENT

Plunkett and Plop-plop were bullfrogs who loved adventure. Since they could leap great distances, they were confident in their ability to escape from danger. So they weren't too worried when they were captured and taken to a laboratory in a large burlap bag.

The professor put Plop-plop in a cage in front of two pots of water. Then, while Plop-plop watched, the professor lowered Plunkett into a pot of boiling water. Instantly Plunkett's brain registered "DANGER! DANGER!" Gathering his strength, he leaped out of the pan and into a dark corner.

Sad about losing sight of his friend, Plop-plop wasn't paying much attention when the professor lowered him into a pot of lukewarm water. "Oooooh, this feels good," he thought to himself. "Plunkett doesn't know what he's missing!"

Plop-plop was so lost in thought that he didn't notice the professor slowly turning the heat up. By the time the water reached the boiling point, it was too late! Poor Plop-plop!

◆ THINKING ABOUT DISCERNMENT

Plunkett quickly realized he was in danger. But when Plop-plop realized what was happening, he could no longer leap to safety.

We live in a world that is not always what it seems to be. Sometimes the spiritual dangers of our world are as obvious as boiling water. But other times the dangers we face are not quite so clear. So God's children need to develop the character quality of spiritual discernment. This verse shows how necessary that is:

"How do you know I got this dirt on me? Maybe I'm biodegrading."

● KEY VERSE ON DISCERNMENT
The man without the Spirit does not accept the things that come from the Spirit of God . . . because they are spiritually discerned (1 Corinthians 2:14).

▲ LOOKING AHEAD
Discernment is **the ability to see people and situations the way they really are, not merely as they appear to be.** We'll see how this is possible in our complex world.

After you read Proverbs 19:25, think of at least two ways a discerning person benefits when someone corrects him.

Would you think you were in danger if . . .
• a friend invited you to learn a mind-control technique he'd been practicing?
• your state legislature passed a law saying parents could no longer see their children's school records?
• your physical education class at school began teaching yoga?
• your friend encouraged you to go ahead and take something because the department store would never miss it?
• you were offered some pills to take at a party?
• you frequently listened to music with lyrics that encourage you to do things God's Word says are wrong?
• the TV programs you watch each week consistently showed violent or immoral acts?

◆ TAKE A LOOK / Acts 13:2-12

Some of those situations are like the boiling water Plunkett found himself in yesterday. But others are like the "lukewarm water" that trapped Plop-plop.

Unless we have discernment, it's hard to see Satan's evil intentions. Even Eve, after walking with God in the Garden of Eden, did not recognize evil when the serpent spoke to her (Genesis 3:1-5). The Bible describes Satan as crafty (Genesis 3:1) and a liar (John 8:44). Paul the apostle says this about him:

The god of this age has blinded the minds of unbelievers, so that they cannot see the light of the gospel of the glory of Christ (2 Corinthians 4:4).

Discernment is what helps us see through Satan's crafty tricks. You'll see discernment in action in the lives of Barnabas and Paul when you read Acts 13:2-12.

▲ TAKE A STEP

We know that Satan's evil works are destructive. But unless we recognize them, our lives may be in danger. Elymas the sorcerer may have looked like other men, but Paul and Barnabas discerned that the spirit within him was Satan's.

Look once more at the situations at the top of the page. Remembering that Satan is a crafty liar who tries to keep you from seeing him at work, tell how each situation may be spiritually dangerous. In such situations, which of these questions can help you be more discerning: "Is everyone else doing it?" Or, "Does this agree with God's Word?"

If you don't see danger, you won't run to safety

Q

Why do I need to be a discerning person?

A

Discernment keeps me from falling into Satan's evil traps.

PARENT:
Another area of spiritual danger is the occult. Find an opportunity to discuss this danger with your older children.

Open my eyes that I may see

"**W**ell, son, it's up to you to decide," Howard's dad told him at the end of their discussion.

Howard was trying to decide which softball team to join. The Chargers, last year's league champions, had invited Howard to play with them. But the Christian school Howard attended needed one more player to be eligible to join the league.

Howard went outside and sat on the porch. He knew it was an honor to be asked to play with the Chargers. They were sure to be in the play-offs this year. In fact, they might even win the championship again! And everybody knew the school team didn't have much of a chance. Besides, he could always play for them next year. It would be fun to be on a winning team. But still . . .

After much thought, Howard went back inside. "Dad, I think I see the situation clearly now. I've decided to play on the school team. You know, if I played for the Chargers, I'd be doing it just to get a trophy—not to glorify God. I'll be playing on the school team for the right reasons."

What should a spiritual person discern?

◆ **TAKE A LOOK** / Psalm 119:125; 1 Corinthians 2:14; Philippians 1:10

Because Satan is so crafty and deceitful, we need to be able to discern his threatening traps so we can avoid them. But Christians need to discern other things besides danger. As you read the following three verses, write on the blank line what each verse tells you to discern:

This verse tells me . . .	that I must discern:
Psalm 119:125	_____
1 Corinthians 2:14	_____
Philippians 1:10	_____

Discernment helps me know what God wants me to do in any situation.

▲ **TAKE A STEP**

You can begin to discern God's Word by reading it regularly and applying it in your life.

You can discern spiritual truths as you study God's Word and learn to rely on Him in every situation.

In today's story, Howard had to make an important choice. He needed to discern what God wanted him to do—not merely what he wanted to do. Think of a choice you had to make recently (maybe you're in the middle of making such a decision). What steps did you take to make that decision? Looking back, do you feel you discerned what was best? If not, what can you do to be more discerning in future decisions?

Dwayne, come here right now!" Mr. Danby bellowed as he lifted his suitcase out of the trunk.

Dwayne hurried into the garage, wondering why in the world his father was so furious—apparently at him.

"Look at this garage," Mr. Danby steamed. "I told you it had better be cleaned out when I got back. But just look at it!"

"But Dad—"

"Don't give me any excuses. I told you to clean out the garage, and you didn't. And that's all there is to it."

Just then Mrs. Danby stepped out of the kitchen. "Harry, I know you're tired from your long trip, but there's something you need to know. Your brother had an accident on the tractor last Monday. Dwayne's been out there every day until well past dark doing Jim's chores and keeping things going. I told him the garage could wait till things settled down."

Mr. Danby let loose a big sigh. His wife continued with a mischievous grin, "Honey, why don't you back out of the driveway, come in again, and we'll start all over!"

◆ TAKE A LOOK
Romans 14:10; 1 Corinthians 2:15

Because he didn't take the time to discern the facts, Mr. Danby made a snap judgment which wasn't fair to his son. In order to become a more discerning person, we need to learn the difference between discerning and judging.

The Bible sometimes uses the word *judge* to describe discerning actions. But in other verses, the word *judge* means "to condemn." Judge in Romans 14:10 has a different meaning than judgment in 1 Corinthians 2:15. Which one do you think means "to condemn"? Which one means "to discern"?

▲ TAKE A STEP
The spiritual man makes judgments about all things (1 Corinthians 2:15)

A spiritually growing person is always discerning. He observes, listens, investigates, and evaluates the situations he's in so he can respond in a godly way.

Mr. Danby condemned before he discerned. Mrs. Danby could have done the same thing by accusing her husband of being unfair. Instead, she was discerning and helped to settle the problem.

If Mr. Danby had tried to be more discerning in this situation, what do you think he could have said to Dwayne after seeing the mess the garage was still in?

Getting the facts straight can prevent heartbreak

Q

How can I be more discerning?

A

Discernment involves observing and listening carefully to get the facts straight.

PARENT: Remember, the discerning parent is first and foremost a good listener.

Be on the lookout for opportunities to love

*J*ayne watched her father slump wearily into his
recliner. He hadn't even bothered to pick up the
paper! And Mother didn't seem to have any energy
this evening either.

Jayne knew her parents were deeply concerned
about Granny. She thought about the many trips to the
hospital they had been making after work every day.
"No wonder they're tired," she thought.

Just then the clock chimed eight. Quickly Jayne ran
upstairs and into her little sisters' room. Usually Mom
and Dad bathed the little ones and dressed them for
bed, but tonight she would do it!

Thirty minutes later, a slightly damp six-year-old and
a squeaky clean four-year-old came to kiss their parents.

"Jayne's going to read our story tonight, Daddy,"
one said.

"Yeah," her little sister chimed in. "Jayne says
you're tired, Mommy, and we should let you rest. So
good night!" And they bounced off to bed.

Q

*How
does a
discerning
person
treat
others?*

A

*Discernment
means
treating
others with
love and
sensitivity.*

◆ TAKE A LOOK / 2 Timothy 1:1-8

God's people need discernment to keep out of
spiritual danger. But it's also important that we
discern the needs of people around us.

Even though the apostle Paul was in prison, he
received news from his many friends in the cities
where he had preached. When he heard from his
young friend Timothy, he was able to discern that
all was not well with him.

As a young pastor, Timothy may have felt
timid about teaching and leading older men. Paul
encouraged him (1 Timothy 4:12). Because
Timothy also had some health problems, Paul
instructed him to take better care of himself
(1 Timothy 5:23). As you read the opening of
Paul's second letter to Timothy (1:1-8), look for
clues that tell you Paul discerned Timothy's needs.

▲ TAKE A STEP

Timothy probably felt better about himself and
his work because of Paul's sensitive understanding.
Jayne's parents got a little rest because she discerned their need and worked to meet it.

In the following verse, find the four-letter word
which summarizes how a discerning person should
treat others:

This is the message you heard from the beginning: We should love one another (1 John 3:11).

How will you put that word to work in your
family today?

MISSIONS

*A*fter Jesus arose from the dead, He returned to heaven. A legend tells what might have happened when Jesus met the angel Gabriel. The Lord told Gabriel that His work on earth had been finished.

"And what is Your plan now?" inquired Gabriel. "Will You be sending armies of angels to tell the world what You've done?"

"No," answered the Savior. "It's all up to My disciples."

"The disciples!" Gabriel gasped. "Why, they have no education, no management skills. Not only that, some of them are . . . well, they're just a little bit cowardly."

"What you say may be true," the Lord replied, "but I have confidence in them. Their lives have been changed by My life and resurrection, and now they want everyone to know it."

"But Lord," Gabriel protested, "they're only human. They might fail You. What's Your back-up plan if that happens?"

Jesus answered, "There is no other plan. They must succeed."

◆ THINKING ABOUT MISSIONS

That heavenly discussion never really happened, but it does help us see that God wants His children to reach the whole world with the message of His love.

Just before He returned to heaven, Jesus gave this command:

● KEY VERSE ON MISSIONS

"Go and make disciples of all nations, baptizing them in the name of the Father and of the Son and of the Holy Spirit, and teaching them to obey everything I have commanded you" (Matthew 28:19-20).

▲ LOOKING AHEAD

All believers have a mission or **assigned duty to go and tell others about Jesus.**

Isaiah 6:8 has often been used as a motto for missions. Does that verse describe your attitude?

"I'm going to go by the church and donate this to the missions paper drive. Dad can't object to a donation to the missions paper drive."

Untold millions are still untold

Q

Why is mission work important?

A

Mission work is important because people who do not know Jesus will be separated eternally from God.

The thundering landslide had engulfed the little town. Scarcely a rooftop or tree remained to be seen. The few survivors watched the army equipment roll into place and the soldiers begin digging.

Amazingly, some survivors were found, trapped in buildings where air pockets remained. Everyone was joyous, hoping their friends and relatives would be rescued next.

That evening, after leaving instructions that the digging continue, the general in charge of the rescue operation returned to headquarters. For a while, his troops continued to work. But then they slowed down and finally they quit.

"But what about the people you haven't rescued yet?" the villagers cried. "They need your help!"

"But we need our rest," the lieutenant replied callously. "We will dig again tomorrow morning."

After a long rest and a leisurely breakfast, the rescue crews began digging again. But it was too late. All the air pockets were exhausted. There were no more survivors.

◆ **TAKE A LOOK / Mark 16:15; 2 Thessalonians 1:6-9**

The soldiers should have worked through the night for two reasons: (1) Their general had commanded it, and (2) people were in danger of dying.

When you think about it, those are the same reasons why Christians should take the news of Jesus Christ to the entire world, which is stuck under a landslide of sin. After you read Mark 16:15 and 2 Thessalonians 1:6-9, tell which passage is a command for believers to obey, and which one describes the danger that those who do not know Jesus will face.

▲ **TAKE A STEP**

The people trapped under the landslide didn't have the power to help themselves. Their only hope for survival lay with the rescue unit, but it didn't take seriously the urgency of the mission.

People who have never heard about Jesus must have help from those who do know Him. The verses you just read describe a danger far worse than that of a mere landslide. They describe a time when those who do not know God will be

. . . punished with everlasting destruction and shut out from the presence of the Lord and from the majesty of his power (2 Thessalonians 1:9).

With that verse in mind, how would you answer this question: "Why is missions important?"

*T*est your knowledge of missionaries by matching each description on the left with the name on the right:

1. The shoemaker who is called the "father of modern missions"

2. The person who rescued hundreds of children from temple prostitution in India and founded Dohnavur Fellowship

3. The founder of Wycliffe Bible Translators

4. One of the missionaries killed by Auca Indians in South America

5. The founder of the China Inland Mission

a. Nate Saint
b. William Carey
c. Hudson Taylor
d. Cameron Townsend
e. Amy Carmichael

◆ TAKE A LOOK / Acts 13:1-5

Maybe you've heard this statement before: "Every Christian is a missionary." That's true in the sense that every Christian must do his or her part to tell the Good News to others. But some men and women, by God's leading, are appointed by the church to do that work in a special way, often far away from their homes.

The apostle Paul is often referred to as the first missionary. Read how he and Barnabas became missionaries in Acts 13:1-5.

▲ TAKE A STEP

No professional coach selects his team members by calling for volunteers. Neither does the president select an ambassador to another country from a pool of volunteers. Yet a common way of selecting missionaries today is to wait until somebody volunteers. This wasn't true in the early church. Did you notice this verse in your Scripture reading today?

The Holy Spirit said, "Set apart for me Barnabas and Saul for the work to which I have called them" (Acts 13:2).

Finding and sending out missionaries is the special responsibility of the church. If you feel God is calling you to the mission field, let your pastor know. Ask him to pray for you to determine exactly what God wants you to do.

And if you don't know much about missionaries, check your church library or local Christian bookstore for the biographies of some of the missionaries featured in the quiz today. You're in for an adventure!

The mission of the church is missions

Q

Who carries out God's mission?

A

Missions is the church's most important assignment, involving every believer— including me.

PARENT:
Reading a biography about a missionary will give you and your child a greater understanding and vision for missions.

Answers: 1-b; 2-e; 3-d; 4-a; 5-c.

Missions begins in your own backyard

After Jonathan Goforth accepted Christ in 1877, he witnessed daily in his hometown. Telling people about Jesus became his greatest joy.

Later, when he was in Bible school, Jonathan was invited to speak at a church some distance away. Unfortunately, he had only enough money to get him part of the way there. He would have to leave the train at a station 10 miles short of his destination.

So Jonathan bought a ticket, rode to the last station, and began to walk the remaining 10 miles. After he had covered about eight miles, he passed a crew of men repairing the road. He stopped to witness to them and invited them to the church.

On Sunday, much to his delight, several of the men he had met on the road attended the service. To his even greater joy, one of them accepted Christ as his Savior. Goforth later said, "I would gladly walk 10 miles any day to bring one lost soul to Christ."

Q

How can I spread the gospel without going overseas?

A

Missions starts right where I am as I witness to those around me.

◆ **TAKE A LOOK / Luke 24:45-49; Acts 1:1-11**

Soon after that, Jonathan Goforth journeyed to China as a missionary. But he is best remembered as a witness for Christ wherever he went, whether at home or overseas.

Before Jesus ascended into heaven, He spoke to His disciples about taking the Good News of His life, death, and resurrection to the whole world. He instructed them to wait first for the Holy Spirit to come upon them, and then to go forth as witnesses in His power. As you read Luke 24:45-49 and Acts 1:1-11, try to figure out where the disciples witnessed first.

▲ **TAKE A STEP**

Not all Christians will be sent to other countries as missionaries. But Jesus does expect all believers to be His witnesses, doing what they can right where they are. He says,

"You will be my witnesses in Jerusalem, and in all Judea and Samaria, and to the ends of the earth" (Acts 1:8).

The disciples witnessed first in their hometown of Jerusalem. Jonathan Goforth meant what he said about walking 10 miles to bring one person to Christ. How many lives would you touch if you were to witness only to the people within 10 miles of your home? Make a list of everyone you know in that area. Then ask God to show you how you can be a witness in *your* "Jerusalem."

*B*ut millions are going to hell every day! They need to hear the gospel now," William argued.

His older friend answered calmly, "When the Lord gets ready to convert the heathen, He will do it without your help or mine."

But William disagreed. After all, Jesus had told His followers to go. William was convinced that Christian nations should send missionaries to countries who knew nothing of Christ.

At age 22, William Carey became a preacher. Whenever he had the opportunity, he pleaded with churches to send missionaries. And he prayed for the world, country by country. With all his heart he believed Christ's command:

"Ask the Lord of the harvest, therefore, to send out workers into his harvest field" (Matthew 9:38).

◆ **TAKE A LOOK / 2 Corinthians 8:14-15; 9:11-12; Colossians 4:12-13**

William Carey was concerned about people who had no opportunity to hear about Jesus. In 1792 he started a foreign missionary society. Soon he went as a missionary to India. There he preached for seven years before one person believed. But Carey continued to pray and work, and eventually hundreds came to the Lord through his ministry.

William Carey was first of all a man of prayer, but he knew missionaries could not live and teach in foreign countries unless they were supported by people back home. But money isn't a missionary's only need. Because they preach the gospel of Jesus Christ, missionaries are literally soldiers on the front line of the battle against Satan's forces. They need the prayers of all God's people behind them.

In 2 Corinthians 8:14-15 and 9:11-12, find one reason why God gives us money. Then in Colossians 4:12-13, find two words that describe how we should pray for missionaries.

▲ **TAKE A STEP**

If you can't actually go to another country as a missionary, you can support those who do by giving generously and working hard in prayer for them.

Ask your pastor for the address of one or more missionaries your church supports. Write them and ask for photos and specific prayer requests. Tape the missionaries' pictures to a world map with strings to the countries in which they serve. One day each week, be sure to pray for them.

If you can't go, then help someone else go

Q

How can I help missionaries if I stay at home?

A

Missions should be supported by the gifts and prayers of all God's children.

PARENT: If you give regularly to support missions, include your child in this joy. A special "missions bank" to fill with loose change can be a reminder to pray for "your" missionaries.

GRACE

With the aroma of fried chicken and fresh corn wafting around them, the Potter family sat down to dinner. Mr. Potter asked 10-year-old Randy to say grace. Randy ducked his head and quickly mumbled, "Godisgreat, Godisgood, LetusthankHimforourfood. ByHishandweallarefed, giveusLordourdailybread. Amen. Let's eat."

"Wa-a-ait just a minute," Mr. Potter said. "You may think you've said grace, but I don't feel that I've thanked the Lord for anything. Would you like to pray again, or would you like me to?"

Ashamed of his "automatic" prayer, Randy prayed again. Then while the food was passed, Randy looked perplexed. "Dad, I'm mixed up. We learned a verse in Sunday school that says we're saved by grace. Does that mean we have to say grace to be saved?"

◆ THINKING ABOUT GRACE

When you hear the word *grace*, you may think of mealtime prayers. But grace means much more than that.

The Bible uses the word *grace* in two ways. One way refers to God's undeserved blessing of salvation; the other refers to the help God gives us to live each day. Put those two ideas together and you'll see that grace is **God's willingness to respond in love to the needs of undeserving people**.

God deals graciously with everyone by providing for life's daily needs—including food, shelter, air, water. And believers experience grace when He gives us strength to face difficult situations. But even more important, grace is God's favor extended to sinful people who don't deserve anything but His wrath. As the Bible says:

"I have a math test tomorrow, Sir, and I could use Your help multiplicationwise."

● KEY VERSE ON GRACE

For it is by grace you have been saved, through faith—and this not from yourselves, it is the gift of God (Ephesians 2:8).

▲ LOOKING AHEAD

Grace may be hard to understand. But it's not hard to experience—a fact you'll learn this week.

Reread the definition of grace (in bold type above); then tell how Randy's familiar dinnertime prayer really does describe God's grace.

*I*n 1946 a young scientist was carrying out experiments in the brand-new field of atomic science. To determine the amount of nuclear fuel needed for a chain reaction, he would push two small mounds of uranium together. Just as the mass was ready to explode, he would push them apart with his screwdriver, instantly stopping the chain reaction. He had performed that experiment many times.

But one day something unexpected happened. His screwdriver slipped, the mounds of uranium touched, and instantly the room was filled with a dazzling blue haze. Almost without thinking, the scientist tore the two piles of uranium apart with his hands, stopping the deadly chain reaction.

Immediately he realized he would die from exposure to the radiation. But even then he was concerned about the seven other scientists present. Quickly he diagrammed their positions on the blackboard so doctors would know how much radiation each had received. If he hadn't acted sacrificially, those others would have been fatally exposed. Nine days later he died in agony.

◆ TAKE A LOOK
Romans 5:17; Ephesians 1:7-8; 2:4-9
The scientist stopped the deadly chain reaction of atomic power at the cost of his own life. Almost 20 centuries ago, God's Son Jesus deliberately walked into an even more deadly "chain reaction" when He allowed the curse of sin to fall on Him and take His life. Though He didn't deserve to die, Jesus gave His life to stop the deadly chain reaction of sin. Why did He do it? Because of God's grace.

Romans 5:17 and Ephesians 1:7-8, and 2:4-9 talk about God's grace in our lives. How many things can you find in those verses that are possible only by the grace of God?

▲ TAKE A STEP
Salvation, redemption, forgiveness, righteousness, eternal life, and much more—only God's grace makes these things possible, because God's sinless Son paid the terrible price for our sin. God is indeed gracious.

In him we have redemption through his blood, the forgiveness of sins, in accordance with the riches of God's grace that he lavished on us with all wisdom and understanding (Ephesians 1:7-8).

Close your family time today by specifically thanking God in prayer for the many ways He has lavished His grace on you.

Grace = God's riches at Christ's expense

Q
What is God's grace?

A
Grace is God's loving provision of salvation through His Son Jesus.

Grace is having my name written in God's Book

*A*mazing grace! how sweet the sound,
   That saved a wretch like me!
I once was lost but now am found,
   Was blind, but now I see.

'Twas grace that taught my heart to fear
   And grace my fear relieved;
How precious did that grace appear
   The hour I first believed.

Through many dangers, toils, and snares
   I have already come;
'Tis grace hath brought me safe thus far,
   And grace will lead me home.

◆ TAKE A LOOK / 1 Timothy 1:12-17

Q

How can I experience God's grace in my life?

The man who wrote the words of that beloved hymn knew God's grace. Though he had been born into a Christian home in England, he was orphaned at age six and placed in the care of an unbelieving relative, who scoffed at what his parents had taught him.

That relative had a bad impact on the boy. As a young man, he enlisted in the Navy and went to Africa, determined to break the laws of God and man. And he succeeded. He experienced sin in many of its most awful forms. He was indeed a wretch! Years later, after many horrible experiences, John Newton cried out in repentance to the God he remembered from his childhood. He knew he deserved punishment and death. But by God's grace, he experienced forgiveness. He had been lost in the darkness of sin, but now he was found by God's gracious love.

A

Grace is experienced personally when I receive Jesus Christ as my Savior.

John Newton would heartily agree with the words of the apostle Paul in 1 Timothy 1:12-17. As you read those verses, you'll find that grace and mercy are two sides of the same coin.

▲ TAKE A STEP

As John Newton, the apostle Paul, and millions of others have discovered, no sin is too great for the grace of God to forgive.

After reading this page, you might want to sing the hymn "Amazing Grace" together. Discuss what you think the writer meant each time he used the word *grace.*

The grace of our Lord was poured out on me abundantly, along with the faith and love that are in Christ Jesus (1 Timothy 1:14).

*T*he prisoners met once a week for Bible study. Tonight the group leader read this verse, paused, then read it again:

" 'But he said to me, "My grace is sufficient for you, for my power is made perfect in weakness" ' " (2 Corinthians 12:9).

"Most of you know me," he began slowly. "You know what I've done. But I can tell you that God's Word is true. His grace is sufficient.

"When I was convicted and sentenced to life imprisonment, I didn't believe God existed. All I knew was that I was miserable and didn't want to go on living. But my cellmate began talking to me about Jesus. Before long, I understood what it meant to repent of my sins and accept Jesus as my Savior. And He has made all the difference to me."

"What difference?" someone sneered from the back. "You're still in prison, ain't ya?"

"Yes, you're right—I'm still in prison," the man replied. "My body is behind bars and always will be. But my spirit is free. I know God has forgiven me. I've learned to accept what I cannot change, and to live for the Lord even in this place. That's what I mean when I say God's grace is sufficient."

◆ TAKE A LOOK / Job 13:14-16; 19:23-27

Job wasn't in prison like that man, but he too learned the lesson that God's grace is sufficient for any situation. He lost his family, his property, and the support of his wife. He got terrible sores all over his body. Friends who should have comforted him instead criticized him.

Job was angry, in pain, full of questions, and ready to give up. But still he experienced the grace of God, as you'll see when you read Job 13:14-16 and 19:23-27.

▲ TAKE A STEP

God's grace is not a magic wand that changes our circumstances or gets us out of tough situations. Instead, His grace strengthens our faith to believe His promises. By His grace the Holy Spirit assures us that God loves us and is working in our lives—even in times of difficulty.

Read Job 13:15 and 2 Corinthians 12:9 in as many different versions of the Bible as you can. As a reminder that God gives grace for every situation, print those verses from the translation you like best on an index card and give it to the family member (or members) facing a tough situation today.

God's grace keeps me going day by day

Q

How does God's grace strengthen me?

A

Grace helps me face the tough situations in my life.

Say, you're looking more and more like Him!

Q

What does it mean to "grow in grace"?

A

Grace is evident in my life when I become more like Jesus.

Ed, you married the best cook in Williams County! Ellen, that dinner was fantastic," Joe said, leaning back in his chair. Joe was visiting his younger sister and her family.

"Well, an old bachelor like you is not too hard to please," Ellen said grinning as she began to clear the table. Quickly, 11-year-old Kevin got up and began to help. Uncle Joe watched in amazement as Kevin scraped the dishes and carried them to the sink. "I'll take the trash out when you're finished cleaning up, Mom," he said cheerily as he left the room.

"I'm not believing my eyes, Ed!" Joe said. "The last time I visited, you literally had to threaten Kevin every evening to get him to take the trash out. Now he's even volunteering to help with the dishes. What made such a tremendous change?"

"I guess he's growing up," Ed replied. "I don't know what—"

"Oh, it's more than just growing up," Ellen interrupted. "He wants your approval, Ed, so he's trying to be like you. I'm just glad he's got such a good model to follow."

◆ TAKE A LOOK / Titus 2:11-14

Kevin's mom was right. Kevin admired and loved his dad so much that he not only wanted to do things that pleased him, he also wanted to grow up and be just like him!

Human beings are born to grow. And so is anyone who is "born again" (John 3:3) as a baby in God's family. As we grow physically as children, we often resemble our parents. As growing Christians we should

grow in the grace and knowledge of our Lord and Savior Jesus Christ (2 Peter 3:18).

You can learn more about what it means to "grow in grace" by reading Titus 2:11-14.

▲ TAKE A STEP

As a Christian you need the spiritual nourishment of God's Word, fellowship with God through prayer, and relationships with other Christians. But to grow in grace—to become even more mature as a believer—means to become more and more like Jesus.

Just as Kevin modeled his life after his earthly father, God wants His children to model their lives after His Son Jesus. As you reread Titus 2:12, think back over Jesus' life. How did He "say no to ungodliness and worldly passions"? What are some things you've had to say no to lately?

GRANDPARENTS

A n energetic, mischievous young boy, Billy Frank knew the stories about the heroism of his grandfather, Ben Coffey—a one-eyed, one-legged Civil War veteran, who worked harder than most men who had two legs and eyes. When he returned from the war and began raising a family, he made daily Bible reading and prayers a regular part of the family routine. His grandson, Billy Frank, benefited from the example set by Grandfather Ben Coffey when his own mother and father followed that godly pattern.

Billy became a Christian after hearing a sermon by a Southern evangelist. But the example his grandparents set had already prepared him by pointing him in the right direction.

Maybe you've heard of Billy—his last name is Graham. *

◆ THINKING ABOUT GRANDPARENTS

These days you may not find Grandma in the kitchen baking goodies for her many grandchildren. Instead she may be going to college. And it's just as likely that you'll find Grandpa working out at the health club as sitting on the banks of the fishing hole. But the kind of relationship Grandfather Ben had with his family is still possible—and much needed—today.

Grandparents can spoil you, spank you, praise you, or pray for you. But most of all they love you without any strings attached.

Though it's hard to believe if you're still young, becoming a grandparent may be **one of God's special blessings for you when you grow older.** The psalmist says:

● KEY VERSE ON GRANDPARENTS
May the LORD bless you from Zion all the days of your life; . . . may you live to see your children's children (Psalm 128:5-6).

▲ LOOKING AHEAD
This week we'll investigate the special relationship between grandparents and their grandchildren.

"Ask Mom for Sweet Chunk cookies. If she says no, ask Grandma."

*From Grandparents Can by Dale Evans Rogers with Carole C. Carlson. Copyright 1983 by Dale Evans Rogers. Published by Fleming H. Revell Company. Used by permission.

Grand-parents know the "inside story"!

Q

Why are my grand-parents an important part of my family?

A

Grand-parents who are strong in their faith encourage me to grow in my faith.

Why can't you be neater?" Marcia's mother frowned at her daughter's messy room. "At least make your bed!"

"Well, I'll just mess it up again tonight," Marcia grumbled.

"I don't care if nobody sees it but you and me—your bed must be made. And I mean it, Marcia," her mother said firmly.

Grandma Langdale, whose room was next to Marcia's, walked in the room chuckling. "Edith, you certainly do have a poor memory," she said to Marcia's mother.

"Uh-oh. I think I feel a story coming on," Marcia's mom groaned. Marcia perked up, ready to listen.

"Marcia, when your mother was growing up, she shared a room with your Aunt Marlene, who was very tidy. But your mother was a bit messy and would never help make up their bed.

"Well, Marlene finally got tired of making the whole bed by herself. So I'd go into their room after they'd left for school and find Marlene's half of the bed neatly made, and your mother's side still rumpled! So I'm not sure your mother has much room to talk."

Marcia's mother grinned. "We can always count on Grandma to tell the 'inside story'! But that's no excuse, Marcia—you still have to make your bed!"

◆ TAKE A LOOK / 2 Timothy 1:4-7

Looking back, most grandparents can see things they would have done differently in raising their children. And they realize their children will not be perfect parents either. But by providing acceptance, love, and wise advice when it's needed, grandparents can often bridge the gap between parent and child.

Grandparents have an important teaching role too. Read the opening words of the apostle Paul's second letter to his young friend Timothy (vv. 4-7). Then try to figure out who influenced Timothy to become a Christian.

▲ TAKE A STEP

Paul recognized that Timothy's sincere faith
. . . first lived in your grandmother Lois and in your mother Eunice (2 Timothy 1:5).

Have each family member share one thing a grandparent has done that has made a spiritual contribution to his or her life. If you have grand-parents who are not believers, close your family time by praying for them.

*W*hat a Grandmother Is," by Patsy Gray (age 9): "A grandmother is a lady who has no children of her own, so she likes other people's little girls. A grandfather is a man grandmother. He goes for walks with boys and they talk about fishing and tractors and stuff like that.

"Grandmas don't have to do anything except be there. They are old, so they shouldn't play hard or run. It is enough if they drive us to the market where the pretend horse is and have lots of dimes ready.

"They don't have to be smart, only answer questions like why dogs chase cats or how come God isn't married.

"They don't talk baby talk like visitors do, because it is hard to understand. When they read to us they don't skip words or mind if it is the same story again.

"Everybody should try to have a grandma, especially if you don't have television, because grandmas are the only grown-ups who have got time."*

◆ TAKE A LOOK / Ruth 1:19-22; 4:13-21

People often judge other people by the way they look and the abilities they have. But those things really aren't important to grandparents. To them, you're special!

The book of Ruth introduces us to a typical grandparent. As the story begins, Naomi and her two daughters-in-law are the only ones left in the family. One daughter-in-law returns to her own family. But the other one, Ruth, journeys with Naomi to her mother-in-law's home country. Read about how Naomi felt about their discouraging situation in Ruth 1:19-22.

But circumstances change . . . especially when God is in control. When you have time—maybe this weekend—read the entire book aloud to one another. You'll see how Ruth eventually meets and marries a man named Boaz and has a son, Naomi's grandchild. But right now, read Ruth 4:13-22 to learn more about the relationship possible between grandparents and grandchildren.

▲ TAKE A STEP

What Naomi's friends said about little Obed was true:

"He will renew your life and sustain you in your old age" (Ruth 4:15).

Can you think of three things you can do to "renew the life" of your grandparents?

Grandparents help us bridge the generation gap

How do my grandparents help me?

Grandparents help me by making me feel special, and I can do the same for them.

*Used courtesy of Glendale (CA) NEWS PRESS

Letters can send smiles across the miles

Hey, Dad, I didn't know we had important people in our family," Dwight said, bounding in clutching a letter. "How come you never told me?"

"Well, everybody in our family is important. But nobody's famous, if that's what you mean," Mr. Sayer responded.

"Oh, I'm not talking about now—I mean a long time ago. Gramps and I have been writing to each other, and he's been telling me about how things were when he was a boy. Did you know his great-grandfather was a Civil War hero? There's even a street named after him in his hometown."

"I didn't know that! What else did Gramps tell you?"

"A lot! I'm going to keep those letters for my own kids. You know, Gramps is pretty neat. I'm glad we started writing!"

Q

What can I do if my grandparents live far away?

A

Grandparents and grandchildren need to keep the lines of communication open.

◆ **TAKE A LOOK / Exodus 20:12; Leviticus 19:32**

In Bible times, children and grandparents often lived in the same house, so they spent a lot of time together. But today, cross-country moves have separated many families. So it may take a great deal of effort for children and grandparents to get to know each other. But there are many ways to do that. For instance, Dwight and his grandfather built an airmail bridge!

Wise King Solomon recognized the importance of grandparents and grandchildren when he wrote:

Children's children [grandchildren] are a crown to the aged (Proverbs 17:6).

Exodus 20:12 and Leviticus 19:32 give God's commands about your relationship to your parents. After you read these verses, tell how they might apply to your grandparents as well.

▲ **TAKE A STEP**

When children and grandparents live far apart, it's important to keep in touch. Postcards, phone calls, letters, and handmade gifts can be exchanged. Using old photos, your grandparents could put together a booklet called "My Life with Your Father (or Mother)." And your parents could take pictures of you for a book called "A Day in the Life of Me!"

Sharing a hobby is another way to develop a stronger relationship with your grandparents. Tell them in a letter about your hobbies, and ask them about their own. Then help each other pursue those hobbies. For instance, if Granddad collects stamps, be on the lookout for interesting ones to send him.

L isten as two grandfathers introduce themselves:
"My name is Oki Shikoru. I am 75 years old, and I
live in Japan. I have seven children, 15 grandchildren,
and five great-grandchildren. When I retired, I came to
live with my oldest son. 'On' is the special Japanese
word for the debt children owe their parents for raising
them. Every Japanese child knows the saying, 'On is
higher than the mountains and deeper than the seas.'
Family is very important here in Japan. My son has a
very small home and we are very crowded. But my
children and grandchildren are the most important
people in my life."

"My name is Albert Parson. I am 81 years old and I
live in the United States. I have four children, nine
grandchildren, and two great-grandchildren. I live in a
nursing home. Sometimes I get very lonesome. My
children are very busy and come to see me some
Sundays. But they don't stay very long. I haven't seen
any of my grandchildren in almost a year. The people
here are good to me, but I miss my family very much."

◆ TAKE A LOOK / Psalm 71:9-18

It's sad, but Mr. Parson's situation happens all
too often. In Bible times, older folks were nearly
always the center of family life and were honored
for their wisdom and experience. Children and
grandchildren asked them for advice. The nation
itself turned to older leaders, priests, and judges for
guidance. Even the warriors were experienced men,
not the very young.

Psalm 71 is the prayer of a man who is aware
he's growing old. According to verses 9-11, what
are some of the fears older people have? After you
read verses 12-18, tell what you think is the
greatest strength older people have.

▲ TAKE A STEP

Our society seems to revolve around young
people, so sometimes we overlook the wonderful
contributions our older citizens make. But God
never overlooks anyone's worth. He promises:

"Even to your old age and gray hairs I am he, I
am he who will sustain you. I have made you
and I will carry you; I will sustain you and I will
rescue you" (Isaiah 46:4).

As they grow older, grandparents need your
continued care and respect for their wisdom and
experience. Before you see them or talk to them
again, think of ways you can show them respect.
Then be sure to do it!

My grandparents deserve my respect and care

Q

*What do my
grandparents
need as they
grow older?*

A

*Grandparents
need—and
deserve—my
continuing
respect and
care.*

PARENT:
*Involve your
children in your
parents' lives.
Don't overlook
any opportu-
nity to do so.
Remember, you
are setting the
pattern for how
your own
grandchildren
will relate to
you.*

FAIRNESS

It's not fair," the student complained angrily. "I should have been sent to the state competition. But someone in the office goofed up my grade point average. And now it's too late."

• "I should have won!" the wrestler protested to his coach. "The ref made a bad call and it cost me the match. It's not fair."

• "She never lets me play with her dolls when I go to her house, Mommy. But you always make me share. It's not fair!"

• "The doctor made a mistake in his diagnosis, but we still had to pay for that extra office visit. It really isn't fair."

• "That hit-and-run driver nearly ruined my life, and he got away scot-free. It isn't fair at all!"

◆ THINKING ABOUT FAIRNESS

Everyone wants to be treated fairly. As citizens, we expect our national government to be just, upholding the rights of each person equally. In sports, we want everyone to play by the rules, so no one gets special treatment. We want doctors, lawyers, and business persons to put the welfare of others above their own personal interests. And in our relationships with others, we expect to be treated fairly.

But no matter how we're treated ourselves, God expects us to act in fairness—by **treating others with justice, equality, and honesty**. Solomon explains how we can learn to be more fair:

● KEY VERSE ON FAIRNESS

My son, if you accept my words and store up my commands within you, . . . then you will understand what is right and just and fair—every good path (Proverbs 2:1, 9).

▲ LOOKING AHEAD

This week we'll see how important fairness is. Have someone read Deuteronomy 16:18-20 aloud. Think about what that says concerning the importance of justice (on a national scale) and fairness (on an individual basis). Find out the names of the judges in your town, county, or district, and post their names on a bulletin board as a special prayer reminder this week!

"This isn't evenhandedness. It's fifteen minutes to herself."

*T*he cake was frosted, the punch was made, and Pam was sure her tenth birthday party would be perfect!

For the next few minutes, the doorbell rang again and again. As each girl handed her a beautifully wrapped gift, Pam exclaimed, "I'm so glad you could come! This gift is so pretty, it's almost a shame to open it." After she placed the present on a table, she led each friend to the refreshments.

But when Barbara arrived, Pam reacted differently. Barbara handed her a card instead of a gift. As Pam took it, she pointed to the table and said curtly, "Come in. Refreshments are over there."

As the party went on, Pam's mother noticed that Barbara was left out of the conversations and seemed very unhappy. Pam's mother pulled her daughter aside and whispered, "Pam, honey, how do you think you'd feel right now if you were Barbara?"

Ashamed of her behavior, Pam's eyes filled with tears. After a moment, she returned to her friends . . . and made an extra effort to include Barbara in the fun.

◆ TAKE A LOOK
Leviticus 19:15; Acts 10:34; James 2:9
In the classroom the "teacher's pet" gets special treatment. On the playground the "super athlete" always gets to play the longest. Many people play favorites. And that's just not fair.

If you know how it feels to be on the receiving end of an unfair action, then you know why God wants believers to avoid treating others that way. As you look up the following verses, see if you can find one reason in each verse why it's important to be fair (just, equal, and honest) in all your relationships with others.

Leviticus 19:15   Showing partiality perverts
_____ .

Acts 10:34   _____ does not
show favoritism

James 2:9   If you show favoritism, you
_____ .

▲ TAKE A STEP
Paul's instruction to the young preacher Timothy is good advice for anyone who wants to please God:

Keep these instructions without partiality, and do nothing out of favoritism (1 Timothy 5:21).

Think of a situation you faced recently with friends, family, classmates, or fellow workers in which you could have played favorites. Would you do anything differently now?

Fair play is a good way to make somebody's day

Q

Why is it important that I be fair?

A

Fairness means I don't "play favorites" but treat each person equally.

PARENT:
Making an effort to give all your children equal love and attention will encourage them to do the same for others.

God sets the standards for a godly life

Q

Who determines what is fair?

A

Fairness means I practice God's principles of justice in my everyday life.

"**H**ey! I threw doubles so I get another turn," Marilee yelled.

"That's not the way my family plays Parcheesi," Joy replied.

"Well, you're at my house now. And that's the way we play, so I'm taking another turn!"

Marilee threw a six and moved her marker. "I capture your man," she exclaimed. "You have to go back to the start."

"But you can't," Joy protested. "My man is on a space with a circle. That's a safety zone and you can't capture there."

"Yes, I can! Playing with safety zones slows the game down too much. So I'm moving your man."

Just then Marilee's mother came into the room to see why the girls were arguing. "Mom, Joy keeps changing the rules and I keep telling her that's not how we play," Marilee exclaimed.

"Girls, girls!" Marilee's mom sighed. "There's no need to argue. The rules are all clearly written here on the box lid. Let's read them together so we'll all know exactly how to play."

◆ TAKE A LOOK
Proverbs 21:3; Isaiah 56:1; Romans 13:7

Winners and losers often have different ideas about what's fair. Losers may blame their loss on the referee's "unfair calls," while winners praise that same referee for a job well done! It all depends on your perspective.

Many people have a hard time "playing fair," even though they know the rules. But God wants His children to treat others fairly. And we have the help we need to do that, because God has given us His rulebook—the Bible—and the Holy Spirit to help us understand and apply God's Word. Find out what the Bible says about treating others fairly: Proverbs 21:3; Isaiah 56:1; Romans 13:7; and Colossians 4:1.

▲ TAKE A STEP

Through the prophet Isaiah, God declares: "I, the LORD, love justice; I hate robbery and iniquity" (Isaiah 61:8).

Try to remember a recent situation in which you had a hard time deciding what was the fair thing to do. Then answer this question honestly: "Did I have a hard time deciding because I really didn't know what was right . . . or was it hard because I was afraid I might look bad or be laughed at if I did what I knew was fair?"

I'll get even with Candy if it's the last thing I do!"
Monica thought as she glared at her classmate.

Monica passed a note to her friend Evelyn which
said, "Candy cheated on the math test. She'll get an A
she doesn't deserve."

After Evelyn read the note she wrote back: "How do
you know? Candy's smart. Why would she cheat?"

But by recess time, the rumor had spread—and
even Candy had heard it. She and her friends stood
whispering and glaring at Monica and her group. Then
one of Candy's friends went inside.

Later, the teacher motioned Monica into the hall.

"Monica," she said, "Someone has reported that
you cheated on the math test. It's unusual for anyone
to get all the answers right, as you did, so I think we'd
better talk about it."

Monica couldn't believe what she was hearing! The
rumor she started had boomeranged! But she knew
who the culprit was that got her in trouble.

"Just wait," she thought, "I'll make things so bad
for Candy and her gang, they'll wish they'd never
tangled with me!" Then she said sweetly to her teacher,
"Mrs. Archer, someone is just trying to get me in
trouble. I never cheat!"

◆ **TAKE A LOOK / Romans 12:17-21**
Revenge never evens the score or ends a conflict. It only makes things worse. When you try to
get even with someone who treated you unfairly,
you hurt him. Then he feels you've hurt him worse
than he first hurt you, so he must get even with
you. Soon you're locked into a circle of hurtfulness.

But God has designed a way for you to escape
from the destructive path of revenge. You can discover what it is when you read Romans 12:17-21.

▲ **TAKE A STEP**
*Do not be overcome by evil, but overcome evil
with good (Romans 12:21).*

A person who helps the one who treated him
unfairly doesn't have time to hate.

Evil people will eventually be repaid for what
they do—by God, not by you. So instead of getting
even with those who hurt you, try to do something
nice for them—and see how they respond. It may
change their lives!

Suppose for a moment that you were Evelyn,
the girl who first received Monica's note about
Candy. From what you read today, how would you
suggest that Monica treat Candy?

Revenge is not the way to fair play

Q

Should I try
to get even
when
somebody
hurts me?

A

Fairness
means
reacting to
hurts with
love, not
revenge.

Do I really care if something isn't fair?

I hope I make it," Jerry whispered as he and David jogged to the gym. The coach had just posted the list of players who would be on the freshman football team. David was the first-string quarterback, so his place was assured. But Jerry was competing with two other guys.

"Aw, Jerry, nobody has worked out harder or practiced more than you. You're in for sure," David replied.

When they got there, a group of guys had already gathered around the bulletin board. They inched their way closer and quickly scanned the list. David spotted his own name and was looking for Jerry's . . . when he saw his friend quickly turn away.

Again David read the list. "There must be some mistake!" he muttered to himself. "How could Curt beat Jerry for that position? Curt missed half the practices and never worked out!"

"I'll tell you why," another teammate spoke up. "Curt's dad gave several thousand dollars toward the new weight room, so the principal told Coach that Curt had to be on the team. It's not fair, but that's the way it is."

Should I try to make others be fair?

Fairness means I must stand up for the rights of others.

◆ **TAKE A LOOK / Amos 5:1, 7, 10-12, 14-15**

David wasn't unfairly treated, and his position on the team was secure. But it was hard for him to see someone else treated so unfairly.

Many Old Testament prophets reveal God's great concern for justice. In Amos 5:1, 7, 10-12, and 14-15 you'll see one reason God judged the Israelites was for their lack of justice.

▲ **TAKE A STEP**

Have you ever witnessed a situation where someone was treated unfairly? When such things happen, many people decide not to get involved.

But injustice—whether on an individual, national, or international scale—will never be stopped unless someone stands up for the rights of those who are unfairly treated and cannot help themselves. The Bible says:

The righteous care about justice for the poor,
but the wicked have no such concern
(Proverbs 29:7).

We've thought a lot about fairness on an individual basis. Now think for a moment about fairness on an international scale. Name a situation in the world today in which certain people are unjustly treated because of their race or religion. How could your family learn more about that situation? What could you do to show that you care?

STUDYING

-O *LOGY is a suffix that means "the study of" something. See how many of the following "-ology" words on the left you can match with the meanings on the right:**

1. anthropology
2. ornithology
3. entomology
4. conchology
5. numismatology
6. theology
7. epidemiology
8. geology
9. zoology
10. biology

a. study of the earth
b. study of coins and medals
c. study of mankind
d. study of God and religion
e. study of birds
f. study of diseases and epidemics
g. study of animals
h. study of living things
i. study of insects
j. study of mollusks and shells

◆ THINKING ABOUT STUDYING

Maybe you groaned when you heard this week's topic. After all, you may feel you already know everything you need to know about studying. But don't close your ears—or mind—just yet. Studying doesn't have to be a drudgery, and it offers some rewards.

Studying is **one of the ways people learn life's important truths**. It usually involves reading, observation, and research. A wise person will make learning a high priority throughout his life. Solomon, who is famous for his wisdom, said this:

● KEY VERSE ON STUDYING

*Let the wise listen and
add to their learning
(Proverbs 1:5).*

▲ LOOKING AHEAD

This week we'll study the "whys" and "hows" of opening your life to new ideas.

To get started with your study, read Proverbs 1:1-4, 7. Why do you think Solomon said "the fear of the LORD is the beginning of knowledge" (Proverbs 1:7)? Do you think it's possible to know the truth without knowing the One True God?

"Why do we have to memorize Lincoln's Gettysburg Address? Isn't it in the Gettysburg phone book?"

*Answers: 1-c, 2-e, 3-i, 4-j, 5-b, 6-d, 7-f, 8-a, 9-g, 10-h.

The Bible is God's answer Book for life

Q

Q

Why should
I study
God's
Word?

A

Studying
the Bible is
important
so I can
confidently
and
respectfully
stand up
for my
faith.

PARENT:
The Institute
for Creation
Research
(2100
Greenfield Dr.,
El Cajon, CA
92021) offers
materials for
all ages on
the subject of
biblical
creation.

Dad, uh—there's something I've got to tell you,"
Ian said slowly as he walked into the den. "I got
thrown out of social studies class today. I don't know if
I can go back."

"Maybe you'd better tell me exactly what
happened," Ian's dad replied as he set his Bible aside.

"Well, all week we've been reading about ancient
civilizations and how they got started. Today Mr.
Kramer started talking about evolution, and he said,
'You know, of course, that we all descended from
monkeys.' Well, I opened my big mouth and blurted,
'Mr. Kramer, you may have come from a monkey, but I
didn't.' Mr. Kramer turned real red and yelled at me.
He said I shouldn't treat the Bible as if it were a science
book. He said it was only a bunch of stories and fables,
so I shouldn't just swallow everything it says. I said, 'I
know the Bible isn't a science book, but everything it
says is true—even the scientific things.' Well, he sent
me out of class for creating a disturbance. I don't
know, Dad—it was like he was afraid for anyone to
hear my view. Now he doesn't want me in his class."

◆ **TAKE A LOOK**
1 Peter 3:15-17; 2 Peter 3:1-7, 17

Like Ian, you may one day face a direct
challenge to your beliefs. One reason for studying
the Bible now is to prepare yourself to meet those
attacks when they come.

*Always be prepared to give an answer to
everyone who asks you to give the reason for
the hope that you have. But do this with
gentleness and respect, keeping a clear
conscience (1 Peter 3:15-16).*

As you read 1 Peter 3:15-17 and 2 Peter 3:1-7,
17, prepare to respond to others in a confident yet
respectful way by answering these questions:

1. Which verse tells you that Peter wanted his
listeners to study the Scriptures and think for
themselves?

2. In which verse does Peter warn his hearers to
guard against false teachers?

3. Which verse describes people who leave God
out of their theories?

▲ **TAKE A STEP**

Even though Ian was frustrated and angry, he
should have been more respectful in the way he
spoke to his teacher.

Which one of the verses you read today would
you use to advise him how to answer someone who
was attacking his faith in God?

*W*ell, Mom and Dad got that one right, too," Clifford sighed to his sister. "Give 'em another question." The four Harper children had challenged their parents to a trivia game. But somehow it wasn't working out as well as they'd hoped.

Sherri asked the next question. "What is the annual salary of the president of the United States?"

Mr. and Mrs. Harper didn't even have to confer on this one. They knowingly nodded to each other, then replied, "$200,000."

"But how did you know that?" Sherri asked in exasperation.

"You two can answer five or six questions and we miss most of ours the first time."

Mr. Harper looked across the top of his bifocals at his children and replied, "Well, after all, your mother and I do have years of experience behind us! But really, I think it's because we read. When you four are glued to the tube watching reruns of 'Gilligan's Island,' your mother and I are in the den reading. Naturally we remember some of it."

◆ **TAKE A LOOK** / Matthew 2:1-12

If you've ever played a trivia game with your parents, you may have felt kind of dumb. Actually, your I.Q. has little to do with learning trivia. Continual exposure to a wide range of information does.

Understanding how our world works comes through the process of study—sometimes by our own observation, but often by reading about discoveries made by others.

You've probably learned about many famous scientists whose discoveries have changed our lives. Some of them were Christians who realized as they studied creation how great the Creator is. As you read Matthew 2:1-12, think what the Magi would have missed if they hadn't taken the time to study the stars (v. 2) and biblical and historical information (vv. 5-6).

▲ **TAKE A STEP**

You no doubt find some things to be more interesting than others. For instance, you may be excited about rocks or stars, while birds or flowers make you yawn. In any case, you should respond to your study in the same way the wise men did:

They saw the child with his mother Mary, and . . . bowed down and worshiped (Matthew 2:11).

Think of a subject you enjoy in school, or just for the fun of it. What does it tell you about your great God?

Q

What should I study in addition to God's Word?

A

Studying parts of God's creation gives me more reasons to praise Him.

You'll never learn by studying that way!

Why is studying sometimes so hard to do?

Studying is hard work because it takes total concentration.

PARENT:
Evaluate your own study habits. Do you spend time studying God's Word each day? Do you keep up with current events? Remember, you set study standards for your home!

Go upstairs, Gary," Mr. Brookins ordered as he walked into the room. "You can't study for that science test in front of the TV."

Reluctantly Gary pulled himself up off the family room floor, gathered his books, and went to his room.

When Mr. Brookins checked on his son thirty minutes later, he found him sprawled on his bed with the stereo playing loudly.

"Gary, turn down that stereo!" he yelled above the noise. "That's better. Now, Gary—" he began, but the ringing of the phone interrupted him. "I'll get it," Gary shouted as he ran down the hall to answer. "Oh, hi, Bobby. Yeah, I've got a minute."

Then Gary felt his father scowling at him. "Uh— listen, Bobby, I can't talk now. See ya."

"Gary, go in your room, stay off the phone, turn off the stereo, keep away from the TV, and sit at your desk properly. You're meant to be studying, not goofing off."

"But Dad," Gary replied, "I am studying!"

◆ **TAKE A LOOK / Ecclesiastes 1:13; 12:9-14**

Parents and children sometimes have different ideas about what it means to "study." Some students think studying is skimming through the assigned material once or doing one or two problems. Parents and teachers, on the other hand, want you to do whatever it takes to get that subject into your head. That may mean taking notes in class, outlining, carefully reading the book two or three times, creating self-tests, reviewing with a partner, or doing practice exercises. Most of all, they want you to spend your study time wisely by concentrating without distractions.

King Solomon devoted much time to studying (read Ecclesiastes 1:13). As you read his conclusion in Ecclesiastes 12:9-14, you may notice what seems to be a negative statement about studying. Do you really think that Solomon—who also wrote the book of Proverbs—thought studying is not worthwhile?

▲ **TAKE A STEP**

Much study wearies the body (Ecclesiastes 12:12).

But so do hard work, sports, and many other things usually considered to be "fun." Studying is difficult; it sometimes makes you tired. Think of three things you could do for a quick break if you got tired while studying.

Distractions which keep you from concentrating make studying harder. What was keeping Gary from studying? Do you ever have a problem with any of those distractions?

Mrs. Winston jumped up from the dinner table to answer the phone. "Hello? . . . Yes, Mrs. Wilkins, this is Kimberley's mother. . . . Oh, she did? I'm sorry to hear that, but I'm glad you told me. I'll talk to her about it. . . . Okay. Thank you for calling."

That conversation sounded like trouble to Kimberley. "What's wrong, Mom?" she asked as her mother hung up the phone.

"That was your English teacher, Mrs. Wilkins. She's concerned about your grades. She said you do all your homework and class assignments, but you do poorly on the tests. She wondered if you're regularly reviewing the material, and studying for the tests the way you should."

"But, Mom," Kimberley protested. "I studied for that test. Ask Margie—we studied together for a whole hour the night before!"

◆ **TAKE A LOOK / Luke 2:41-50**
Kimberley assumed that, since she spent a whole hour "studying" with a friend, she knew the material she would be tested on. But the success of your study time is measured not by the amount of time you spend, but by the results you achieve.

Do you remember the story about Jesus in the temple when He was 12 years old? As you read that story in Luke 2:41-50, listen carefully for clues that tell you Jesus was a good student. What two things did He do to help Him learn?

▲ **TAKE A STEP**
Mary and Joseph found Jesus
. . . sitting among the teachers, listening to them and asking them questions (Luke 2:46).

Of course the next verse says everyone was amazed at Jesus' answers. After all, He was God's Son! Even so, if Jesus listened and asked questions, think how much more we need to do the same in order to learn!

Try this experiment:
Concentrate on what your teachers say.
Don't let yourself be distracted by other students.
Take good notes on class lectures and textbook readings; pay attention to the way the material is organized.
Then, if you still don't understand, ask questions.
With these simple steps, you may find you're learning more than you ever thought you could!

The best things in life take time

Q

How can I become a better student?

A

Studying is more beneficial when I listen carefully and ask questions.

DEPENDABILITY

*I*t propels rivers and streams and pulls rain from the clouds. It gives direction to tree trunks and flower stems as they grow.

It determines the shapes of galaxies and the orbits of planets. But even though it is always there, we are rarely conscious of it.

We win over it when, as a baby, we first lift our wobbly head to peer around. We win again when we stand up, ride a bicycle, climb a mountain, or clear a hurdle. It wins every time a plane crashes, a tower topples, a child falls down, or a piece of toast drops to the floor—jelly-side down.

It keeps our feet firmly planted on the earth. It fills all of space and cannot be turned off. It passes through every kind of material, affects all matter equally, and has no opposing force. There's no way to shield against it. Do you know what this totally dependable force is?*

◆ THINKING ABOUT DEPENDABILITY

Because it is always there, doing what God designed it to do, the natural force of gravity illustrates the key quality of dependability.

There is no specific Bible verse that says, "Thou shalt be dependable." Instead, God uses other words to show us that **doing what others are counting on us to do** is an important quality to develop. See if you can pick out a synonym for dependability in this verse:

"It's a good thing history repeats itself. It sure can't depend on me to do it."

● KEY VERSE ON DEPENDABILITY

The fruit of the Spirit is love, joy, peace, patience, kindness, goodness, faithfulness, gentleness and self-control (Galatians 5:22-23).

▲ LOOKING AHEAD

As believers, we're responsible to be dependable—or faithful—to God and to others.

The dependability of nature is crucial to our lives and our universe. Can you find four verbs in Job 38:31-32 which describe the force of gravity in everyday language? What would it be like to live in a universe in which gravity was not dependable?

*These concepts adapted with permission from Rainbows, Snowflakes and Quarks: Physics and the World, by Hans C. VonBaeyer, published by McGraw-Hill Book Co., 1984.

*T*he phone rang just as Melissa was drying the last supper plate. Instantly she recognized the voice. It was Roger, star football player, "A" student, and all around good-looking guy!

"Hey, Melissa, I got some tickets to the play at the Civic Center, and I was wondering if you could go with me tonight?"

Melissa's heart hit the floor. After all this time, Roger had finally asked her out—and she couldn't go! "Oh Roger, I promised the Thompsons weeks ago that I'd baby-sit for them tonight. They're really counting on me!"

"Why not tell them an emergency came up and you can't babysit?" Roger suggested. "They'll never know the difference."

"No, I couldn't do that," Melissa replied. "It's not right. And it's too late for them to get someone else. But keep me in mind for another time." As Melissa hung up, a question slipped into her mind: "If that's the way Roger thinks, I wonder if I could ever really depend on him anyway?"

◆ TAKE A LOOK / Psalm 15

Though she would much rather have gone to a play, Melissa knew it wouldn't be right to back out of her baby-sitting commitment. Keeping her word was more important to her than personal pleasure. For Melissa, being dependable meant being reliable and honest. It meant accepting responsibility and keeping commitments—things that weren't very important to Roger.

In Old Testament times, David knew something about dependability. In Psalm 15 he lists the qualities of a person whose behavior pleases God. Though David doesn't use the word *dependability*, one of his phrases describes a dependable person. Can you find it?

▲ TAKE A STEP

God wants His followers to be dependable even when it costs us something. He describes a dependable person as one

. . . *who keeps his oath even when it hurts* (Psalm 15:4).

Like Melissa, you may have to choose between keeping a commitment and doing something more fun that comes along. But a dependable person will keep his or her word—even when it hurts. Have each person write the phrase "even when it hurts" on a small slip of paper. Tape it to the family activities calendar to remind you what a dependable person would do if a schedule conflict arises!

It's a great ability to have depend- ability

Q

Why do I need to be dependable?

A

Dependability means keeping my word even when it hurts.

Can I depend on anyone?

Read through the following examples thoughtfully. They all point to one big problem. What is it?
- Because an employee didn't follow instructions, a printing shop loses thousands of dollars to reprint a job.
- A child is disappointed because her daddy decides to work late instead of coming to her kindergarten program.
- The government loses millions of dollars because its contractors charge them for things they shouldn't.
- A scuba diver dies in the ocean because his air tanks weren't properly filled.
- A three-year-old falls down a flight of stairs while his babysitter is talking on the phone.

What happens when people aren't dependable?

A

Undependability ruins personal relationships.

PARENT: Can your children count on you to take part in their school activities, help with homework, or just to play? Your dependability can illustrate God's dependable love for them!

◆ TAKE A LOOK / Romans 1:28-32
Some people just aren't dependable. They put their own pleasure or convenience before their responsibilities to others. Today's motto seems to be "Me first. My pleasure, my success, my happiness come before any other person. I'll keep my commitment to you only if it's convenient to me." From home to school to office, people are hurt because others let them down.

God has designed human beings to be dependent on Him and on one another. When people leave God out of their lives, they become self-centered. And when whole societies act that way, chaos results.

In Romans 1:28-32, the apostle Paul paints a dismal picture of what happens when people and societies turn away from God's ways. Can you find in those verses a word which suggests that such people become undependable?

▲ TAKE A STEP
When people refused to obey God,
. . . he gave them over to a depraved mind, to do what ought not to be done. They have become filled with every kind of wickedness (Romans 1:28-29).

In Paul's list of evil attitudes and actions, you'll find the word *faithless*. That describes people without faith in God who, as a result, are undependable in their dealings with others.

Do the opening examples bring to mind a time you weren't dependable? Perhaps it was a school activity, family chore, or work project you let slide. If you've caused someone to suffer because of your selfishness, don't let another day pass before you ask forgiveness and try to correct the damage you caused.

"C ome on, Barney, get in the car," Terry coaxed the old beagle gently. But Barney didn't want to get in the car. He knew all too well the only places he ever went in the car were to the animal hospital, or the kennel, or the pet shop to get bathed and dipped. And he could do without those trips.

When Terry finally got Barney in the back seat, he climbed in beside him and cradled the dog's head on his lap. It wasn't long before tears welled up in his eyes. "Honey, are you worried about Barney surviving the heartworm treatment?" Terry's mom asked.

"Uh-huh," Terry sniffed. "He's too old and he might not pull through. And it's all my fault. He wouldn't have gotten these old worms if I'd just kept on giving him his medicine every day like the doctor told me to. I did for a while, but then I kept forgetting. I just thought it was too much trouble."

Tears streamed down Terry's cheeks. "It's my fault you're sick, Barney," he said, stroking the dog's fur. "I wish I could do it over again. I'd never miss a day giving you your medicine."

◆ TAKE A LOOK / Luke 12:41-48

Sad as it was, Barney's plight was Terry's fault. Barney's very life had depended on Terry doing what others counted on him to do. As a result of undependability, Terry was not the first person to wish for a second chance.

Hopefully you've not had such a heartbreaking experience, but you may have had some pretty close calls. Maybe you, like Terry, desire to become more dependable.

You won't find a chapter in the Bible entitled "How to Develop Dependability." But you can find guidelines and principles to help you do just that. As you read the teaching of Jesus in Luke 12:41-48, think about this question: What is the major difference between a faithful servant and an unfaithful servant?

▲ TAKE A STEP

"It will be good for that servant whom the master finds doing so when he returns" (Luke 12:43).

You can do almost anything one step at a time—including becoming more dependable! Think about a specific area of your life in which you need to be more dependable. Then write this note to yourself and tape it to your mirror: "Today is the first day of the rest of my life to become more dependable by _____ !"

"You can depend on me . . . some- times . . . maybe!"

Q

How can I develop dependability in my own life?

A

Dependability grows as I fulfill my responsibilities one day at a time.

Great is Thy faithfulness, O God my Father,
    There is no shadow of turning with Thee;
Thou changest not, Thy compassions, they fail not;
    As Thou hast been Thou forever wilt be.

Summer and winter, and springtime and harvest,
    Sun, moon, and stars in their courses above,
Join with all nature in manifold witness
    To Thy great faithfulness, mercy, and love.

Pardon for sin and a peace that endureth,
    Thy own dear presence to cheer and to guide;
Strength for today and bright hope for tomorrow,
    Blessings all mine, with ten thousand beside!

How does the Bible describe God's dependability?

◆ **TAKE A LOOK / 1 Corinthians 1:8-9; 10:13**
No human being is totally dependable. Somewhere along life's way, someone will think you let him or her down. And you in turn will feel let down by someone you counted on.

But you can always count on God! As you've probably already guessed from the words of the hymn you just read, *faithfulness* is the word the Bible uses to describe God's complete and continual dependability.

Psalm 145:13 proclaims this wonderful truth: *The LORD is faithful to all his promises and loving toward all he has made (Psalm 145:13).*

After you look up the following Bible verses, write on the line at the right what God can be depended on to do:

Faithfulness is the word that describes God's dependability.

This verse shows that . . .	God is faithful to:
1 Corinthians 1:8-9	_____
1 Corinthians 10:13	_____
1 Thessalonians 5:23-24	_____
1 Peter 4:19	_____
1 John 1:9	_____

▲ **TAKE A STEP**
Praise God for His faithfulness by singing (or reciting together) the first verse of the hymn above. Then close with these words of its familiar chorus (and by the way, how has God shown His faithfulness to you this week?):
Great is Thy faithfulness!
    Great is Thy faithfulness!
Morning by morning new mercies I see;
    All I have needed Thy hand hath provided—
Great is Thy faithfulness, Lord unto me!

PARENT: Check out Lamentations 3:22-23. Those are great verses for your family to memorize!

WRITING

*E*ach day of your life, you may read the writings of 50 people or more! Perhaps you begin your day reading the Bible, maybe using a devotional guide. Then you glance at the morning paper and check the instructions on the box of toaster waffles. Later you read textbooks in school or reports at work. You may order lunch from a sign over a take-out grill or from an eight-page menu. You may see many billboards on your way home.

After you come home, you look through your mail. Perhaps you read a bedtime story to the youngest member of the family. If you're a student, you read and write homework assignments.

Before you go to bed you may write a letter to a friend or jot down a page or two in your diary. Perhaps you spend a few minutes reading a chapter in a book by your favorite author. And sometime—right now in fact—you read this devotional guide!

Without a doubt, writing is an important part of your everyday life. What other things have you read today?

◆ THINKING ABOUT WRITING

From ancient hieroglyphics to modern computer printouts, every form of writing is **human communication put in a visible form**. Writing links us to people of the past, the future, and to many around the world in the present.

Writing also links us to God, our Creator. He has revealed Himself to us through the written record called the Bible. God's written history of His people still has this purpose:

● KEY VERSE ON WRITING

These things happened to [the Israelites] as examples and were written down as warnings for us, on whom the fulfillment of the ages has come (1 Corinthians 10:11).

▲ LOOKING AHEAD

Throughout much of their history, the Jewish people have been called "the people of the Book." Why do you think that is? Could that description be applied to your family?

"I did have an eventful day, but nothing, in my opinion, to write home about."

From scribbles and scrawls to paragraphs and pages

Q

Why is writing an important skill?

A

Writing helps me remember and learn from the past.

PARENT:
Encourage each child to keep a journal at his own pace. Blank books are available at many bookstores.

On her 13th birthday, Anne Frank started a diary with these words: *"I want to write, but more than that, I want to bring out all kinds of things that lie buried deep in my heart."*

Almost daily for the next two years she shared not only the events of her life, but also her innermost thoughts and feelings, her family conflicts, and the news she heard about World War II, which was sweeping the outside world.

To escape persecution by the Nazis, Anne and her family hurriedly went into hiding in a secret annex of a house in Holland. There they spent many difficult months waiting and hoping.

As the frightening months passed, Anne wrote: *"The brightest spot of all is that at least I can write down my thoughts and feelings; otherwise I would be absolutely stifled."*

Anne's diary ends abruptly on Tuesday, August 1, 1944, when the Nazis raided their hiding place and sent everyone to concentration camps. Anne Frank died in one of those camps. But her wish—*"to go on living even after my death"*—has come true: Her diary survived and, through it, her memory lives on.

◆ **TAKE A LOOK / Psalm 45:1, 17**
Anne Frank was an ordinary teenager living in extraordinary times. For her, writing became a way to organize her thoughts and emotions. And, as you may know if you've read her diary, writing has made her memory live on.

Giving people a way to remember the past is an important function of writing. God has recorded the history of His people because that record can teach us important truths—such as the trustworthiness of God, and our need to depend on Him totally. Read Psalm 45:1 and 17 to see why we need to remember how God worked in the past.

▲ **TAKE A STEP**
The psalmist claimed that
My tongue is the pen of a skillful writer
(Psalm 45:1).

Like Anne Frank or the writer of Psalm 45, you too may have thoughts you'd like to record. Purchase a small spiral notebook for each family member in which he can record daily events, life's lessons, dreams, and prayer requests and answers. Encourage one another to write entries regularly. But remember: A diary is private property unless willingly shared!

Match the kinds of writing on the right with the definitions on the left.

1. An ancient word-picture language still used today by about one-fourth of the world's population.

A. 𓏏 𓅓 𓂝 𓆓 (ancient characters)

2. Wedge-shaped characters used by the ancient Sumerians, Akkadians, Assyrians, and Babylonians.

B. ◁ 𓆟 △ 𓅱 (hieroglyphic characters)

3. The ancient Egyptian system of writing in which figures or objects are used to represent words or sounds.

C. בראשית

4. The language—still in use today—in which the Old Testament was written.

D.

◆ **TAKE A LOOK / Genesis 11:1-9, 31**

Though scholars have worked long and hard to unravel the mysteries of ancient languages, no one knows exactly when human writing was first developed. The earliest known writings were excavated at the ancient site of Uruk (called "Erech" in Genesis 10:10). The clay tablets discovered there were written about 3,000 B.C.!

The Chinese, Mayas, Sumerians, Egyptians, and other ancient civilizations all wrote—though their cuneiform and hieroglyphic writing styles aren't much like today's.

Studying ancient languages is important because they help us understand more about Bible lands and people. Read Genesis 11:1-9 and 31 to find out how the many ancient languages began. Do you recognize the name of a very important Old Testament character in one of those verses? See if you can find Ur or Babylon on an Old Testament map in the back of your Bible.

Since Abraham was from Babylonia, which language shown above do you think he could read and write?

▲ **TAKE A STEP**

The LORD confused the language of the whole world (Genesis 11:9).

Many language groups in the world today still have no system of writing. So Bible translators learn to write those languages and then teach the people to read translated portions of the Bible in their language. Find out why their work is so important and exciting by reading Revelation 5:9-10.

Q

What does writing teach me about the Bible?

A

Writing of ancient peoples helps me understand Bible lands and times better.

Answers: 1-d, 2-a, 3-b, 4-c

Parables and proverbs, poetry and prose

History and biography, poetry and prose—you can find all those forms of writing on the shelves of your local library. But you can also find them in the pages of your Bible! Match the kind of writing on the left with the example of it on the right to see what kind of "literary critic" you are!

1. Narrative poem—a long poem that tells a story
2. Heroic narrative—a story built around the life of a specific character
3. History
4. Parable
5. Letter
6. Short poem

a. 2 Samuel—the life of David
b. Psalm 23
c. The book of Galatians
d. Luke and Acts
e. The book of Job
f. The story of the good Samaritan

Q

Why are there different styles of writing?

A

Writing communicates truth in different ways from the author's heart to mine.

Answers: 1-e; 2-a; 3-d; 4-f; 5-c; 6-b

◆ **TAKE A LOOK / Psalm 2:1-5, 10-12; Jude 3-7**

You may think of the Bible as one big book. Actually it's a collection of 66 individual books written over a period of about 1,500 years—a whole library in one volume.

Because the Bible is God's Word, all 66 books work together to give us God's total message to humankind. The different styles of writing the many authors used under His guidance perfectly matched the message He was sending, touching the lives of those who heard it.

In Psalm 2:1-5, 10-12, and Jude 3-7, you will find a strong warning written in two different styles. The first is poetry, which appeals to the heart. The second is a forceful letter appealing to the mind. If you received both a clear, straightforward letter and an inspirational poem encouraging you to do something, which one would make a bigger impression on you?

▲ **TAKE A STEP**

God wanted His children to get His message that *In the past God spoke to our forefathers . . . at many times and in various ways, but in these last days he has spoken to us by his Son* (Hebrews 1:1).

God sent Jesus as the living Word (John 1:1), bearing the message of forgiveness. Today this same message is being sent into the world as God's Word is translated into more and more languages. But the message also goes out every day in another way. You'll discover what it is by reading 2 Corinthians 3:2-3. What message does your life communicate?

Many think of writers as people who spend their whole lives scribbling away in an attic, never getting out to experience life. But good writers don't hide from life. Instead, they enter into life wholeheartedly . . . and invite us to do the same.

Anyone—including you—can become a better writer simply by practicing. And you'll be better still if you learn to train and sharpen all your senses to experience the world around you.

Have you heard the expression, "Keep your eyes peeled"? Well, if you want to be a better writer, you'll do just that—and more! For fun, try these "eye-peelers" to help you really see the things you look at every day:

Viewpoints—Bend down and look through your legs backwards and upside down. What do you see?

Camouflage—Have someone hide a number of things in plain sight, but in unexpected places. (For instance, bran flakes sprinkled in the dirt of a potted plant.) Give everyone a list of the items "hidden." The one who spots them all first wins.

Objects—Put a dozen objects on a tray to show everyone. Then take them away. Have each person write down as many objects as he or she can remember.

Three Days to See—Imagine that you have only three days before you lose your eyesight. Share with the others the things you'd like to store in your memory for the rest of your life.

◆ **TAKE A LOOK / Ephesians 1:17-18**
Whether it's a journal, an essay for school, letters home, or notes to your best friend, writing is a skill that will bring pleasure to you and others. And writing can help you remember the great things God has done for you.

In his letter to the Ephesians, the apostle Paul prays
> that you may know him better . . . that the eyes of your heart may be enlightened in order that you may know the hope to which he has called you, the riches of his glorious inheritance in the saints, and his incomparably great power for us who believe (Ephesians 1:17-18).

▲ **TAKE A STEP**
Has Paul's prayer been answered in your life? Set aside time in your schedule today to write a poem, story, or descriptive word sketch of something you've seen with the "eyes of your heart." Talk about it together now to get some ideas (Paul's prayer in Ephesians 1 may help). Plan to share your "creations" together at dinnertime on Sunday.

Awaken my eyes— and my ears and my nose

Q

How can I become a better writer?

A

Writing skills improve as I practice and become more aware of my world.

PARENT:
Try to get in the habit of using a dictionary to help your younger children build their vocabulary.

DISCIPLES

*H*ow many of Jesus' 12 disciples can you name in one minute? Try right now and see. Ready—go!

Your family may have started out like this: "Matthew, Mark, Luke, and John . . . no, that's not right. It's Peter, Andrew, James, and John . . . Matthew . . . Judas . . . uh . . . Thomas . . . uh . . . " and then you faded out. If you named more than seven, you did pretty well!

◆ THINKING ABOUT THE DISCIPLES

We do not know the method Jesus used to choose the twelve specially trained disciples, or **learner/followers**. But the following verses show that Jesus made His decision after much prayer and for a specific purpose:

● KEY VERSES ON DISCIPLES

One of those days Jesus went out into the hills to pray, and spent the night praying to God. When morning came, he called his disciples to him and chose twelve of them, whom he also designated apostles (Luke 6:12-13).

When Jesus had called the Twelve together, he gave them power and authority to drive out all demons and to cure diseases, and he sent them out to preach the kingdom of God and to heal the sick (Luke 9:1-2).

▲ LOOKING AHEAD

The disciples were Jesus' approved representatives.

You'll find their names listed four times in the Bible: Matthew 10:2-5; Mark 3:16-19; Luke 6:13-16; and Acts 1:13. Read the list in Luke and then the one in Acts. (Matthew and Mark call Judas, son of James, by another name, "Thaddaeus.") Can you identify who is missing from the list in Acts? Do you know why?

"That's right, Beverly. They gave up everything. Not just spelling and long division."

*I*f you had lived in Galilee during the time of Christ, any one of the disciples might have been your next door neighbor. They were ordinary men who generally lived ordinary lives. They had an average education and average talents, normal personalities and normal jobs. Take a minute to see if you can match some of these average, ordinary Israelites with their descriptions:

1. Simon Peter	a. Jewish tax collector for the Romans
2. John	b. Meditated under a fig tree
3. Andrew	c. Wanted to judge things for himself
4. Matthew	d. Brought his brother to Jesus
5. Nathanael (Bartholomew)	e. Impulsive fisherman, who dared to walk on water
6. Thomas	f. He and his brother wanted a place of honor
7. James	g. Jesus gave His mother into this disciple's care*

◆ **TAKE A LOOK**
Acts 1:21-26; 2:43; Mark 3:14-15
As we learned from Luke 6:13—this week's Key Verse—Jesus had many disciples. But only 12 of those disciples were made apostles. A disciple is a learner—someone who follows and imitates a teacher. An apostle, on the other hand, is an authorized representative who is personally sent out for a particular purpose.

As you read Acts 1:21-26, you will find two qualifications of an apostle. Can you find others in Acts 2:43 and Mark 3:14-15?

▲ **TAKE A STEP**
Everyone was filled with awe, and many wonders and miraculous signs were done by the apostles (Acts 2:43).

Jesus Himself specifically chose 12 men to lay the foundation of the church and spread the Good News of salvation throughout the world. Their power to work miracles proved that their message was from God. Furthermore, to be an apostle one must have personally witnessed the resurrection of Jesus Christ.

According to the Bible's definition, no one alive today qualifies to be an apostle. But anyone who trusts in Jesus for salvation can be His disciple.

Reread the definition of a disciple above. Are you following your "Leader," Jesus Christ? Would your friends, neighbors, fellow students, and co-workers agree?

The world's most famous fisherman's club

How are disciples today like Jesus' apostles?

A

Disciples today are those who imitate and follow Jesus.

PARENT:
Jesus' eleven disciples were also apostles, but there were other apostles too. Examine the apostleship of Paul using Galatians 1–2; 2 Corinthians 10-12.

*Answers: 1-e; 2-g; 3-d; 4-a; 5-b; 6-c; 7-f.

Twelve who turned the world upside down

*T*ime for another quick quiz about the 12 disciples! *(No groaning, please—it'll be fun!)*

Many of today's professional athletes are known by their nicknames. Some of Jesus' disciples also had nicknames, or were frequently described in a certain way. How many can you match?

1. Peter	a. The Zealot
2. Andrew	b. Levi, the tax collector
3. James	c. Nathanael, the guileless
4. John	d. The Rock
5. Philip	e. The disciple Jesus loved
6. Bartholomew	f. The Doubter
7. Thomas	g. Judas, son of James
8. Matthew	h. The Less
9. James	i. Son of Thunder
10. Thaddaeus	j. Iscariot, the Traitor
11. Simon	k. Peter's brother
12. Judas	l. Witnessed to Nathanael*

What special job did the disciples have?

◆ **TAKE A LOOK / Matthew 28:16-20; Acts 1:8**

Professional athletes are selected to become members of a team. Using their individual skills, they work together to win games. In much the same way, when Jesus picked His disciples, He knew their strengths and weaknesses. He also knew the job He wanted His "team" to do.

You'll find the disciples' "job description" in Matthew 28:16-20 and Acts 1:8. Can you put it into your own words?

A

Disciples spread the Good News of Jesus throughout the ages and around the world.

▲ **TAKE A STEP**

The disciples were just plain people. In fact, they were sometimes selfish and bad tempered. The key is they personally knew the risen, living Jesus. And as a result they—and their world—were changed. Jesus once said to His disciples:

"As the Father has sent me, I am sending you" (John 20:21).

History tells us the disciples did their job well. By the end of the first century (less than a hundred years after Jesus lived,) Christianity was already a major force in the world.

If the disciples had not gone when they were sent, would you be a Christian today?

It's exciting to know that the disciples did their job and spread the Good News around the world. But remember—the work is not finished. As a disciple yourself, what will you do today to lead someone else to Jesus?

Answers: 1-d; 2-k; 3-i or h; 4-e; 5-l; 6-c; 7-f; 8-b; 9-i or h; 10-g; 11-a; 12-j.

No one knows for sure exactly where the disciples traveled after Jesus ascended, or how they died. But historical tradition gives us some ideas:

Peter traveled to Rome and was crucified upside down.

Andrew was crucified in Greece on an X-shaped cross.

James started many churches around the Mediterranean Sea. Beheaded by Herod in Jerusalem, he was the first disciple to die.

John survived being put into a boiling cauldron, but was then banished to the Island of Patmos. He returned to Ephesus and died a natural death as an old man.

Philip was stoned to death in Asia Minor.

Bartholomew was flayed alive and beheaded in Armenia.

Matthew was killed by the sword in Mesopotamia.

Thomas was pierced with a spear after building several churches in India.

James the Less was killed by being sawed in two.

Thaddaeus was shot with arrows in Mesopotamia.

Simon the Zealot was killed by an angry mob.

Judas Iscariot committed suicide after betraying Jesus.

◆ TAKE A LOOK
Acts 1:4; 2:1-6, 14, 22-24, 32-33, 36-38

The disciples would never have been voted "Most Likely to Succeed"! While Jesus was on earth they let Him down many times. They even had a hard time understanding His teachings. And after Jesus' resurrection, they were the ones who couldn't quite believe it! Yet Jesus chose these 12 to get His message to the rest of the world. Read how they did this in Acts 1:4; 2:1-6,14, 22-24, 32-33, and 36-38.

▲ TAKE A STEP
All of them were filled with the Holy Spirit (Acts 2:4)

The disciples lived with Jesus for three years. Slowly but surely, their lives were transformed by His teaching, His character, and His presence. And after His ascension they were filled with the power of the Holy Spirit. They succeeded in doing His work because they did it in His strength—not in their own.

Share a time you sensed God's power at work as you witnessed for Christ. If you can't think of one, is it because you've been trying to be a disciple in your own strength instead of God's?

The power of Pentecost is present in you!

How do disciples fulfill their assignment?

A

Disciples do their work for God by the power of the Holy Spirit.

PARENT:
For dinnertime discussion, imagine the decisions Peter and Andrew may have had to make to become a disciple. What reactions would you have if a family member quit college or a good job in order to work in a ministry?

Not super saints, just people like me!

Q

What does it cost to be Christ's disciple?

A

Disciples must be willing to follow Jesus whole-heartedly.

PARENT: Some of this week's information was drawn from The Twelve, by Leslie B. Flynn.

Answers: 1-c; 2-d; 3-a; 4-b; 5-f; 6-e.

When you hear names like "Saint Peter" and "Saint John," it's easy to think the disciples must have had halos. Not at all! As we've learned, the disciples were just ordinary people. In fact, all believers are called "saints" (Romans 1:7). And our "halos" are a godly lifestyle and a winning, gracious spirit.

Even so, early painters often showed the disciples with halos so people would know who they were supposed to be. Sometimes artists even represented a disciple with a symbol which stood for a significant event in his life or showed how he died. For instance, Judas is often represented by a hangman's noose.

Quickly review this week's quizzes (especially Tuesday's and Thursday's) and see if you can figure out which symbols represent these six apostles:

1. 3 Keys
2. 3 Scallop Shells
3. A Carpenter's Square and Spear
4. 3 Purses
5. A Fig Tree
6. A Saw

a. Thomas
b. Matthew

c. Peter
d. James
e. James the Less
f. Bartholomew*

◆ **TAKE A LOOK / Matthew 16:24-27**

The book of Acts tells the thrilling story of how the disciples started spreading the gospel. But we have to turn to history books to find out more about the disciples themselves.

Early church history indicates that the disciples went separate ways to spread the gospel and organize churches. Yesterday's review showed where each one probably traveled. All of them were persecuted because of their faith.

Jesus taught His men about the cost of being a disciple. Many times during their lives they must have remembered His words. If you had been one of Jesus' disciples, how do you think Jesus' words in Matthew 16:24-27 would help you?

▲ **TAKE A STEP**

"Whoever loses his life for me will find it" (Matthew 16:25).

There's more than one way to "lose your life for Jesus." For the disciples, it meant giving up their whole lives.

What do you think this verse means today? Think about the places in the world where people are persecuted or forbidden to worship because of their faith. Could Christian discipleship bring death even today?

CONSCIENCE

*B*ecause he longed for a son, the poor woodcarver Geppetto lovingly fashioned a puppet-boy he named Pinocchio. He was amazed when Pinocchio came to life and moved around freely.

But though Pinocchio could move and talk, he mocked Geppetto, showing no respect at all. He pulled one prank after another and got himself—and Geppetto—in all sorts of trouble.

In the Walt Disney cartoon version of this old story, a tiny character named Jiminy Cricket plays a major role. So small as to be almost invisible, Jiminy constantly chirps at Pinocchio to do the right thing—to stay out of trouble, to treat others kindly, to think of others. But Pinocchio rarely listens to Jiminy, and so lands in some very bad situations. But Jiminy Cricket continues chirping no matter what. He will not be silent, for he knows his job. He's Pinocchio's conscience!

◆ THINKING ABOUT CONSCIENCE

Your conscience is **that "voice" within you that approves when you do right and accuses when you do wrong.** You can argue with it, ignore it, and harden it, but you cannot escape it.

Your conscience compares your actions with the standards of behavior you are taught, and lets you know how they measure up. People around the world may have different standards of right and wrong, but the "voice" of conscience is something everyone has.

The highest standard for any conscience is God's Word. When we believe in Jesus we have the opportunity to start over with a clean conscience, which can be trained to that high standard.

● KEY VERSE
How much more, then, will the blood of Christ . . . cleanse our consciences from acts that lead to death, so that we may serve the living God!
(Hebrews 9:14)

▲ LOOKING AHEAD
This week you'll study your own "Jiminy Cricket."

Can you remember the story of the first time people heard their consciences speaking? (Hint: Read Genesis 3:7.) Share the last time your conscience spoke to you. How did you respond to it?

"I had a very nice time Mrs. Benson. Really!"

The little voice with the big message

Q

How does my conscience work?

A

Conscience lets me know when my actions, thoughts, or attitudes are missing God's standards.

PARENT:
You may want to read Pinocchio or watch the cartoon version together, and then talk more about how Jiminy Cricket acted as Pinocchio's conscience.

Look, there'll be so many kids at the Christmas conference that we won't even be missed," Brad declared as he turned the car around and headed east. "Besides, my sister is going to get us copies of the program." Gary chimed in. "And as long as we're back home about the same time the church bus gets there, no one will ever know."

"Yeah, I'd much rather ski four days than listen to a bunch of boring old conference speakers," Brad agreed.

But Jeff had a worried look on his face. Finally he blurted, "But what if something happens to one of us and we need help? Or worse yet, what if something happens to one of our folks and they try to get in touch with us?"

"Jeff's right," Kirk agreed. "We may not have gotten caught during spring break, but I've felt guilty about that ever since. Our parents would never agree to this. Maybe we ought to go to the conference and see if we can go skiing another time."

"You're such a chicken," Brad taunted. "We're going skiing."

◆ **TAKE A LOOK / Acts 24:16; 1 Timothy 1:18-19; 1 John 3:19-22**

Unlike animals, birds, and fish, human beings are more than just bodies. We are made "in the image of God" (Genesis 1:26-27), and so we have the ability to distinguish right from wrong.

The apostle Paul explains that all people have

> . . . the requirements of the law . . . written on their hearts, their consciences also bearing witness, and their thoughts now accusing, now even defending them (Romans 2:15).

Conscience plays an important part in your life. Read Acts 24:16; 1 Timothy 1:18-19; and 1 John 3:19-22. Which passage describes the importance of your conscience in: (1) your relationships with others? (2) your prayer life? (3) your ability to keep believing?

▲ **TAKE A STEP**

Your conscience is God's gift to you. Your conscience will give you an inner prompting when your actions, thoughts, or attitudes are out of line with God's Word.

In the opening story, which boys had a tender conscience? Which boys were trying to ignore their consciences? If you can remember a time you ignored the "still, small voice" of your conscience, share what happened.

*A*ny other time he would have really enjoyed the beautiful brisk weather and the opportunity to enjoy skiing. But right now Kirk was miserable.

"If only I'd been driving we wouldn't be here," he muttered to Jeff as the two settled down for the night. "Brad and Gary keep talking about friendship and loyalty, and how we have to support each other. What he means is how we have to cover up for each other. I mean, friendship is important, but so is obedience. I don't like to deceive my parents."

"Yeah, I know," Jeff agreed. "This hasn't been half as much fun as I thought it would be."

"Well, I've got another problem, too," Kirk confided. "My mom made me promise to call her tonight. If I don't, she may try to get in touch with the conference director and have me paged tomorrow morning. But if I do call her, she'll ask me questions about what we're doing. And if I tell the truth, we'll all get in trouble. But I really hate to lie to my mom. It's just a humongous mess. What do you think I should do, Jeff?"

◆ **TAKE A LOOK**
1 Corinthians 4:4; 8:7; 1 Timothy 1:3-6
In the following verses you'll see that the Bible talks about many kinds of consciences. For example . . .

1 Corinthians 4:4 mentions a _____ conscience.

1 Corinthians 8:7 describes a conscience that is both _____ and _____ and 1 Timothy 1:3-6 shows the importance of a _____ conscience.

God's Word also teaches that a good conscience helps us to be victorious in our warfare against Satan (1 Timothy 1:18-19). And it helps us to be honorable in all the things we do (Hebrews 13:18). But most of all a good conscience works to keep us on the path God has designed for our lives. Paul explained it this way:

Our conscience testifies that we have conducted ourselves in the world, and especially in our relations with you, in the holiness and sincerity that are from God (2 Corinthians 1:12).

▲ **TAKE A STEP**
Yesterday and today you read of four boys who were deceiving their parents. Based on what you've read, do you think the boys had a good conscience? Why do you think Brad and Gary weren't feeling as guilty as Kirk and Jeff? Together, try to figure out what advice you'd give Kirk.

Keeping on the straight and narrow path

Q

How can my conscience help me?

A

Conscience can help me live an honorable, victorious, and godly life if I listen to it.

*What
causes an
evil
conscience?*

*Unless I
take sin
seriously,
my con-
science can
become
hardened
and evil.*

C '*mon, Kirk! You're ruining everybody's fun. So we're
not telling our parents what we're doing. What's
the big deal?*"

"*Look, Brad,*" *Kirk snapped,* "*I let you talk me into
this and now I'm sorry. My mom and dad have always
trusted me, but if they ever find out I deceived them
about spring break and now about going to this
conference, they may never trust me again.*

"*And not only that, it's just plain wrong to lie to your
parents. But what I don't understand is why I'm the only
one feeling so guilty. What's the matter with you guys?*"

"*Hey, we haven't done anything really wrong,*"
Brad stated emphatically. "*It's just like we asked
permission to go to Big Chef for a hamburger and then
changed our minds and went to the Burger Barn
instead. You think they're gonna care about that?*"

Sorrowfully Kirk shook his head. "*It's over 500
miles difference between where we're supposed to be
and where we are. Yeah, I think they're gonna care.*"

◆**TAKE A LOOK / 1 Samuel 15:12-35**
We learned yesterday that a good conscience
constantly works to keep us in line with God's way
of doing things. But an evil conscience begins to
develop when a person doesn't take sin seriously;
his heart becomes hardened. Treating sin and its
results lightly shows disrespect for our holy God,
who cannot tolerate sin.

Saul, the first king of Israel, was instructed to
totally destroy the Amalekites and everything they
owned. But he didn't take God's commands
seriously, and his partial obedience eventually led
to an evil conscience. Trace Saul's steps to an evil
conscience by reading 1 Samuel 15:12-35.

You'll see Saul (1) playing with sin by lying
(vv. 12-13); (2) making excuses instead of
confessing (v. 15); (3) trying to convince himself
his sin wasn't very bad (v. 20); (4) blaming others
(v. 21); and (5) making a weak confession only
because he was concerned about what others
might think (v. 30). (Do you think he would have
confessed if he hadn't gotten caught?)

▲ **TAKE A STEP**
People who have an evil conscience are seldom
bothered by the wrong things they do. Now that
you've seen in Saul's life how an evil conscience
can develop, what evidence do you see in Brad's behavior that shows he might be on the same path?

Do you need to guard against following in the
same path?

*T*he public service announcement was sandwiched between the soft drink commercial and the final football game of the season. The TV announcer smoothly but firmly said, "If you are 18, you are required by law to register for the Selective Service. Pick up the forms at your local post office."

Troy suddenly stopped chomping on his apple. He realized that his 18th birthday was only a month away.

"Dad," he said softly, "I'll have to do that, won't I?"

"Yep," his father answered, "you sure will."

"Does that mean I might get drafted if we get into a war? I might actually be shot at in some little country somewhere! Seems to me 18 is a dangerous age. Maybe I should sign up as a 'conscientious objector.' What do you think?"

◆ **TAKE A LOOK / Exodus 1:15-22**

Avoiding duties required by law because you don't like them is not the same as opposing them because you believe they are morally wrong.

The Bible clearly says believers are to submit to the government. Yet throughout history some people—from America's founding fathers to today's leaders of resistance movements—have felt led by conscience to oppose their governments.

When the Israelites were living as slaves in Egypt, a group of courageous women deliberately disobeyed Pharaoh, the powerful ruler of Egypt, and then lied to cover up what they had done. Yet God blessed their "disobedience." See if you can discover why as you read Exodus 1:15-22.

▲ **TAKE A STEP**

To some, the Bible seems to contradict itself about obeying the government. Paul wrote,

Everyone must submit himself to the governing authorities, for there is no authority except that which God has established (Romans 13:1).

Yet Peter deliberately disobeyed the authorities, saying,

We must obey God rather than men! (Acts 5:29).

Was one of these great apostles wrong? No! But when a government makes laws that directly oppose God's laws, believers must obey God's laws and work to change human laws. Even so, we must face the consequences of those laws just the same, even if it means death.

Are you willing to obey God's laws—no matter what? What issues would you be willing to die for?

Standing for right when laws are wrong

Q

What if my conscience differs from my nation's laws?

A

Conscience says I must put God's law above human law.

PARENT: *Civil disobedience is an important issue in the church today. Ask your pastor to recommend resources, and take the time to discuss the subject with your family.*

BIBLE STUDY

Of all the people who say they believe the Bible, only 12 percent actually read it every day! How much do you know about what's in the Bible? Take this quiz and find out!

How many books are in the Bible?_____

What is the third book in the Bible? _____

What is the last book in the Old Testament? _____

What is the last book in the New Testament? _____

Who wrote at least 13 of the 27 New Testament books? _____

Name one of the kings of Israel or Judah. _____

Quote the first of the Ten Commandments._____

Quote one of the Beatitudes.*_____

◆ THINKING ABOUT THE BIBLE

Because the Bible is **God's message to mankind**, it's the world's most important book. Long ago, Jewish fathers taught their children the ways of the Lord by telling stories about their nation's past and explaining the laws, feasts, and sacrifices God had established.

Today many families—like yours—still spend time together learning God's truths. But it's just as important to spend time studying the Bible individually. This week's key verse will encourage you to do just that!

"I'm very familiar with the Bible . . . King Jim Version."

● KEY VERSE ON BIBLE STUDY

Do your best to present yourself to God as one approved, a workman who does not need to be ashamed and who correctly handles the word of truth (2 Timothy 2:15).

▲ LOOKING AHEAD

Studying God's Word personally may sound like a hard job. But this week we'll make it easier and more meaningful for you.

What do you think is the first thing you need to study God's Word effectively? Find out by reading Psalm 119:16, 20, 72, and 143. Then pray for that as a family right now!

*Answers: They're in the Bible —have fun looking for them!

Mom, I can't stand being fed this way," Robert grimaced. "I'd almost rather not eat at all." He jerked his head to the side, turning away from the next forkful of meat his mother held.

"Robert, we've been through this before," his mother said unsympathetically. "Nobody likes having both arms broken, but we're just thankful you weren't killed in that accident. Now turn around and eat this before it gets cold."

"But Mom," Robert complained again, "it's just that I feel like a baby. I can't do anything for myself."

"Well, I'll be as glad as you are when the casts come off next week. It's harder to feed a 14-year-old than it is a baby. But in one way you're no different than you were then—you still eat everything I can shovel in. Now, how about some apple pie?"

◆ TAKE A LOOK / Psalm 1:1-3

Because of his two broken arms, Robert was in the awkward position of having to be spoon-fed. And as an independent teenager, he didn't like that one bit.

Strange as it may sound, many Christians are in exactly the same position as Robert. They rely on what other people say about God's Word rather than feeding themselves through regular Bible study. Both kinds of "feeding" are important for healthy spiritual growth.

Physical babies need milk to grow, and spiritual babies need the nourishment of God's Word. But just as babies grow and learn to feed themselves, spiritual children must also learn to feed themselves through regular Bible study.

The psalmist David grew spiritually because he studied God's law. As you read Psalm 1:1-3, look for two important reasons for studying the Bible.

▲ TAKE A STEP

The person who studies God's Word
*is like a tree planted by streams of water. . . .
Whatever he does prospers (Psalm 1:3).*
Studying the Bible for yourself helps you put down deep roots in God's truth, giving you a strong basis for your faith. In a world filled with confusing and often wrong ideas, studying God's Word on a regular basis can keep you from going astray.

Ask yourself: "Do I love God enough to spend time by myself each day studying His Word?" Help one another think through daily schedules to carve out a specific time for Bible study. Answer that question with actions, not just words!

Will it be feast or famine? It's your choice!

Q

Why should I study the Bible for myself?

A

Bible study on my own is a vital way for me to get spiritual nourishment.

PARENT:
Your child can find practical help for personal Bible study in Off the Shelf and Into Yourself *by Terry Hall.*

Use the right tools for rewarding reading

Q

Why are tools important for Bible study?

A

Bible study can be made easier and more meaningful with the help of proper tools.

PARENT:
Your older child might enjoy and benefit from having his or her own study Bible.

For a long time Shawn had wanted a bookshelf to hang over the desk in his room. His dad had promised to help him make one. Now, at last, they had bought the wood from the lumber supply store and were unloading it in the basement.

"Can we start right away, Dad?" Shawn asked excitedly. "Maybe we can even finish it today!"

"Not so fast," his dad replied. "We need a few more tools."

"But we've got a hammer," Shawn pointed. "And here are the saw and the nails. What else do we need?"

"To do a first-class job, we'll need a square to make the corners fit smoothly, and a plane and sander for smoothing the boards. And we'll need a jigsaw to cut that fancy pattern on the top shelf. I asked Mr. Bowen if we could use some of his wood working tools, and he said to come over this afternoon."

Shawn looked surprised. "Wow. I didn't know it took so many tools to build a little bookshelf. It looked so easy in the magazine!"

◆ TAKE A LOOK / Psalm 119:94

Look around your house and you'll discover, as Shawn did, that many tasks—from cooking a meal, to doing minor repairs on the family car, to caring for your fingernails—are easier because you have the right tools.

Over the years, scholars have developed many "tools" to help you "mine" the truth in God's Word. Some of these helpful tools have been added to various editions of the Bible.

Instead of reading a Scripture passage today, take time to look at two or three of the Bibles your family members own. You may have what is called a "study" Bible, which includes notes, references, and other helpful features such as introductions to each book, a concordance, maps, lists, articles, and charts. Take a few minutes to "study" what's included in your Bible. You may find some tools you didn't know you had!

▲ TAKE A STEP

I have sought out your precepts (Psalm 119:94).

To help you search out the meaning of God's Word, a Bible concordance and a Bible dictionary are probably the most useful tools. Several fine editions of each are available. Ask your pastor or Sunday school teacher to recommend a couple, or plan to browse at your local Christian bookstore or church library. The right tools make the job easier!

I don't ever again want to be lost downtown in a strange city at night during a thunderstorm!" Mr. Patrick told his host, Mr. Mitchell, as they pulled into the driveway. "St. Louis must be the most confusing city in America."

"Hey," Mr. Mitchell chuckled, "it's not so bad."

The next morning the Mitchell and Patrick families drove back downtown to the waterfront. There before them, gleaming in the sun, stood the Gateway Arch. After riding up one leg of the arch in small capsules, they stood at the top—630 feet above the ground. Below, the mighty Mississippi River looked like a mere ribbon. They spotted the stadium and remembered how lost they had felt when they drove around it twice the night before.

"After seeing the city from this view, I can better understand the way it's laid out," Mr. Patrick commented. "You may not have to send out a search party again tonight after all!"

◆ TAKE A LOOK / Luke 6:46-49

Just as Mr. Patrick benefited from his panoramic view of St. Louis, getting an overview of the whole Bible will help you feel more comfortable as you study portions of God's Word.

But whatever methods of study you use, remember that God gave His Word so we can know Him better and obey His commandments.

And this is love: that we walk in obedience to his commands (2 John 6).

After you read the words of Jesus in Luke 6:46-49, tell why you think this statement is true: "The key to successful Bible study is to do what we learn."

▲ TAKE A STEP

These techniques will help you better understand God's message to you:

• Decide on a study plan (such as a chapter a day).

• Think up a chapter title of not more than four words for each chapter you read.

• Take brief notes on who, what, when, where, why, and how for each chapter.

As you read, wear some special SPECS. Ask yourself: Does this passage show me a **S**in to forsake, a **P**romise to claim, an **E**xample to follow, a **C**ommand to obey, or a **S**tumbling block to avoid?

Close each time of Bible study by asking the Lord, "Now what should I do with what I know?"

Get the big picture with a wide-angle lens

How can different Bible study methods help me?

Bible study methods show me how to be more obedient.

PARENT: *Walk Thru the Bible Ministries offers seminars to help your church family get the "big picture" of the Bible. For information, write P.O. Box 80587, Atlanta, GA 30366.*

Regular review is good for you! (Meditation too!)

Q

How can I get the most out of what I study?

A

Bible study has lasting results if I meditate on what I've studied.

C andace walked into the den with her head in a book. "Dad, what does 'deux heures de l'apres-midi' mean?"

"That's French for '2:00 P.M.,' " Mr. Compton replied.

"Oh yeah! Thanks. Say, didn't you tell me that you and Jill's mother both took French in the same class in college?"

"Yes, we did. Why do you ask?"

"Well, Jill told me her mother doesn't remember a bit of French. She can't help Jill at all. But you speak French beautifully and help me all the time. It just seems strange."

"I think the difference comes from how we've used what we've learned," her father replied. "I've made it a point to keep up with French because my business takes me to Paris several times a year. Since I use it so much, it's become a part of me."

◆ TAKE A LOOK
Psalm 119:15, 23, 48, 78, 97, 99

If you're learning a second language, you know you must continually hear that language and practice speaking it until you can use it almost as easily as your own native language.

In the same way, if you want to get the most out of personal Bible study, you must also get the meaning into your mind, will, and emotions.

The psalmist understood how to make God's Word a part of his life. Can you identify how he did this by reading Psalm 119:15, 23, 48, 78, 97, and 99?

▲ TAKE A STEP
David knew God's blessings would come to anyone who fit this description:

His delight is in the law of the LORD, and on his law he meditates day and night (Psalm 1:2).

One of the ways David meditated was to turn the truths he had learned about God into prayers, many of which are recorded as psalms. You too can meditate on God's Word by using Scripture passages as prayers. For instance, when someone you care for needs comfort, you can pray this prayer based on Psalm 23: "Lord, thank You that You are _____ 's shepherd and that he lacks nothing. Make him lie down in green pastures. Lead him beside quiet waters. Restore his soul. . . ."

Another way to meditate is to memorize verses and think about them often. Can you think of another way to meditate on God's Word? Maybe today's story will give you a hint!

MUSIC

C an you imagine . . .
 - *a football game without "The Star-Spangled Banner"?*
 - *never whistling, humming, or playing an instrument?*
 - *a baby without a lullaby?*
 - *a wedding without the "Bridal March"?*
 - *movies without soundtracks?*
 - *teenagers without radios?*
 - *a worship service without hymns and anthems?*
 - *a Christmas without carols?*
Can you imagine a world without music?

◆ THINKING ABOUT MUSIC

There are as many different styles of music as there are different kinds of people! In one form or another, music is an important part of every known human society. Just about everybody enjoys some kind of music. What are your favorites?

Music is a vital part of human life. And it's important to God, too. Through the psalmist, God commands us to . . .

● KEY VERSE ON MUSIC

Shout for joy to the LORD, all the earth, burst into jubilant song with music; make music to the LORD with the harp, with the harp and the sound of singing (Psalm 98:4-5).

▲ LOOKING AHEAD

Music is **a pleasing sequence of sounds that communicates a message or emotion.** Just as our eyes are light receptors and our ears are sound receptors, scientists now believe that each person also has a music "receptor" in his brain. If that's true the question arises, "Why is it there?"

Begin your study of music by reading Psalm 150. Then take stock of the musical "instruments" in your house (including tape players, radios, and each person's voice). Finally, put your voices together in song with the chorus "This Is the Day That the Lord Hath Made."

A. THOMAS
PIANO
LESSONS
←

"It's not easy playing eighty-eight keys with just ten thumbs."

From zithers and lyres to electric guitars

B elow are pictures of some instruments mentioned in the Bible: harp, flute, drum, cymbals, horn, and lyre. Can you identify them?*

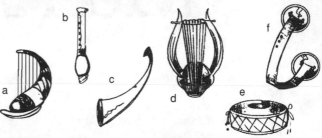

◆ TAKE A LOOK
Genesis 4:17-21; Revelation 5:11-13

Because tape recorders didn't exist in Bible times, we don't really know how ancient music sounded. Even so, we do know that ancient peoples enjoyed music as much as we do. They played a variety of instruments and mentioned music often in their writings.

Read Genesis 4:17-21 to find out how early music became a part of civilization. Then turn to Revelation 5:11-13 to discover the major role music will play throughout eternity. Music always has been, and always will be, part of life!

▲ TAKE A STEP

God enjoys music. He created many birds and other creatures so that they could sing melodiously. He gave people the ability to sing, to compose, and to perform music as well. He even gave His people many songs and hymns to sing. The Bible makes it clear that God Himself is extremely interested in the music His creatures make. In fact, the prophet Zephaniah speaks of a time when God Himself

> . . . will take great delight in you, he will quiet you with his love, he will rejoice over you with singing (Zephaniah 3:17).

Think about the words, harmonies, rhythms, and purpose of the music you listen to most. If Jesus personally came to your home or rode in your car while that music was playing, do you think He would enjoy it . . . or be offended by it?

Illustrations of musical instruments taken from *Zondervan Pictorial Encyclopedia*, vol. 4. Edited by Merrill C. Tenney, 1975 by the Zondervan Corporation. Used by permission.

When did music begin?

Music is as old as humankind, because our ability to make it was created by God.

*Answers:
a-harp,
b-flute,
c-horn,
d-lyre
e-drum,
f-cymbals.

Mr. Winthrop handed the news magazine to his wife. "Here, hon. Read this article on rock music."

"I had no idea rock music was so sexually explicit! We've got to have a family meeting about this."

A few minutes later, Mr. and Mrs. Winthrop entered their sons' room where the stereo was going full blast! "Please turn that down," Mr. Winthrop said. "We need to talk to you."

As the decibel level dropped, Mr. Winthrop continued. "Your mother and I just read some really shocking things about the X-rated lyrics in rock music."

"Dad, there's nothing to that. We don't pay any attention to the words—just the music," Reid replied calmly. Phil added, "I don't think any of our friends really listen to the lyrics."

With that the matter was dropped. But a few days later Mr. Winthrop casually asked his sons, "Have you boys heard the song 'Relax'?" Without thinking, his sons started singing that song, which is performed by a group that openly supports homosexuality.

◆ **TAKE A LOOK**
Psalm 101:3; Romans 12:2; Colossians 2:8
If you're a teenager, you may very well be thinking, "Oh, no—not another sermon on the evils of rock music!" But wait a minute before you close your mind. Jesus said,

"For out of the overflow of the heart the mouth speaks. The good man brings good things out . . . and the evil man brings evil things out of the evil stored up in him" (Matthew 12:34-35).

Through his music, a musician sends out a message either for good or evil. As you listen, those ideas and philosophies seep into your mind—sometimes without your even realizing it. Is God honored when a Christian saturates his or her mind with messages about violence, immorality, and sexual perversions? To determine the answer, look up Romans 12:2; Colossians 2:8; Psalm 101:3; and Ephesians 5:3-7.

▲ **TAKE A STEP**
Christians shouldn't allow their lives to be "conformed" or shaped by the world; instead their lives should be "transformed" by God's power.

When that happens, your renewed mind can "test" what God's will is concerning all kinds of things, including rock music. From the Scriptures you read today, come up with three principles for testing the music you listen to.

The beat goes on . . . and so do the words

Q

How does music affect my life?

A

Music can influence me for good or evil.

PARENT:
If your teenager's musical diet is primarily rock, visit a record store together and look at cassette and CD covers and lyrics of current performers. Then discuss 1 Timothy 4:1-2 and Ephesians 5:3-7.

Godly guidelines for good music

Q

How can I decide what music to listen to?

A

Music that encourages me to sin does not honor God or help me to grow.

PARENT: Media Update *offers information regarding the rock music scene plus reviews of Christian music. For information write* Menconi Ministries, P.O. Box 306, Cardiff, CA 92007.

"Y ou really made me mad last Sunday," Daphne admitted to the youth minister as she entered the Sunday school classroom.

"I knew you were angry, Daphne," he said with a smile. "I think what I said about music upset a lot of people."

"Yeah. I guess I was mad because I didn't want to believe what you said. But when you explained how a person's basic philosophy affects everything he does, and how the immoral lifestyles of so many rock stars are reflected in their music, I knew deep down it was true. I just didn't want to believe it."

"I see. But something must have changed your mind . . ."

"Well," Daphne continued slowly, "when you talked about how a kid who's been real committed to Christ can change when he listens regularly to rock music, I could see how I'd begun to change. I didn't enjoy my quiet time as much, and when I prayed it was just words. In fact, I didn't even want to have a quiet time. I wasn't a very happy Christian. So I did what you said—I checked out what I was listening to. And I got rid of a lot of stuff. And you know what? My time with the Lord this week has been really great. And I'm playing my Christian music again!"

◆ **TAKE A LOOK / Proverbs 4:23-24; 3:31; Philippians 4:8; James 4:4**
The discerning heart seeks knowledge, but the mouth of a fool feeds on folly (Proverbs 15:14).

If you want knowledge that will help you choose good music, read these verses: Proverbs 4:23-24; 3:31; James 4:4; and Philippians 4:8. Add to the list you started yesterday any new principles you discover for testing your music "diet."

▲ **TAKE A STEP**
If you're willing to reject the sinful music that floods the airwaves today, write out Ephesians 5:3-7 on a piece of notebook paper along with these guidelines for choosing music:
1. *Consider the lyrics.* What values are presented? Do they have content Christ would commend? Do they mock God? 2. *Look at the musicians.* What are their values, morals, and lifestyles? What do their videos portray? 3. *Ask yourself,* Would Jesus listen to this music? Does this music make me a partner with sin?

With these guidelines in mind, check out the tapes and discs you own. Then ask God to help you do what you need to do.

C ome, let us sing for joy to the LORD;
   let us shout aloud to the Rock of our salvation.
Let us come before him with thanksgiving
   and extol him with music and song.

For the LORD is the great God,
   the great King above all gods.
In his hand are the depths of the earth,
   and the mountain peaks belong to him.
The sea is his, for he made it,
   and his hands formed the dry land.

Come, let us bow down in worship,
   let us kneel before the Lord our Maker;
For he is our God and we are the people of his
   pasture,
the flock under his care (Psalm 95:1-7).

◆ TAKE A LOOK / Psalm 150

You may never have pictured God as a
musician, but the Bible makes it clear that He is
indeed the Master Musician. At creation, He gave
human beings musical ability and filled the world
with wonderful sounds. Through human authors
He gave us the Psalms, and He desires that we sing
them in praise to Him.

Through the apostle Paul, God gives us this
command:

Speak to one another with psalms, hymns and
spiritual songs. Sing and make music in your
heart to the Lord (Ephesians 5:19).

As you'll learn when you read Psalm 150, we're
to use all our musical resources to praise our
worthy God.

▲ TAKE A STEP

You may worship in a large cathedral where
the choir sings great anthems accompanied by the
swelling tones of a magnificent organ. Or you may
meet in a less formal setting where a piano or
guitar is the only instrument, or songs are sung "a
cappella." No matter how you worship, remember
that God Himself is a Musician who appreciates
well-prepared music that is sung from the heart.

The songs you sing on Sunday morning are not
intended primarily to make you feel good, or to
display a performer's talent. They should be sung
to glorify God and give Him pleasure. Knowing
that, how will you sing differently in church this
week?

God is the ultimate "Minister of music"

Q

*Why should
I worship
God with
music?*

A

*God is a
musician
who enjoys
being
praised
with music.*

PARENT:
*Many
churches
have a choir
program for
all ages. If
yours does,
encourage
your children
to get
involved.*

HONOR

*E*ight-year-old Danielle and her mother were walking down the busy sidewalk looking for a good place to watch the parade, when Danielle noticed something unusual. "Mommy, why are those ladies selling those little red paper flowers?"

"Well . . . " her mother began, "do you remember how I explained that today is Memorial Day?"

"Oh, yeah. That's why we're having a parade," Danielle exclaimed excitedly. "Davy's dad is in the parade 'cause he was in a war before Davy was born."

"That's right, the parade is a way to honor the soldiers who fought and died for our country. There's a famous poem* about the burial ground of the soldiers from World War I that mentions poppies growing on their graves. Since then, a red poppy has been the symbol for the soldiers who died in wars."

"Mom, I want everybody to know I'm thankful for our soldiers too," Danielle perked up. "Can we go back and get a poppy?"

◆ THINKING ABOUT HONOR

Memorial Day, May 31, and Veterans Day, November 11—are the days officially set aside to honor American soldiers. We hope you'll take time to say "thank you" to friends, neighbors, and family members who served in the military.

The word *honor* can be used in two ways. As a verb it refers to **the action of showing deep respect for others.** As a noun it means a person's good reputation, or the respect he deserves.

"I don't have the most cavities in the history of his practice, but I get honorable mention."

● KEY VERSE ON HONOR
Honor one another above yourselves (Romans 12:10).

▲ LOOKING AHEAD

God wants us to honor many people—not just soldiers. This week we'll explore just how to do that.

You already know one of God's commandments to honor someone. If you can't remember what it is, a quick look at Exodus 20:12 will remind you!

*"In Flanders Fields," by John McCrae, can be found in many anthologies.

When you think about it, honor is an important concept—even in everyday life. How many of these phrases have you heard or said yourself lately?

- My word of honor
- Graduate with honor
- The honor system
- The seat of honor
- Scout's honor
- The honorable senator from the state of . . .
- The honor roll
- Your honor, we beseech the court . . .

Can you think of any more "honorable" phrases?

◆ TAKE A LOOK
Matthew 23:1-3, 5-7, 23-28, 33

The Bible often encourages us to honor God and certain other people. But oddly enough, there is no general command for us to "be honorable people." When we live a godly lifestyle, however, that's exactly what we'll be. To be an honorable person means you always keep your actions in line with your character and values.

Another word describing personal honor is *integrity*. A person of integrity is upright, honest, and sincere.

One way to understand personal honor better is by looking at its opposite. When Jesus was on earth, the Pharisees seemed to be honorable people. But Jesus recognized they weren't really what they seemed to be. As you read Matthew 23:1-3, 5-7, 23-28 and 33, find a word meaning the opposite of personal honor.

▲ TAKE A STEP

The Pharisees were dishonorable men, or hypocrites, because their actions didn't match their words. Jesus rightly condemned them when He said,

"On the outside you appear to people as righteous [good] but on the inside you are full of hypocrisy and wickedness" (Matthew 23:28).

People can't see into your heart and mind to understand your motives. But God can—and does. And it pleases Him when your words and deeds correspond with His Word.

Reread the first few verses of Matthew 23 and try to find a good slogan for being honorable. (Hint: Check the title of today's devotional!) Then, on a slip of paper write the letters "P W Y P" to remind you to do just that today!

Be honorable —practice what you preach!

Q

What does it mean to be an honorable person?

A

Honor means I keep my word by doing what I say I will do.

PARENT: Discuss with your older child why he or she thinks today's popular "heroes" are honored. Are they really honorable? Who are some truly honorable people you know?

Who fills the number-one place in your heart?

With a puzzled look, Aunt Janet walked with her nephew to the family car in the church parking lot. Finally she asked, "Jake, why aren't you going on the mission trip? The kids who signed up seemed to be about your age."

"I'm saving my money for a car," Jake answered defensively.

"Oh," his aunt murmured. "So tell me: What are you planning to do after you graduate next June?"

"Well, I'm not going to be stuck here like the rest of this family—doing nothing but working and going to church. I'm moving into an apartment. And I'm going to buy some scuba diving gear and go diving every chance I get. And I'll do a lot of fun things, too."

They stood in silence by the car, waiting for the rest of the family. Then Aunt Janet said gently, "You know, Jake, you're describing a totally self-centered lifestyle—one that doesn't honor God at all. You may think you'll be happy, but you won't be until you see that God's plans are more important than your own."

◆ TAKE A LOOK
Deuteronomy 11:1, 13-21, 26-28

Since God created the entire universe, it's logical to conclude that He rules it. So in order to honor God, nothing in your life should fall outside of His lordship. That includes the way you spend your time, what you talk about with friends, where you go to school, whom you date and whom you'll marry, what kind of car you drive (and where), how you spend your money, and much more.

The laws God gave the nation of Israel emphasize how important it is to honor God in every area of life. As you read Deuteronomy 11:1, 13-21, and 26-28, what four-letter word can you find to summarize how God's people—then and now—can honor Him?

▲ TAKE A STEP

Honoring God means obeying Him in love, and putting Him first in your life. As Moses said,

Love the LORD your God and keep his requirements, his decrees, his laws and his commands always (Deuteronomy 11:1).

The first commandment is to have no other gods before God (Exodus 20:3). What was Jake putting before God that kept him from loving and obeying God wholeheartedly? Look at your own schedules and interests. Do you have the same kind of problem?

Q

What does it mean to honor God?

A

Honoring God means I don't put anything ahead of Him in my life.

"**O**h, Mom, you should have seen it. It was a riot!" Jill was laughing so hard she could hardly talk. "You know Amy Long, the girl who's always wearing low-cut tops, and jeans so tight she looks like she's poured into them?"

"Oh, yes," her mom replied. "What did she do that was so funny?"

"Well, this morning we were all getting ready to leave Meg's house after the slumber party. And you should have seen Amy putting on her jeans. She had to lie on the floor on her back! She literally wiggled into them inch by inch," Jill giggled. "And then it must have taken her five minutes just to pull the zipper up! If she keeps that up, she'll cause brain damage from a lack of oxygen!"

"Well," Jill's mom sighed, "You may think it's funny. But I think it's sad that she feels she has to dress that way."

◆ **TAKE A LOOK / 1 Corinthians 6:13-20**
One of the clear commands of Scripture is this: *You are not your own; you were bought at a price. Therefore honor God with your body (1 Corinthians 6:19-20).*

How can you honor God with your body? Take a minute to think of as many ways as you can.

If your answers include eating a balanced diet, exercising properly, and getting adequate rest, then you're on the right track. And everyone knows that habits such as smoking, drinking alcohol, overeating, and taking drugs ultimately destroy the body and do not honor the Lord.

But did you think of the way to honor God with your body that Paul talks about in 1 Corinthians 6:13-20? What is it?

▲ **TAKE A STEP**
Sex is a physical expression of love that God designed for the marriage relationship. But many people feel God's laws about sex are old-fashioned. They see sex simply as a physical function, with no feelings, no closeness, and no responsibilities.

And so they see nothing wrong with dressing immodestly, in a sense advertising their bodies—like Amy in today's story. But while society's views about sex have changed in the past few decades, God has not changed His mind about sin.

One of the most important ways to honor God with your body is to keep from sexual sin. Together, think of three ways to keep from getting caught in Satan's deception that sex outside of marriage is okay.

If I don't own me, then who does?

How can I honor God with my body?

A

Honoring God with my body means taking care of it as though it belongs to Him, because it does.

PARENT: Guard your child from sexual traps by offering biblical information and keeping communication open. For younger teens we recommend Preparing for Adolescence *by Dr. James Dobson.*

The only honor that will last forever

*T*he pastor stood in the pulpit and began his sermon. "Only a few of you attended yesterday's funeral for Miss Grace Newsome. But this entire congregation will miss her greatly."

In surprise, people glanced around curiously, listening attentively as he continued.

"Miss Grace was a member of our congregation for 82 of her 88 years. For the last fifteen years, she hasn't been able to attend, so a lot of you folks didn't know her. But she knew you—and she prayed for you. She prayed for every baby born, every couple married, and every person who entered the hospital. When a new Christian was baptized, Miss Grace prayed for his growth. Every time I preached, she was praying for me. She prayed for our missionaries, our elders, our Sunday school teachers, our choir. She served God—and others—day after day. And even though her work wasn't known by many other people, you can be sure she entered the gates of heaven with honor."

Q

Whom does God honor?

A

God honors and rewards those who serve Him with a pure heart.

◆ **TAKE A LOOK / Psalm 58:11; Matthew 25:34-40; Revelation 22:12**

People can be honored in many ways. Presidents and prime ministers honor men and women who have served their nation in a special way. The military honors those who have been heroic in battle. Schools honor distinguished graduates. But none of the honors the world gives can compare with the honor God will bestow on His children who have served Him well. Jesus said:

"Whoever serves me must follow me; and where I am, my servant also will be. My Father will honor the one who serves me" (John 12:26).

After you read Psalm 58:11 and Revelation 22:12, tell when God is going to reward His servants. Then read Matthew 25:34-40 to see what kind of service God honors.

▲ **TAKE A STEP**

In Old Testament times, God often blessed those who served Him by giving them material possessions. But making lots of money in this life does not mean you will automatically receive honor when Jesus returns. Instead, showing love, compassion, mercy, and kindness to those in need is the kind of service that pleases God.

Why do you think the pastor said Miss Newsome entered heaven with honor? Think of two activities you're involved in as an individual, as a family, or in church that may earn God's honor. Now, can you think of one more to do?

GOD'S ATTRIBUTES

E ight-year-old Mandy perched on the arm of Grandpa's recliner.
"Grandpa," she said thoughtfully as he closed his Bible, "will you tell
me who God really is?"

The old man drew his granddaughter onto his lap and gave her a
hug. "Mandy, my child, I'll give you the answer I learned long ago: 'God
is a Spirit, infinite, eternal, and unchangeable in His being, wisdom,
power, holiness, justice, goodness, and truth.' " He paused in thought,
then said, "You know, I've been getting to know the God those big words
in the catechism describe ever since I was a boy."

"The cat-a-what? Grandpa, what do all those big words mean? Will
you teach me so I can know God too?"

◆ THINKING ABOUT GOD

Because God is different from His creation, we as His creatures
sometimes have difficulty finding adequate words to describe all His
perfections and powers.

As a child, Mandy's grandfather learned the catechism, a series
of questions and answers which taught the basic truths of the
Christian faith in an organized way. Some churches still use the
catechism to teach their young people.

This week as we learn more about God's character, why not
memorize this verse as well as one answer from the catechism:

● KEY VERSE ON GOD

*As for God, his way is
perfect . . . (Psalm 18:30).*
Who is God? **God is a
Spirit, infinite, eternal, and
unchangeable in His being,
wisdom, power, holiness,
justice, goodness, and truth**
(From the Westminster Shorter
Catechism).

▲ LOOKING AHEAD

This week we'll learn more
about four of the attributes or
perfect characteristics of our
wonderful God.

Begin now to memorize the
question and answer above. Let
each family member have a
turn to both ask and answer the
question.

*"And Adam and Eve were naked,
and they had to leave the garden . . . "*

Holy, holy, holy—that's what God is wholly

Q

What is
God's
holiness?

A

God's
holiness sets
Him apart
from all
created
beings
because
He is totally
pure and
perfect.

PARENT:
Spend some
extra minutes
this week
meditating on
the holiness of
God. As a
resource you
may enjoy
The Holiness
of God by
R. C. Sproul.

*A*fter years of preparation and study, the day arrived when young Martin Luther would perform his duties as a priest for the first time. His father and twenty friends rode their horses to the monastery for the joyous celebration.

Such a solemn occasion always made the young priests nervous, but Martin had been an excellent student. He recited the opening words of the ceremony confidently. But when he came to the words, "We offer unto Thee, the living, the true, the eternal God . . . " he froze. He couldn't utter another sound! As the congregation grew restless and uncomfortable, the young priest finally returned to his seat, embarrassed and fearful.

His father was furious; his superiors were puzzled. What had happened? Later in life Martin Luther explained: "At those words I was . . . terror-stricken. I thought to myself, 'Who am I, that I should lift up mine eyes or raise my hands to the divine Majesty? . . . For I am dust and ashes and full of sin, and I am speaking to the living, eternal and the true God.' "

◆ **TAKE A LOOK / Isaiah 6:1-8**
Martin Luther was not the first person to be overcome by an insight into God's holiness. As you read Isaiah 6:1-8, imagine yourself in Isaiah's place, seeing the God of all creation seated on His throne. How would you have reacted?

▲ **TAKE A STEP**
Compared to many other people, Martin Luther and the prophet Isaiah were good and upright men. But when they caught a glimpse of God's holiness and were measured against His goodness, they both realized they were nothing but sinful human beings.

God is holy; that means He is above and beyond any of His creatures, totally pure and perfect. God's holiness will not allow Him to overlook human sin. And it's important that we as His creatures be reminded of that fact. That's why the seraphim, the angels around His throne, constantly cry out,

"Holy, holy, holy is the LORD Almighty; the whole earth is full of his glory" (Isaiah 6:3).
Now that you've caught a glimpse of God's holiness, look at your own life. What do the experiences of Isaiah and Martin Luther teach you about the "little, secret sins" in your life? Perhaps this is a good time to put 1 John 1:9 to work!

"**W**e read a sermon by Jonathan Edwards in American Lit today," Stu announced at supper. "I've never heard so much discussion!"

"What was it about?" Mr. Simonson queried.

"Well, the sermon was called 'Sinners in the Hands of an Angry God.' It was like a horror story—about how angry God is with sinners, and how people are dangling over a bottomless pit by a slender thread. One guy said it wasn't fair to lay a big guilt trip on people, because nobody's perfect. But most of the students said a loving God wouldn't send people to hell."

"What do you think?" Mr. Simonson asked.

Stu thought a moment. "Well, that sermon scared a lot of people back then. But modern people don't want to hear sermons about hell. Maybe it is better just to preach about God's love."

"You're right about people," Mr. Simonson replied. "But the real issue isn't what people want to hear; it's what God wants us to know. And one thing He wants us to know is that His attitude toward sin hasn't changed."

◆ TAKE A LOOK / Revelation 15:1-8

The great preacher Jonathan Edwards knew that God never has changed His mind about sin— and He never will. Because God is just, He must judge and punish sin. People need to know they are in eternal danger unless they turn to God in faith.

Sinful people don't like to think about that. They'd rather focus on God's love and mercy. God wants to forgive our sins; but if we do not ask Him to, then we must pay the penalty.

God will not "overlook" sin forever. Revelation 15:1-8 describes the time when God's mercy will end and His justice will begin to fall on the world.

▲ TAKE A STEP

Long ago, God allowed a whole generation of Israelites to die in the wilderness because of their sin. As their children assembled to hear Moses' last sermon before they entered the Promised Land, they learned this:

[God] is the Rock, his works are perfect, and all his ways are just. A faithful God who does no wrong, upright and just is he (Deuteronomy 32:4).

God is just, so sin must be punished. To avoid experiencing God's justice firsthand, each of us must accept the salvation God offers through His Son Jesus. Have you done that? Why not tell a friend!

God acts according to His own perfect rules

What is God's justice?

God's justice means that, because He is perfect and holy, He cannot overlook sin.

Because God is truthful, He is trust-worthy!

Q

Why is God's truthfulness important?

A

God's truthfulness gives me confidence to trust Him with my life.

PARENT:
Children often cannot distinguish verbal teasing from honest communication. Be careful not to undermine a child's confidence in you.

Edward loved to tease his four-year-old cousin. Once when little Cary wasn't looking, Edward swiped his cookies off the plate. When Cary found them gone, Edward said, "Your cookies? Oh, the Cookie Monster ate 'em!"

When Cary asked for his "security blanket" before naptime, Edward upset him by saying, "That old thing? I thought it was just a rag. You didn't really want it did you?" And when Cary looked around for his mother, Edward made him howl by teasing, "She's gone to Alaska. She may be back next week."

Before long, Cary didn't trust Edward. He didn't want Edward as a baby-sitter. If Edward was around, Cary just wouldn't have a snack. And he never let his security blanket out of his sight.

Every time Edward came to visit, the question Cary repeatedly asked was, "Mommy, is Edward teasing me?"

◆ TAKE A LOOK
Titus 1:2; Psalm 119:151; Hebrews 10:23

Truthfulness is an important personal quality. A truthful person is reliable, sincere, stable, and trustworthy. Unlike Edward, whose teasing and lies raised doubts in Cary's mind, our God is completely truthful and therefore trustworthy. That's why the psalmist said:

Into your hands I commit my spirit; redeem me, O LORD, the God of truth (Psalm 31:5).

Because God is truthful, His words to us are totally true. What do these verses teach you about the God who is truth?

This verse shows . . .	that the God of truth:
Titus 1:2	does not _____
Psalm 119:151	gives true _____
Hebrews 10:23	keeps His_____

▲ TAKE A STEP

Our truthful God has also shown us the truth about ourselves—that each of us is sinful (Romans 3:23). And He has shown us the truth about the future—that those who believe in Jesus Christ will have everlasting life, and that those who do not will suffer God's wrath (John 3:36). No one who stands before God on Judgment Day will be able to claim, "God, You didn't tell me the truth!"

Think back to Edward's relationship with Cary. Can your friends and family members trust what you say? If not, how can you change your actions to "speak" the truth in everything you do?

*T*he well-dressed couple sat silently, puzzled and hurt, as they waited for the guard to bring their son from his cell.

At last the door clanged shut, and their son shuffled across the room and slumped at the table. For a while no one spoke.

Finally the mother asked, "Are you all right, son?"

"Whadda you care?" he mumbled. "You never cared before."

"How can you say that?" his father asked, trying to hold his anger in check. "We gave you the best home, sent you to the best schools, and you had a car before anyone else in your crowd."

"Yeah, I know all that," the boy muttered without looking up. "You gave me plenty of things. But not love."

"Of course we loved you. And we still do!" the woman cried.

"No," the son shook his head sadly. "If you loved me you would have given me yourself instead of things. And maybe we wouldn't all be here right now." And he motioned the guard to take him back to his cell.

◆ TAKE A LOOK
Romans 5:8; 1 John 4:9; Hebrews 12:10

People have a lot of wrong ideas about love. Some think love is giving things. Others think love is total freedom with no discipline. Some show love only if it has been earned. And many believe that all expressions of physical love must be okay with God, since the Bible says "God is love."

All those ideas about love are wrong. The Bible does indeed say "God is love" (1 John 4:8). But not all love is God's! Love that smothers, love that substitutes things for personal involvement, love that demands performance, and physical expressions of love outside the marriage relationship—all are called "love." But they are not true love.

According to Romans 5:8; Hebrews 12:10; and 1 John 4:9, what are three things God's love causes Him to do?

▲ TAKE A STEP
Skim through 1 John 4:7–5:3 and count how many times the word *love* is used.

This is how we know that we love the children of God: by loving God and carrying out his commands (1 John 5:2).

Can you think of a verse that tells how much God's love for you cost? (Hint: It's a verse John wrote in the gospel that bears his name!)

God's love is an active, costly love

Q

Why is God's love so special?

A

God loves me even though I don't deserve it, and He wants me to love even though it may cost something.

THANKSGIVING

E ach little flower that opens, each little bird that sings,
  He made their glowing colors, He made their tiny wings.

The purple-headed mountain, the river running by,
  The sunset, and the morning that brightens up the sky.

The cold wind in the winter, the pleasant summer sun,
  The ripe fruits in the garden, He made them every one.

He gave us eyes to see them, and lips that we might tell
  How great is God Almighty, who has made all things well.

All things bright and beautiful, all creatures great and small,
  All things wise and wonderful, the Lord God made them all.
                              —Cecil Alexander (1848)

◆ THINKING ABOUT THANKSGIVING

The Jewish people observed a seven-day thanksgiving festival
each year to celebrate God's goodness and thank Him for the
harvest. Americans have officially observed Thanksgiving Day each
year since 1942. But as the hymn above reminds us, God's blessings
are so abundant that thanksgiving
should be our constant attitude.

● **KEY VERSE ON THANKSGIVING**
*Give thanks to the LORD, for he
is good; his love endures
forever (Psalm 107:1).*

▲ **LOOKING AHEAD**
This week we'll think about
God's goodness and learn to give
thanks.
    What can you think of to be
thankful for? Take turns completing
these sentences:
    A beautiful thing I'm thankful
for is _____ .
    A creature that blesses my life is
_____ .
    A wise person I'm thankful for is
_____ .
    A wonderful thing that fills me
with joy is _____ .

*"Sure. He didn't give us any
homework over Thanksgiving,
but he knows we'll be
counting our blessings."*

F or months Randy had looked forward to getting his driver's license on the morning of his sixteenth birthday. When that Saturday finally arrived, he could hardly wait. He ran into the kitchen just as his mother was hanging up the phone.

"I just called the State Patrol office to find out when they open," she said, "and they said to bring proof that you've taken a drug and alcohol course. Do you know what they mean?"

"Oh yeah—I took that course last quarter," Randy assured her, "but my certificate hasn't gotten here yet."

"Well, they're not going to just take your word for it. They said you had to have the certificate with you to take the test."

"What?! It's their fault they're so slow with the paperwork!" Randy raved. "Oh no—and I was going to drive to Heather's party tonight. It's just not fair!"

That evening Randy's dad drove him to the party. On the way, the left rear tire blew out, and they barely missed hitting an oncoming car. While they were changing the tire, Randy's dad remarked, "You know, Randy, I think we can safely say God was in control today. Otherwise, you may have had a wreck the first time you took the car out. I know you were upset, but I'm glad you didn't have your license today!"

◆ **TAKE A LOOK / Revelation 4:1-11**
The people who lived in Bible times were as human as Randy—and as you. Sometimes their dreams and hopes were shattered too. God promised Abraham a son; but at age 99 he was still childless. Joseph looked forward to managing his father's business; instead he spent time in an Egyptian jail. David as a teenager was anointed to be king; yet in his thirties he was a fugitive in the desert. Even so, each one knew that God was in control of his life.

Revelation 4:1-11 gives us a glimpse of the God in whom Abraham, Joseph, and David placed their trust. Can you find a phrase in verse 9 which reminds you that God is in control?

▲ **TAKE A STEP**
The living creatures give glory, honor and thanks to him who sits on the throne (Revelation 4:9).
Close your eyes and think of a situation that's making you anxious today. Now picture the King of heaven sitting on His throne issuing orders about that situation. Finally, do what you're told to do in 1 Thessalonians 5:17-18.

God's on His throne and all is well

Q

Why should I be thankful that God is on His throne?

A

Thanksgiving overflows when I realize that God is in control.

PARENT:
Thanksgiving is a time to share your blessings. Invite someone in your church or neighborhood to dinner this week.

The best Thanksgiving Day Parade ever

"**G**randma, were you and Grandpa married during World War II?"

"Yes, we were, Katherine," her grandmother answered. "And after three months your grandfather went to fight in Europe. Your mother was born while he was gone. But why are you asking?"

"I have to report on VE day—that's 'Victory in Europe' Day. From the pictures we saw in class, it seems like everyone went berserk. What were you doing when you heard the news?"

"I'll never forget it. I was out strolling your mother—she was a terribly cranky baby—and a girlfriend of mine came rushing up to me shouting, 'Evelyn, Evelyn, the war is over! Our boys are coming home!' I hurried to her little apartment and we listened to the newscasts on the radio—we didn't have TV then. Soon other friends came over and we were whooping and hollering. By then the whole neighborhood was in the street. For the first time in years it seemed a weight had been lifted off my shoulders. I knew your grandfather was coming home."

What is the victory we have in Christ?

◆ **TAKE A LOOK / 1 Corinthians 15:51-57; Colossians 2:13-15**

People in your grandparents' generation celebrated at the end of World War II, just as we recently did at the end of the Gulf War. All over the country, confetti, bells, musical bands of every size and kind, and throngs of people proclaimed that the enemy was defeated, peace was restored.

As Christians, we ought to be just as excited—and thankful—over the victory Jesus has won for us in a battle many of us didn't know we were fighting. You'll learn what that victory is all about in 1 Corinthians 15:51-57. Then Colossians 2:13-15 explains how victory over sin and death was won.

A

Thanksgiving is possible because Jesus won the victory over sin and death for me.

▲ **TAKE A STEP**

Thanks be to God! He gives us the victory through our Lord Jesus Christ (1 Corinthians 15:57).

Because of sin, human beings were at war with God. But by His death on the cross, Jesus brought about peace. God and man are no longer separated by sin; no longer do we have to fear God's wrath. Satan was defeated!

Have you ever celebrated the victory that Christ made possible? Express thanks your sins are forgiven by singing a "victory" march—a verse of "Victory in Jesus" or "When the Saints Go Marching In." And clap a little bit, too!

When Frank Morris opened the door of his parents' modest home, the fragrance of long-remembered Thanksgivings rose to meet him.

The aroma of apple logs in the old wood stove mingled with the slightly bitter smell of the chrysanthemums sitting gloriously on the mantle. A faint hint of lavender rose from the sparkling linen tablecloth, and the candles already burning on the dining room table gave off a scent of sandalwood.

When Frank surprised his mother in the warm kitchen and whirled her around in a huge bear hug, the delectable smells of roast turkey, candied yams, and fresh yeast rolls rising on top of the refrigerator made him glad he'd made the 700-mile journey.

He poked around the tiny kitchen, lifting lids and bending to smell the sage dressing, the spiced apples, the green beans simmering Southern-style in a black cast iron pot. And he knew that even if he didn't eat a bite today, the privilege of being in this aromatic kitchen was reason enough to give thanks!

◆ TAKE A LOOK / 2 Corinthians 2:14-17

Most of us take our sense of smell for granted. But when you use your nose as Frank did, it can give you a great deal of pleasure—especially on Thanksgiving Day, when the fragrance of spices, roasting meat, and baking bread fill the house!

The Bible often mentions fragrant aromas. At God's instruction, the Israelites made sweet offerings to their Lord on the altar of incense. And in the book of Revelation we learn that the sweet incense symbolizes the prayers of God's people rising before His throne (Revelation 8:3).

But while our prayers are a fragrant aroma to God, our very lives put forth a fragrance other people can "smell" as well. Read 2 Corinthians 2:14-17. What do you smell like?

▲ TAKE A STEP

Thanks be to God, who . . . through us spreads everywhere the fragrance of the knowledge of him (2 Corinthians 2:14).

Just as the aromas of a Thanksgiving dinner drift into every corner of the house, followers of Jesus Christ are to provide a divine "fragrance." At home, school, work, worship, and play, our lives are to attract others to our Lord.

As you enjoy the aromas of fall and the fragrances of fine food today, put a bottle of perfume on the dinner table as a reminder that you are to be a fragrance of Christ.

Nothing smells better than Thanksgiving Day!

Q

How does God use my life?

A

Thanksgiving reminds me that I am the fragrance of Christ to the world.

PARENT: *If you are planning to use an advent wreath or calendar this year, make sure you have it ready to use the first Sunday in December.*

Loving care for the flowers of friendship

Growing Friendship
Friendship is like a garden of flowers, fine and rare;
It cannot reach perfection except through loving
   care;
Then, new and lovely blossoms with each new day
   appear—
For Friendship, like a garden, grows in beauty year
   by year.

There's happiness in little things,
There's joy in passing pleasure;
But friendships are, from year to year,
The best of all life's treasure.
—From A CHILD'S TREASURY OF VERSE

Q

How can I
show my
thanks for
friends?

A

Thanks-
giving is a
time to
appreciate
and pray
for my
friends.

PARENT:
Paul's
prayers in
Ephesians
1:17-19 and
3:16-19 are
wonderful
models to
follow in
praying
for your
children.

◆**TAKE A LOOK / Philippians 1:1-11**
Friendship is a treasure. And just as we would
guard a treasure chest of gold or silver, so we
should protect our friendships.

The apostle Paul never really settled down very
long in one place. But even without home or
family, he was a man with many friends. When he
was imprisoned in a Roman jail, Paul knew he
could count on those friends. And though he
wasn't able to be physically present with his
friends, he did all he could to keep those
relationships growing. According to Philippians
1:1-11, what did Paul do for his friends?

▲ **TAKE A STEP**
As Paul sat in prison day after day, he
probably thought of his friends frequently. And as
their names and faces came to mind, he thanked
God for those friends (verse 3) and remembered the
work they had done together (verse 5). He thought
about them affectionately, wishing he could see
them (verse 8). But most of all, Paul prayed for his
friends (verses 9-11).

Don't let this Thanksgiving week pass without
remembering your friends. Take turns rereading
Paul's prayer, substituting the name of one (or
more) of your friends when it's your turn to read:

"I pray that _____ 's love may abound
more and more in knowledge and depth of insight,
so that he or she will be able to discern what is best
and may be pure and blameless until the day of
Christ. I pray that _____ may be filled with
the fruit of righteousness that comes through Jesus
Christ—so that God would be glorified and praised
through his/her life."

··HOSPITALITY····

Mrs. Carlson was browning the last piece of chicken when her nine-year-old daughter, Rosemary, gave her a hug. "Mom, can I invite Lydia for dinner tonight? She loves fried chicken."

"Oh, honey, I'd really rather not tonight," Mrs. Carlson replied casually. "I don't want the extra bother right now."

"But Mom," Rosemary persisted, "I'll set the table and do the dishes. Just please let me ask Lydia. She needs to come."

Mrs. Carlson paused in thought. Though Lydia Eaton and her mother had been living two houses away for over a month, she still hadn't gotten acquainted. She knew Mrs. Eaton worked long hours. In fact, she had remarked how glad she was that she didn't have to leave Rosemary alone after school. "Oh, Lord," she prayed silently, "forgive me for not caring." Turning to her daughter she said, "Let's invite Lydia and her mother over."

Later that evening as Mrs. Eaton put on her coat, she turned to Mrs. Carlson and smiled warmly. "Dinner was wonderful, but just being with you all was even better. Thank you so much!"

◆ THINKING ABOUT HOSPITALITY

Have you ever heard of "etiquette books"? They explain good manners and rules for entertaining. But helping people experience the love God has given us to share is more than mere entertainment. That takes true hospitality.

Hospitality is **opening your home and your heart, generously sharing what God has given you with guests He sends your way**. Through the apostle Paul, God has given us this command:

● KEY VERSE ON HOSPITALITY

Share with God's people who are in need. Practice hospitality (Romans 12:13).

▲ LOOKING AHEAD

In ancient times, travelers often stayed in guest houses called "hospices." Read 2 Kings 4:8-37 to discover which Old Testament prophet had a hospice built for him. What exciting miracle happened there?

"Your mom sure knows how to make the company feel at home."

The door is always open; the welcome mat is out

Q

Why should Christians practice hospitality?

A

Hospitality is one way for God's children to share His love with others.

PARENT: Our word "welcome" means "I desire guests." If you don't have a welcome mat at your door or a plaque in your entryway, buy or make one this week.

*T*he registration line for the Christian growth seminar was moving slowly. Mrs. Powell had just about run out of ways to amuse her two preschoolers when the young man in front turned around and leaned over to talk to them.

Soon Mrs. Powell was included in the conversation. As they talked she learned that the young man, Richard, had only recently become a Christian. Because of some deep hurts in his life, his pastor had recommended this seminar.

"But where are you staying on such short notice?" she asked. "The reasonably priced places were booked months in advance."

"I could only get a room for tonight," he replied. "I'll try to find something else tomorrow."

Instantly, Mrs. Powell thought of the three empty bedrooms at her father's house—and her father was standing only a few feet away! As soon as they had registered, she made the introductions and proposed her plan. And so it was that Richard stayed that week with Mr. Benson. Ten years later, he was still calling Mrs. Powell's father "Dad Benson."

◆ **TAKE A LOOK / Acts 8:26-40**

Hospitality is a practical way to express God's love. But it's also a direct commandment:

Do not forget to entertain strangers, for by so doing some people have entertained angels without knowing it (Hebrews 13:2).

The word for *angel* in Greek (the language in which the New Testament was first written) simply means "messenger." In Acts 8:26-40 you'll read the story of two messengers—a heavenly one and a human one named Philip. Philip was able to share the gospel with a confused Ethiopian official when that official's curiosity caused him to extend his hospitality to Philip. Can you discover how?

▲ **TAKE A STEP**

Philip wouldn't have lasted long jogging beside the chariot in the desert heat! But it was the Ethiopian official who truly benefited when he "invited Philip to come up and sit with him."

In a similar way, Mr. Benson's hospitality brought about a rich friendship. Has anyone in your family ever had a "divine appointment" such as Philip's, when he just knew he was in a certain place for a reason? If so, share that story. And if you can, invite the other person involved for dessert to hear the same story from his or her viewpoint.

In the early 1950s, an American pastor and his wife left a comfortable parsonage in St. Louis and moved to Switzerland with their children. They wanted to share the reality of Jesus Christ with young Europeans, whose faith had been shattered by the recent World War, and by years of being taught that God didn't exist and the Bible could not be trusted. Before long, young people were gathering frequently in the Schaeffers' mountain home for Bible study, where they heard honest answers to their questions about Christianity.

The Schaeffers trusted God daily to meet their needs to feed and house all the young people who came their way. Their hospitality and dependence on God through prayer demonstrated to their guests that God really is there—and that He cares about them. Today thousands of people around the world can say they came to know Jesus because of the Schaeffers' hospitality in their home called L'Abri or "The Shelter."

Sharing your shelter, sharing your faith

◆ **TAKE A LOOK / Luke 14:1, 12-14**
Sharing meals and friendship was the Schaeffers' way of expressing God's love to those who came their way. Their home became a place of teaching and acceptance for young people who did not know God cared for them. Even though Mrs. Schaeffer and her daughters sometimes had to work long hours preparing meals, they were obedient to this command:

Offer hospitality to one another without grumbling. Each one should use whatever gift he has received to serve others (1 Peter 4:9-10).

Once when Jesus was eating at the home of a prominent religious leader, He was watched very carefully. What important truth about hospitality do you learn in Luke 14:1 and 12-14?

▲ **TAKE A STEP**
A good meal and fun with friends or family is what comes to mind when most of us think of hospitality. But Jesus knew that genuine warmth and acceptance found in an open and loving home is what draws people to Him.

Think for a moment about the people you've had in your home or shared a meal with (even if it was in a restaurant) during the past six months. Are you showing hospitality only to those who are already your friends . . . or are you making new friends? Why not invite some new friends for a meal this weekend?

Q

How does hospitality demonstrate my faith?

A

Hospitality shows others I trust God to meet my needs.

Hospitality should be a family affair

Q

What are some practical ways to show hospitality?

A

Hospitality means more when it's demon-strated simply and sincerely in fun and friendly ways.

PARENT:
Though we're encouraging hospitality, you should warn your children not to talk with strangers unless you are present.

I *'ve invited that new family, the Gibsons, over for dinner today," Mrs. Craig announced as the family climbed into the car after church. "So when we hit the front door, run and make your beds and straighten your rooms. And Tiffany, I'll need you to help me in the kitchen."*

"The Gibsons? Yuck!" twelve-year-old Tiffany wailed. "Charles is so weird. And their twins can be just awful!"

"Twins? What twins?" Mrs. Gibson asked in surprise, turning around in the seat. "I thought Charles was their only son."

"Oh, no. The twins are four years old. They stay in the nursery where I help during church," Tiffany replied.

Now it was Mrs. Gibson's turn to wail! "Oh, honey," she asked her husband, "where are we going to put them all? What if I don't have enough food?"

"How much food can two four-year-olds eat?" Mr. Craig replied calmly. "We're not trying to put on a show or serve a gourmet meal. We'll treat 'em like part of the family, and there'll be plenty to go around. You'll see."

◆ **TAKE A LOOK / Matthew 25:34-40**

Jesus didn't actually own a house where He invited guests. Even so, He is our example of hospi-tality. And He gave the best rule for practicing hos-pitality:

"All men will know that you are my disciples if you love one another" (John 13:35).

Accepting your guests as they are, making them feel at home, and loving them as brothers and sisters . . . that's hospitality. In the opening story above, who wasn't demonstrating a heart of hospitality?

According to the story in Matthew 25:34-40, how many groups of people need your hospitality?

▲ **TAKE A STEP**

After you've read the practical hints below, brainstorm together and come up with three more simple, fun ways to show hospitality:

1. Invite another family over for dessert or offer to bring dessert to their home.

2. Give newcomers a tour of a historical site in your town.

3. Have a game night geared to the skill level of the children involved. Serve only simple refreshments—or ask your guests to bring a favorite snack or dessert to add to yours.

Now pick two of the six ideas and put them on your calendar!

T *he last time I was here—five years ago—my whole
life changed," the speaker said in a lilting accent,
her lovely brown face glowing with the inner light that
only Jesus gives. "Being from a nation where black
people are discriminated against by the white race, I felt
all white people must be bad. In fact, I could hardly
believe that any white person could really be a Christian.*

*"But when I came to America, I was accepted by a
white family as a sister. I stayed in their home, enjoyed
their food, and felt their love. I was accepted as an
equal. I knew their love was sincere. Being here that
week really changed my views of white people; it was
really my 'Damascus Road.'*

*"And our Lord was good. When I went back to my
country, my bitterness was gone. I could no longer work
for a violent revolution. No matter what, I knew God
wanted me to teach my people that we must love our
enemies—not become as bad as they."*

◆ TAKE A LOOK / Acts 9:10-21, 26-28

Years ago, when the white American family
opened their home in hospitality to a black African
woman, they didn't expect anything in return. But
the rewards of hospitality turned out to be great.

They were enriched by a warm, loving
friendship. And they had the joy of knowing they
had made a difference in another person's life.

God doesn't promise rewards such as money
and possessions to one who shows hospitality. But
He does say:

*"Whatever you did for one of the least of these
brothers of mine, you did for me" (Matthew
25:40).*

Ananias was an early disciple of Jesus whom
God told to offer hospitality and healing to a man
who had been his enemy. Read his dramatic story
in Acts 9:10-21 and 26-28.

▲ TAKE A STEP

If you were Ananias, how would you have felt
when you first approached Saul—the man who
had the authority to imprison Christians? What
would you have said or done?

Look at your own life. How do you treat those
people who seem to be your "enemies"—the
teacher who doesn't like you . . . the classmate who
gossips behind your back . . . the neighbor whose
dog messes up your lawn . . . the co-worker who
doesn't carry his load? How can you be hospitable
to them?

"For one of the least of these brothers of mine"

Q

*What
are the
rewards of
hospitality?*

A

*Hospitality
is rewarded
when I
serve others
as if I were
serving
Jesus.*

PARENT:
*For ideas
about how to
make your
home hospi-
table, we
recommend*
Hidden Art
*by Edith
Schaeffer and*
Open Heart,
Open Home
*by Karen
Mains.*

CHRISTMAS

Christmas Everywhere
Everywhere, everywhere, Christmas tonight!
Christmas in lands of the fir-tree and pine,
Christmas in lands of the palm tree and vine,
Christmas where snow peaks stand solemn and white,
Christmas where corn fields stand sunny and bright.
Christmas where children are hopeful and gay,
Christmas where old men are patient and gray,
Christmas where peace, like a dove in his flight,
Broods o'er brave men in the thick of the fight;
Everywhere, everywhere, Christmas tonight!
For the Christ-child who comes is the Master of all;
No palace too great, no cottage too small.
—Phillips Brooks

◆ THINKING ABOUT CHRISTMAS CELEBRATIONS

Nearly two thousand years ago, Jesus was born in the tiny town of Bethlehem. And His whole life—His words and deeds, His death and resurrection, His ascension and promise to return—proves He is indeed God's Son.

Wherever men and women have heard and believed that message, they have devised **unique ways to honor Christ's birth**. Believers around the world have a variety of ways to take part in the joyous celebration which the angel began when he announced:

● KEY VERSE ON CHRISTMAS CELEBRATIONS

"Do not be afraid. I bring you good news of great joy that will be
for all the people"
(Luke 2:10).

*"We had this **last** year."*

▲ LOOKING AHEAD

Thinking about the different ways Christians around the world observe the birth of Christ may give your family some new ideas for your own celebrations this year. But first read Colossians 1:15-20 to discover just who this Baby in a manger was!

By December 16, most Mexican homes have been colorfully decorated with lanterns and flowers. Families set up a nativity scene with the cradle purposefully left empty.

On the night of the 16th, Mexican children set out on the first of nine processions called "posadas." (Posada is the Spanish word for "inn.") These processions portray the attempts of Mary and Joseph to find shelter in Bethlehem.

Led by two children carrying figurines of Mary and Joseph, the children carry lighted candles from house to house (or from room to room in their own home) singing a song which begs shelter for Mary and Joseph. Time after time they are told there is no room. But finally they find a home where they are invited to stay.

The final posada comes on Christmas Eve. On this night the child who leads the procession carries a figure of the infant Jesus. When the right posada has been found, a special hymn is sung and the figure is placed in the manger. Families then go to church at midnight to welcome the birth of Jesus.

◆ **TAKE A LOOK / Colossians 2:6-10, 16-18**

Traditions like the Mexican posada give children the opportunity to do something they enjoy. Year after year they never tire of the same activity.

In fact, the familiarity of these celebrations brings comfort and security as they bring back memories of all the Christmases before.

Many families have their own traditions, or special ways of celebrating year after year. But those traditions must never become more important than the truth of Jesus Christ. See if you can tell why after you read Colossians 2:6-10 and 16-18.

▲ **TAKE A STEP**

Therefore do not let anyone judge you . . . with regard to a religious festival. . . . These are a shadow of the things that were to come; the reality, however, is found in Christ (Colossians 2:16-17).

Your family probably doesn't celebrate Christmas with elaborate processions like the Mexican posadas, but you may have more traditions than you realize.

Brainstorm together to think of all the Christmas traditions your family has observed— worship times, gift-giving, special activities, foods, getting together with friends, decorating the house and tree. What do your traditions tell you about the "reality . . . found in Christ"?

There was no room in the posada

Q

How is Christmas celebrated in Mexico?

A

Christmas celebrations such as the "posada" encourage me to think about Jesus.

Looking in the darkness for places to serve

In Sweden, the Christmas season officially begins on December 13, which the Swedes call St. Lucia's Day.

Lucia was a follower of Jesus who lived during the time of Diocletian, the Roman emperor who ruled from A.D. 284 to 305. In those days Christians were cruelly treated. Lucia often helped believers who were hiding in caves. In order to have both hands free to carry food and drink, she wore a crown of candles on her head to light her way.

Eventually Lucia was caught and killed by Roman authorities. But her story continues to brighten dark winter nights in Sweden. On December 12, families bake special "Lucia buns." Very early the next morning, before the sun rises, one of the daughters of the house dresses in a long white dress and red sash. Wearing a wreath of lights to show the way, she serves coffee and newly baked "Lucia buns" to the other family members while they are still in bed!

Q

What does St. Lucia's Day encourage me to do?

A

Christmas celebrations such as St. Lucia's Day encourage me to serve others.

◆ **TAKE A LOOK / John 13:12-17**

Just as Lucia served the Christians hiding in the caves of Rome, so Jesus Himself came to serve humanity. He

"did not come to be served, but to serve,
and to give his life as a ransom for many"
(Matthew 20:28).

Shortly before His death, Jesus ate a Passover meal with His disciples. During that time, Jesus—the Master, Teacher, and Miracle-worker—took off His outer clothing, wrapped a towel around His waist, and washed the dusty, dirty feet of His disciples. When He finished He explained what He had done. After you read John 13:12-17, agree on one word you feel should summarize the Christmas spirit.

▲ **TAKE A STEP**

Perhaps the word your family chose was *love, service,* or *humility.* Whatever it was, make that your family's theme for this holiday season! Just as St. Lucia did, reach out in service to others and brighten their path.

Here's an idea to start your "service" tradition. Decide to help an older acquaintance in your neighborhood or church during the holiday season. For example, as a family, volunteer to do some heavy chores such as cleaning the oven or scrubbing bathroom and kitchen floors. Or offer your services as a chauffeur on shopping trips or other outings during the season. Brainstorm some more and you'll come up with good ideas of your own!

Moravia, which was once a part of the country of Czechoslovakia, is the home of a small Protestant denomination founded in 1722. The missions-minded Moravian believers eventually came to America, settling in Pennsylvania in the winter of 1741. They named their settlement Bethlehem.

To celebrate Christmas, the Moravians have a special love feast on Christmas Eve to emphasize the fellowship Christians can enjoy with each other.

While the choir sings, the congregation enjoys a very simple meal—coffee and buns. Dressed in white, the women of the church quickly and quietly pass the baskets of soft buns; the men follow serving mugs of hot coffee.

At the end of the evening, the women give each person present a lighted beeswax candle. Holding their candles high, the people rededicate their hearts to Christ, Light of the World, whose coming is celebrated on Christmas Day.

◆ **TAKE A LOOK** / John 6:35-40; 8:12

Almost everyone notices the lights of Christmas. Advent wreath candles . . . decorative lights strung on windows and eaves . . . tiny blinking bulbs circling the family tree—all the different lights of Christmas give the season a special glow. But the beautiful lights of Christmas are meaningless and artificial unless a person's heart is lit by the Light of the World.

The Moravian love feast reminds us that Jesus is both the Bread of Life and the Light of the World. As you read John 6:35-40 and 8:12, ask yourself if you've "eaten" that bread and had your life "illuminated" by that light.

▲ **TAKE A STEP**

Deep inside each person is a hunger to know what the purpose and meaning of life is.

The only truth that can fill that inner "emptiness" and shed light on all the questions is knowing God through His Son Jesus Christ. This is what Jesus meant when He said,

"I am the light of the world. Whoever follows me will never walk in darkness, but will have the light of life" (John 8:12).

If you've not yet had your "hunger" filled or your life "enlightened," why not accept the gift God gave on that first Christmas so long ago—the gift of His Son! If you already know the Savior, with whom could you share the Good News this month?

Sharing the Bread of Life in the season of light

Q

What does a Moravian love feast demonstrate?

A

Christmas celebrations such as the love feast tell me that Jesus brings light and life.

Celebrate Christmas with a "tube steak" dinner

Yu gat haumas Krismas?" In the Pidgin language of Papua New Guinea, this phrase means "How many Christmases do you have?" To many natives, Christmas is just a way of counting the years one has lived.

To others like the Suena, who live on the West Coast of Papua New Guinea, it's a time to return to home villages, to forget about work, to beat drums and learn new dances, and to sit around gossiping. At Ambunti, where the river dominates daily life, the people take great pride at Christmastime in racing their swift canoes —and in using their newly acquired outboard motors.

But the gospel has come to many areas of Papua New Guinea, and with it have come new customs to help celebrate the true meaning of Christmas. Caroling from village to village—not with our familiar carols but with native songs of the faith—is one popular activity, as is attending village worship services.

And not to be forgotten is the Christmas feast with missionaries: Hot dogs cooked underground in a stone pressure cooker, then joyfully shared with all who attend!

Q

What do Papua New Guinea's celebrations remind me to do?

A

Christmas celebrations mean more if I do something for those who have never heard about Jesus.

◆ **TAKE A LOOK / John 3:16; Revelation 5:9-10**

As English-speaking people, it's easy for us to think that Christmas is "our" holiday. But we must never forget that from God's viewpoint, the birth of Jesus was

"good news of great joy that will be for all the people" (Luke 2:10).

God desires that men, women, boys, and girls all over the world hear about Jesus. Read John 3:16 and Revelation 5:9-10. According to those verses, why does God desire that?

▲ **TAKE A STEP**

Having hot dogs in Papua New Guinea is a bit different from eating the traditional Christmas turkey! But whether you're a tribe member in Papua New Guinea or a "native" of the melting pot of America, God's truth still has the power to conquer sin and bring eternal life.

Honor God's purposes by doing what you can to make sure the "news" of Christmas reaches all people. Agree now to spend less on your own celebrations, or to make gifts rather than buy them. Then give the money you save to your church's mission program or another mission agency. Your gift might allow someone in a place like Papua New Guinea to truly celebrate Christmas for the first time next year!

CHRIST'S BIRTH

*T*he Shaws always waited until just a few days before Christmas to decorate their home. Kim and Billy were bubbling with excitement. While Mom and Dad wrestled the tree into its stand in the living room, the children set up the nativity scene on a table. Each year they arranged the hand-painted figures of Joseph and Mary, the animals, the shepherds, the angel, the wise men, and the baby Jesus for all their friends to see.

"Can't you be more careful?" Kim chided her seven-year-old brother, who had knocked the sheep into the cow, which fell over and hit Mary. "You wouldn't want to break Christmas, would you?"

Soon the children stood back to admire their handiwork. "You know," Billy said thoughtfully, "that was just a barn with a bunch of messy animals. Do you think the wise men really knelt down in there? Yuck!"

◆ THINKING ABOUT CHRIST'S BIRTH

Because the events we celebrate as part of Christmas actually took place over a two-year period, we, like Billy, may get confused.

For example, we know the wise men really weren't present on the actual night of Jesus' birth; we don't know exactly how many came to visit later. Yet, as we think about Christ's birth this week, we should have the same attitude toward Him as they did, so we can say:

● KEY VERSE ON CHRIST'S BIRTH

"We . . . have come to worship him" (Matthew 2:2).

▲ LOOKING AHEAD

Billy knew all the characters in the nativity set were somehow connected with Christ's birth. But he couldn't quite fit all the details together.

This week we'll look at the birth of Christ through Billy's eyes and ask questions with him.

You'll get a head start on knowing the answer to Billy's last question by reading Philippians 2:5-11 right now.

"That's right, son. Just gold, frankincense and myrrh. No Nintendo."

"But I thought His name was 'Jesus'!"

Q

Why was Jesus called "Immanuel"?

A

"Immanuel" means God Himself came to be with us on earth.

PARENT:
Over a meal try to think of as many other "names" for Jesus in the Bible as you can. Here are some verses to get you started: Isaiah 9:6; John 1:34; 8:12; 14:6; Acts 10:36; Hebrews 12:2; 1 Peter 5:4; 1 John 1:1; Revelation 1:8; 19:16.

Hey, Kim, I was just thinking," Billy said with a puzzled look. "Why do we have an angel in our nativity scene? I don't remember reading about that in the Bible story."

Kim was used to her little brother asking "dumb" questions, but this one made her wonder, too. She'd heard the Christmas story many times, but she couldn't remember anything about an angel at the manger. "Billy, you've stumped me," she sighed.

Billy held the angel in his hands, studying it intently. He couldn't tell whether it was male or female, but it had a shining face and hair topped with a golden halo. Suddenly, Billy set it down right beside the manger. "An angel must have been there," he said triumphantly. "Angels are everywhere!"

Then after a pause, he asked, "But why did the angel say He would be called 'Immanuel'? I thought His name was 'Jesus'!"

◆ TAKE A LOOK / Matthew 1:18-25

Playing with the nativity scene helped Billy imagine how it was when Jesus was born. Some of his questions might be questions you'd like to have answered, too.

Mary was engaged to Joseph when God told her she would become the mother of His Son. Because she would go through a normal time of pregnancy, God sent an angel to assure Joseph that Mary had not sinned before their marriage, and that he should care for her as his wife. As you read the angel's words to Joseph in Matthew 1:18-25, look for words and phrases that describe this special baby and His special mission on earth.

▲ TAKE A STEP

The angel assured Joseph that Jesus was the Messiah for whom the Jewish people had been waiting for centuries. In fact, He was God Himself, come to earth as a baby.

It may be hard to think of God as a baby, developing inside His mother . . . being born . . . then growing through all the stages people go through. But this was God's plan for Jesus:

> And being found in appearance as a man, he humbled himself and became obedient to death —even death on a cross! (Philippians 2:8).

How would you have answered Billy's last question? Reread Matthew 1:23 to find out what "Immanuel" means. Which verse in today's readings hints that Jesus' birth was the first step to the cross?

B illy's favorite part of Christmas was right after dinner. The adults would linger over a cup of coffee while Dad read the account of Jesus' birth from the book of Luke, reminding the family once again why this day was different. Then Grandpa would read a Christmas story for the children.

This year he read Billy's favorite: "A Certain Small Shepherd," the story of a little boy named Jamie, who couldn't speak. As Grandpa read, Billy brimmed with joy when Jamie was chosen to portray a shepherd for the school Christmas play. He wiggled with frustration when the pageant was cancelled. And he experienced fresh wonder over that little shepherd's Christmas miracle.

When Grandpa closed the book, Billy leaned back and heaved a contented sigh. Then suddenly he sat up straight, mouth open.

"Not another question!" Kim groaned, recognizing the signs.

But Billy looked serious. "Dad, why did God send the angels to shepherds? They weren't very important people, were they?"

◆ TAKE A LOOK / Luke 2:1-20

Being a shepherd was once a noble occupation. Even the great King David had tended sheep in the same village where Jesus was born. But by Jesus' time shepherding wasn't such a glamorous job.

Shepherds were usually country peasants hired to tend sheep owned by someone else. They were rough and uneducated, yet they were the first to hear the news about Christ's birth!

Imagine yourself on that hillside as you read Luke 2:1-20.

▲ TAKE A STEP

The Jewish religious leaders, the king of Judea, and the Roman rulers were only a few miles away. So why did God announce His Son's birth to lowly shepherds?

The Bible doesn't really answer that question. But one answer can be found in the words the angel spoke to the shepherds:

"I bring you good news of great joy that will be for all the people" (Luke 2:10).

Use your imagination to answer these questions: (1) How does the fact that God told shepherds show us that all people are important to Him? (2) If Jesus were born today, whom do you think the angels might tell? (3) What did the shepherds do after they saw Jesus (verse 20)? Why not join them in praising God right now!

We wish everyone a merry Christmas —even shepherds!

Q

Why did the angels appear to shepherds?

A

Christ's birth was good news for all people— especially the lowly and unloved.

PARENT:
Why not follow the example of the family in today's story and read a Christmas story together!

He left a glorious heaven to be born in a barn

Billy couldn't leave the nativity scene alone. He loved to play with the figures, moving them around in different positions and acting out the story of Christ's birth with them.

"This doesn't really look like a stable," he thought as he fiddled with the figures. "But maybe that's what barns were like back then." Suddenly a question slipped out of his mind into the open. "Kim, why was Jesus born in a stable?"

"There you go again, asking questions nobody ever asks but you!" Kim answered, a little perturbed. "It must be because there wasn't any room in the inn, so that was the only place to stay. Besides, God knew what He was doing, so that's fine with me."

"Yeah, I guess so," Billy said, doubt clouding his voice. "But don't you think it's kind of funny for God's Son to be born in a barn? It just doesn't seem right!"

Q

Why was Jesus born in a barn?

A

Christ's birthplace points to His humble life as the Lamb of God who died for me.

◆ **TAKE A LOOK** / Isaiah 53:7, 10, 12; John 1:29

People sometimes criticize the Bethlehem innkeeper for turning away an expectant mother. But in Bible times an inn was designed as much to protect the animals as the people. So, with Mary's need for privacy during the birth, the stable may have been a blessing in disguise. With his carpentry skills, Joseph may even have had time to make the stable more comfortable.

Even so, the fact that God's Son was born in a barn tells us something. The prophet Isaiah gave a clue many years before when he foretold the coming of Christ. What sacrificial animal is Jesus compared to in Isaiah 53:7, 10, and 12? How does John describe Jesus years later in John 1:29?

▲ **TAKE A STEP**

Because God is holy and just, He requires that humanity's sin be paid for. In Old Testament times God commanded people to give the blood of animals as sacrifice—or payment—for their sins. This was a preview of the great, once-for-all sacrifice Jesus made on the cross. Jesus never sinned; He was

. . . a lamb without blemish or defect
(1 Peter 1:19).

God's Christmas gift to all people was the Lamb born so long ago in the stable. Have you accepted His gift? If you have, bow in prayer and thank God for it. If you haven't, why not accept that gift right now? God is waiting for you to say yes to His gift.

Billy knew better than to ask Kim any more questions, but that didn't stop them from tumbling around in his mind. Late at night he lay in his bed trying to figure them out.

"Okay—Jesus had a mother and grew up like any other little boy—just like me," Billy thought to himself. "But God was Jesus' Father. That's not like Dad and me though."

As he lay there, his mom and dad tiptoed into his bedroom for a last goodnight kiss. On the pillow beside Billy's head they spotted the figure of baby Jesus from the nativity scene. "What's that in here for?" Dad chuckled as he tousled Billy's hair.

"Well, I know Jesus isn't still a little baby," Billy replied. "But I learned in Sunday school that, even though He's in heaven, He's with me all the time. This helps me remember!"

◆ TAKE A LOOK / John 1:1-5, 10-14

The truth which Billy was beginning to understand is this: That helpless infant who ate, slept, cried, and needed the constant care of His parents was not an extra-terrestrial creature in disguise. He was—and still is—God.

The apostle John knew that Jesus was God's ultimate message to humanity. In his writings he even referred to Jesus as the Word. As you read John 1:1-5 and 10-14, find one phrase which shows that Jesus (the Word) is God, and another which points out that He was human.

▲ TAKE A STEP

The Word was God. . . . The Word became flesh and made his dwelling among us (John 1:1, 14).

We often think of Jesus as the Christmas baby. But we must never forget that He is God, the King of kings and Lord of lords, who humbly took on human flesh.

Why did God allow Himself to become human? He was moved by love for His lost creation. Love brought Him to earth and took Him to the cross.

Perhaps you've received God's love-gift and would like to give Him something in return. The gift God wants is your obedience, freely given from a heart of love and gratitude.

If you want to give yourself to God, write a description of your gift—how you will serve or obey Him—on a slip of paper. Put it in a box, wrap it, and address it to God. Keep the box where you'll see it often to remind you of His gift to you, and your commitment to Him.

"The Word" became flesh . . . because He loves us!

Q

Was Jesus like any other baby?

A

Christ's birth was like any other baby's, yet He was wholly human and wholly divine.

DECISIONS

*U*sually the Murray family's weekly meetings were spent scheduling chores, planning special projects and outings, and praying together. But this week they faced a decision that was a lot tougher than usual.

A heavy cloud of uncertainty hovered over the family as they anticipated Mr. Murray's return from visiting Grandpa Murray in New England. Since Grandma died, Grandpa had lived alone and far from them. And now, because his cataract surgery wasn't successful, he could no longer look after himself.

While Mrs. Murray and Tracey drove to the airport to pick up Dad, the 15-year-old twins washed the dishes. "I could tell on the phone that Dad had a lot on his mind," Kerry sighed.

"Yeah," Kendall agreed. "It's like he had to decide Grandpa's future, and there just aren't any easy answers."

◆ THINKING ABOUT DECISIONS
Fortunately, most of life's decisions are simple. But as the Murrays discovered, there are no easy answers to the "biggies."

As Christians, we know that God is in control of all circumstances. Yet, we have been given certain responsibilities, and we must make decisions in order to fulfill them. Solomon gives us good advice about making decisions throughout life:

● KEY VERSE ON DECISIONS
Trust in the LORD with all your heart and lean not on your own understanding; in all your ways acknowledge him, and he will make your paths straight (Proverbs 3:5-6).

"Do you want Quaker or Nondenominational?"

▲ LOOKING AHEAD
This week follow the Murray family as they **choose which direction to take** in helping Grandpa.

Perhaps your family faces a big decision this week too. If not, you will sometime soon! Before you start the process, examine each word of Proverbs 3:5-6 above. What do the verses mean? Are they true of your family? Is there a command you need to obey?

*I*n the car on the way home from the airport, Mr.
Murray talked about how much it had snowed and
how cold it had gotten last week in New England. He
asked what the children had been up to, who had won
the basketball game on Friday, if the roof was still
leaking. But he didn't talk much about Grandpa.

Tracey sat in the back seat and stared out the rain-
streaked window. It didn't seem possible that Grandpa
was going blind. Tracey felt so sorry for him. Grandpa
knew his family would have to take care of him some
way. But how?

"If I were Dad, I'd hate to make this decision,"
Tracey thought to himself. "I don't even like to make
the million little decisions I've got to make. Like, should
I do math or my vocabulary first? Should I take that job
delivering the morning newspaper? But Dad's decision
will affect our whole family—plus his own father's
future. I hope he makes the right choice!"

◆ **TAKE A LOOK** / Joshua 24:14-27
Every living creature constantly faces change,
but human beings are the only ones who can
make complicated decisions. God has made us
with the ability—and responsibility—to choose.

Some decisions are easier than others; some are
more important than others. But in all our decisions
—from minor ones like "What should I wear to
church?" to major ones like "Should I repair this old
car or buy a new one?"—we have an opportunity to
obey and glorify God. The choice is ours.

Joshua, who led God's people after Moses died,
understood how important choices are. He saw
clearly that the decisions we make today determine
what we become tomorrow. You'll see that too as
you read his speech to the Israelites in Joshua
24:14-27.

▲ **TAKE A STEP**
*"Choose for yourselves this day whom you will
serve. . . . But as for me and my household, we
will serve the LORD" (Joshua 24:15).*
The months ahead will be full of decisions—
opportunities to choose for God or for yourself.
Joshua set up a stone as a covenant marker to help
the Israelites remember what they had chosen.
Together, find a large, smooth stone and deco-
ratively paint on it, "As for me and my household,
we will serve the Lord." Then use it as a centerpiece
on your kitchen table when you're making family
decisions.

You can see my faith in the choices I make

Q

*Why must
I make
decisions?*

A

*Decisions
give me the
opportunity
to honor
and obey
God by
choosing
His way.*

God has given us guidelines and goals

Q

Why doesn't God show me clearly how to decide?

A

Decisions can be made with freedom when I obey God's Word and seek to glorify Him.

As usual, the Murray family meeting began with Mr. Murray's prayer. He thanked God for the blessings the family had received—that Kerry's sprained ankle was healing, that Tracey did well on his history quiz, that he himself had a safe flight.

Then he took a deep breath. "Lord," he said, "we have a hard decision to make. Please show us . . . " He paused—so long that Tracey peeked at him.

"Dad's usually so in control," he thought to himself, "but now it's almost like he doesn't even know what we are supposed to ask God for."

Then Mr. Murray began again: "Lord, we have a hard decision to make. Right now, we don't know what we are supposed to do. We know Your Word tells us to honor and respect our parents, and we want to do that for Grandpa. We love him and we thank You for him. Lord, please help us decide what's best for him. Amen."

◆ **TAKE A LOOK / Ephesians 1:11-12; 2 Peter 1:3-8**

Sometimes it seems that following God's will would be easier if He would just tell us exactly what to do. But the Bible doesn't give any commands about many of the decisions we face every day: what kind of car to buy and how much money to spend on it; whether to marry Bob or Joe, Sally or Jean; whether to look for a new job or try to transfer within the company; whether to try out for the cheerleading squad or the basketball team.

God does not dictate every detail of our lives, but He does have one basic requirement for everyone. As long as we meet that requirement, and don't break any of His commands, God has given us a wide range of freedom in making wise decisions. You can learn God's goal for His children by reading Ephesians 1:11-12. Then find out what "equipment" He's given us to reach that goal in 2 Peter 1:3-8.

▲ **TAKE A STEP**

God's goal for our lives is that everything we do *. . . might be for the praise of his glory* (Ephesians 1:12).

To make the right decision, you should honestly want to bring God glory and honor through it. And you should consider any biblical command or guideline regarding it.

Close your family time today by pretending you are the Murray family. What commands in the Bible should you consider before deciding what to do about Grandpa? How do you think your decision could glorify and honor God?

*W*ell, kids," Mr. Murray began, "you all know the situation. Since Grandma died, Grandpa has done pretty well. But he is getting older, and it's gotten to the point where he can't live alone. He's in good health except for his eyesight. But—"

"Why can't Grandpa just come and live with us?" Tracey blurted. "He could have my room and I could sleep on the sofa."

"That's one possibility," Mr. Murray said, "but Grandpa really doesn't want to move down here. He was born in the house he lives in, knows lots of people there, and insists he doesn't want to impose on us. We have to consider his feelings."

"Could we hire a nurse to live with him?" Kerry asked.

"Maybe," Dad answered, "but I'm not sure we could afford one. Besides, he's my dad, and I don't want to shirk my duty to him."

"Shirk," Tracey thought. "That's one of my vocabulary words this week, and it fits here—we can't shirk this decision."

◆ TAKE A LOOK / James 1:22

Have you ever felt like ignoring a decision you had to make, hoping it would go away? Not deciding is still deciding—to do nothing! And it usually causes more problems in the long run.

But God's Word can help us over the decision-making hurdle. In the verses below you'll discover seven helps to making decisions. Match each verse with its description on the right:

This verse tells me . . .	these help me decide
1. Romans 8:28	a. Counsel from others
2. Proverbs 15:22	b. Conscience
3. James 1:22	c. Consequences
4. Galatians 6:7-10	d. Clear instruction in the Word
5. Acts 24:16	e. Common sense (wise behavior)
6. Ephesians 5:15-16	f. Contentment or peace
7. Colossians 3:15	g. Circumstances

▲ TAKE A STEP

A major obstacle in decision making is being willing to obey God. Are you putting off a decision right now? Is it because you aren't willing to do what you know you should do? Practice using the seven principles you've learned by helping the Murrays decide. Then use them to make your own decisions!

"C-ing" the path and charting the course

Q

What steps can I take to make wise decisions?

A

Decisions should be made according to the guidelines God gives in His Word.

PARENT:
Today is a good time for you and your children to begin memorizing the "Seven C's" of decision making.

Answers: 1-g; 2-a; 3-d; 4-c; 5-b; 6-e; 7-f

Right decisions bring right results— right?

*A*s the Murrays discussed the decision they faced, they narrowed their options to four: (1) hire a housekeeper for Grandpa Murray; (2) put him into a retirement home; (3) move him down to live with them; (4) move north to live with him.

"I know you don't like that last option," Mr. Murray said to his children. "If we moved, you'd have to leave your friends and your school. And that's an important consideration. But my company will transfer me if I ask, so we have to think about it."

"But how are we going to decide?" Tracey asked, panic rising in his voice. "How will we know we made the right decision?"

"Well, we're not going to make the final decision tonight," Mr. Murray declared. "In our own quiet times, let's think about our own attitudes, and ask the Lord to guide us in making the right decision for Grandpa. When we meet together next week, I believe we'll all know what God wants us to do."

◆ **TAKE A LOOK / Luke 15:11-32**

The Murrays' decision-making process involved learning the biblical principles, exploring the possibilities, examining the circumstances, and specifically asking God to show them the best course. Mr. and Mrs. Murray believed that God would lead them in their decision, but Tracey asked the question many others have asked: "How will we know we've made the right decision?"

God does not want us to be confused or frustrated about making decisions. Instead, He wants us to have a sense of contentment that what we decide to do is His will:

Let the peace of Christ rule in your hearts, since as members of one body you were called to peace (Colossians 3:15).

The parable of the two sons shows clearly how decisions lead either to frustration and confusion . . . or to inner peace and harmony with others. After you read the story in Luke 15:11-32, think through the questions below.

▲ **TAKE A STEP**

Each son made a decision which led to confusion; what were those decisions?

1. _____
2. _____

One son made a second decision which brought him peace; what was it?

What decisions did the father have to make?

Q

How do I know when I'm making the right decision?

A

Decisions made according to God's will bring peace, not confusion and frustration.